Liberating Dylan Thomas

Writing Wales in English

CREW series of Critical and Scholarly Studies
General Editor: Professor M. Wynn Thomas (CREW, Swansea University)

This *CREW* series is dedicated to Emyr Humphreys, a major figure in the literary culture of modern Wales, a founding patron of the *Centre for Research into the English Literature and Language of Wales*, and, along with Gillian Clarke and the late Seamus Heaney, one of *CREW*'s original Honorary Associates. Grateful thanks are due to the late Richard Dynevor for making this series possible.

Other titles in the series
Stephen Knight, *A Hundred Years of Fiction* (978-0-7083-1846-1)
Barbara Prys-Williams, *Twentieth-Century Autobiography* (978-0-7083-1891-1)
Kirsti Bohata, *Postcolonialism Revisited* (978-0-7083-1892-8)
Chris Wigginton, *Modernism from the Margins* (978-0-7083-1927-7)
Linden Peach, *Contemporary Irish and Welsh Women's Fiction* (978-0-7083-1998-7)
Sarah Prescott, *Eighteenth-Century Writing from Wales: Bards and Britons* (978-0-7083-2053-2)
Hywel Dix, *After Raymond Williams: Cultural Materialism and the Break-Up of Britain* (978-0-7083-2153-9)
Matthew Jarvis, *Welsh Environments in Contemporary Welsh Poetry* (978-0-7083-2152-2)
Harri Garrod Roberts, *Embodying Identity: Representations of the Body in Welsh Literature* (978-0-7083-2169-0)
M. Wynn Thomas, *In the Shadow of the Pulpit: Literature and Nonconformist Wales* (978-0-7083-2225-3)
Linden Peach, *The Fiction of Emyr Humphreys: Contemporary Critical Perspectives* (978-0-7083-2216-1)
Daniel Westover, *R. S. Thomas: A Stylistic Biography* (978-0-7083-2413-4)
Jasmine Donahaye, *Whose People? Wales, Israel, Palestine* (978-0-7083-2483-7)
Judy Kendall, *Edward Thomas: The Origins of His Poetry* (978-0-7083-2403-5)
Damian Walford Davies, *Cartographies of Culture: New Geographies of Welsh Writing in English* (978-0-7083-2476-9)
Daniel G. Williams, *Black Skins, Blue Books: African Americans and Wales 1845–1945* (978-0-7083-1987-1)
Andrew Webb, *Edward Thomas and World Literary Studies: Wales, Anglocentrism and English Literature* (978-0-7083-2622-0)
Alyce von Rothkirch, *J. O. Francis, realist drama and ethics* (978-1-7831-6070-9)

Liberating Dylan Thomas
Rescuing a Poet from Psycho-sexual Servitude

Writing Wales in English

RHIAN BARFOOT

UNIVERSITY OF WALES PRESS
2015

© Rhian Barfoot, 2015

All rights reserved. No part of this book may be reproduced in any material form (including photocopying or storing it in any medium by electronic means and whether or not transiently or incidentally to some other use of this publication) without the written permission of the copyright owner except in accordance with the provisions of the Copyright, Designs and Patents Act 1988. Applications for the copyright owner's written permission to reproduce any part of this publication should be addressed to the University of Wales Press, 10 Columbus Walk, Brigantine Place, Cardiff CF10 4UP.

www.uwp.co.uk

British Library Cataloguing-in-Publication Data
A catalogue record for this book is available from the British Library.

ISBN   978-1-78316-210-9 (hardback)
           978-1-78316-184-3 (paperback)
e-ISBN 978-1-78316-185-0

The right of Rhian Barfoot to be identified as author of this work has been asserted in accordance with sections 77, 78 and 79 of the Copyright, Designs and Patents Act 1988.

THE ASSOCIATION FOR
WELSH WRITING IN ENGLISH
CYMDEITHAS LLÊN SAESNEG CYMRU

Typeset by Mark Heslington Ltd, Scarborough, North Yorkshire
Printed by CPI Antony Rowe, Chippenham, Wiltshire

*For the late Matthew Phillips who, like Dylan Thomas,
was a true lover of words*

Contents

General Editor's Preface ... ix
Acknowledgements ... xi
List of Abbreviations ... xiii
List of Permissions ... xv

Introduction ... 1

Part One: '[M]aking deadly whoopee': Dylan Thomas's Jouissance of Influence

Chapter 1 ... 21
Chapter 2 ... 32
Chapter 3 ... 48

Part Two: '[A]nd I am dumb to tell': Presenting and Representing the Unrepresentable

Chapter 4 ... 67
Chapter 5 ... 85

Part Three: 'Toenails and Tumours': Re-routing Abjection, From Pessimism to Parody

Chapter 6 ... 99
Chapter 7 ... 110
Conclusion ... 125

Notes ... 130
Bibliography ... 156
Index ... 163

General Editor's Preface

The aim of this series is to produce a body of scholarly and critical work that reflects the richness and variety of the English-language literature of modern Wales. Drawing upon the expertise both of established specialists and of younger scholars, it will seek to take advantage of the concepts, models and discourses current in the best contemporary studies to promote a better understanding of the literature's significance, viewed not only as an expression of Welsh culture but also as an instance of modern literatures in English worldwide. In addition, it will seek to make available the scholarly materials (such as bibliographies) necessary for this kind of advanced, informed study.

M. Wynn Thomas
CREW (*Centre for Research into the English Literature and Language of Wales*)
Swansea University

ACKNOWLEDGEMENTS

In completing this book I owe a considerable debt of gratitude to my friend Professor John Goodby, for offering generous encouragement, critical insight and personal support over the whole duration of this project. I would also like to extend my thanks to Professor Goodby for generously allowing me access to a number of unpublished papers.

For his help and support during the development and completion of this book I would like to thank Professor M. Wynn Thomas.

Heartfelt thanks to my friends Claire Houguez and Liza Penn-Thomas for their encouragement during the course of this project.

Finally, thanks to my long-suffering partner Alun, to my mother, Margaret and my sons, Richy and Luke, for their patience and support over the years.

List of Abbreviations

Quotations from the poetry of Dylan Thomas are taken from *The Collected Poems 1934–53*, ed. Walford Davies and Ralph Maud (London: Dent, 1988); the abbreviation *CPDT* will be followed by the relevant page number. Quotations from the letters are from *Dylan Thomas: The Collected Letters*, ed. Paul Ferris (London: Dent, 1985); the abbreviation *CLDT* will be followed by the relevant page number.

LIST OF PERMISSIONS

The University of Wales Press gratefully acknowledges the following permissions to reproduce the poetry of Dylan Thomas:

'A process in the weather of the heart' by Dylan Thomas, from *The Poems of Dylan Thomas*, © 1939 New Directions Publishing Corp., reprinted by permission of New Directions Publishing Corp.

'Altarwise by owl-light' by Dylan Thomas, from *The Poems of Dylan Thomas*, © 1939 New Directions Publishing Corp., reprinted by permission of New Directions Publishing Corp.

'Before I knocked' by Dylan Thomas, from *The Poems of Dylan Thomas*, © 1939 New Directions Publishing Corp., reprinted by permission of New Directions Publishing Corp.

'Ceremony after a fire raid' by Dylan Thomas, from *The Poems of Dylan Thomas*, © 1946 New Directions Publishing Corp., reprinted by permission of New Directions Publishing Corp.

'Do you not father me?' by Dylan Thomas, from *The Poems of Dylan Thomas*, © 1939 New Directions Publishing Corp., reprinted by permission of New Directions Publishing Corp.

'Especially when the October wind' by Dylan Thomas, from *The Poems of Dylan Thomas*, © 1939 New Directions Publishing Corp., reprinted by permission of New Directions Publishing Corp.

'Fern Hill' by Dylan Thomas, from *The Poems of Dylan Thomas*, © 1945 by The Trustees for the Copyrights of Dylan Thomas, reprinted by permission of New Directions Publishing Corp.

'From love's first fever to her plague' by Dylan Thomas, from *The Poems of Dylan Thomas*, © 1939 New Directions Publishing Corp., reprinted by permission of New Directions Publishing Corp.

'How shall my animal' by Dylan Thomas, from *The Poems of Dylan Thomas*, © 1938 New Directions Publishing Corp., reprinted by permission of New Directions Publishing Corp.

'If I were tickled by the rub of love' by Dylan Thomas, from *The Poems of Dylan Thomas*, © 1939 New Directions Publishing Corp., reprinted by permission of New Directions Publishing Corp.

'In the beginning' by Dylan Thomas, from *The Poems of Dylan Thomas*, © 1953 Dylan Thomas, reprinted by permission of New Directions Publishing Corp.

'Lament' by Dylan Thomas, from *The Poems of Dylan Thomas*, © 1952 Dylan Thomas, reprinted by permission of New Directions Publishing Corp.

'Light breaks where no sun shines' by Dylan Thomas, from *The Poems of Dylan Thomas*, © 1939 New Directions Publishing Corp., reprinted by permission of New Directions Publishing Corp.

'My world is pyramid' by Dylan Thomas, from *The Poems of Dylan Thomas*, © 1939 New Directions Publishing Corp., reprinted by permission of New Directions Publishing Corp.

'Now' by Dylan Thomas, from *Collected Poems 1934–1953*, eds Walford Davies and Ralph Maud, © 1989 Dent (London).

'Osiris, come to Isis' (1930 Notebook) by Dylan Thomas, from *Poet in the Making: The Notebooks of Dylan Thomas*, ed. Ralph Maud, © 1968 Dent (London).

Poem 8 (1930 Notebook) by Dylan Thomas, from *Poet in the Making: The Notebooks of Dylan Thomas*, ed. Ralph Maud, © 1968 Dent (London).

Poem 42 (1930 Notebook) by Dylan Thomas, from *Poet in the Making: The Notebooks of Dylan Thomas*, ed. Ralph Maud, © 1968 Dent (London).

Poem I (1930–1932 Notebook) by Dylan Thomas, from *Poet in the Making: The Notebooks of Dylan Thomas*, ed. Ralph Maud, © 1968 Dent (London).

Poem XLVIX (1930–1932 Notebook) by Dylan Thomas, from *Poet in the Making: The Notebooks of Dylan Thomas*, ed. Ralph Maud, © 1968 Dent (London).

Poem XXVI (1930–1932 Notebook) by Dylan Thomas, from *Poet in the Making: The Notebooks of Dylan Thomas*, ed. Ralph Maud, © 1968 Dent (London).

Poem (viii) (Typescript Poems) by Dylan Thomas, from *The Notebook Poems 1930–1934*, ed. Ralph Maud, © 1989 Dent (London).

Poem Twenty Three (February 1933 Notebook) by Dylan Thomas, from *The Notebook Poems 1930–1934*, ed. Ralph Maud, © 1989 Dent (London).

Poem Twenty Seven (February 1933 Notebook) by Dylan Thomas, from *The Notebook Poems 1930–1934*, ed. Ralph Maud, © 1989 Dent (London).

'That sanity be kept' by Dylan Thomas, from *Collected Poems 1934–1953*, eds Walford Davies and Ralph Maud, © 1989 Dent (London).

'The force that through the green fuse drives the flower' by Dylan Thomas, from *The Poems of Dylan Thomas*, © 1939 New Directions Publishing Corp., reprinted by permission of New Directions Publishing Corp.

LIST OF PERMISSIONS

'Today, this insect' by Dylan Thomas, from *The Poems of Dylan Thomas*, © 1943 New Directions Publishing Corp., reprinted by permission of New Directions Publishing Corp.

'When once the twilight locks no longer' by Dylan Thomas, from *The Poems of Dylan Thomas*, © 1939 New Directions Publishing Corp., reprinted by permission of New Directions Publishing Corp.

'When, like a running grave' by Dylan Thomas, from *The Poems of Dylan Thomas*, © 1939 New Directions Publishing Corp., reprinted by permission of New Directions Publishing Corp.

Introduction

> Whatever is hidden should be made naked. To be stripped of darkness is to be clean, to strip of darkness is to make clean. Poetry, recording the stripping of the individual darkness, must inevitably cast light upon what has been hidden for too long, and, by so doing, make clean the naked exposure. Freud cast light on a little of the darkness he had exposed. Benefiting by the sight of the light and the knowledge of the hidden nakedness, poetry must drag even further into the clean nakedness of the light more even of the hidden causes than Freud could realise.
>
> – Dylan Thomas, 1934

> I advocated a careful rereading, focusing on the constant reference to language and its functions in Freud's work.
>
> – Jacques Lacan, 1951

Although Dylan Thomas is a major twentieth-century literary figure, with an international reputation to match, there is, surprisingly, a profound absence of serious, recent criticism of his work.[1] Moreover, as John Goodby and Chris Wigginton have argued in the introduction to their pioneering text, *Dylan Thomas: New Casebook* (2001), what does exist, aside from their own study and Eynel Wardi's *Once Below a Time* (2000), 'is almost entirely innocent of the wide-ranging and excitingly various approaches – feminist, New Historicist, psychoanalytic, Marxist, postcolonial, and so on – that have [radically] transformed literary studies over the last thirty years'.[2] Inevitably, then, speculation and rumour have tended to mould Thomas's critical reception, which correspondingly veers towards the biographical at every opportunity. More than sixty years have passed since his premature death in 1953, yet the personal myth that surrounds Thomas continues to envelop his writing in a critical climate where, predominantly, he is still seen variously as 'consummate artist, crippled genius, erudite metaphysical or psychological curiosity'.[3] Thus, it seems that the divided response with which his work has been met has been generated explicitly by the continued problem of separating the biographical persona, and correspondingly the excess of his lifestyle, from the apparent excess of the writing. As such, Thomas has always faced ad hominem readings that neglect the complexity of his challenge at the level of language, identity, gender and nationality. This is perhaps why, curiously, given the density and brilliance of his stylistically radical writing, and his implicit relevance to issues central to contemporary psychoanalytic and literary theory itself, Thomas, more possibly than any other canonical writer of stature, has, until very recently, remained virtually untouched by contemporary critical activity. Prejudices against him, not infrequently based on disapproval of his life and character, persist as an influential shaping factor in the reception of his work. Whilst this may change over the course of time, for the moment critical discourse remains largely, and regrettably, dogged by the kind of moral assumptions that have generated recurrent misreadings of Thomas. In particular, an entire range of reductive Freudian interpretations, dating back to the 1960s and 1970s, have been applied, and these are characterized most notably by David Holbrook's sustained use of the now somewhat dated classical model of applied psychoanalysis. Here attention is directed explicitly towards the personal, so that the work is treated as an expression of early infant trauma. For Holbrook, Thomas's most tenacious and rebarbative opponent, the poet is something of a 'psychic cripple', morally dubious and the epiphon of his own neuroses. To give some idea, then, of the ideological perspectives that motivate his infamous three-volume attack on Thomas, it is, perhaps, worth quoting Holbrook at length:

> Dylan Thomas sought to disguise from himself, as many of us do, suffering from greater or lesser neuroses, the nature of adult reality. Unconsciously he desired to return to the blissful state of suckling at the mother's breast ... Because of the nature of the world – our twentieth-century society – its immaturity, and its reflection on his [own] neuroses, he was able to find acceptance and popularity because of his very immaturity. He invented a babble language which concealed the nature of reality from himself and his readers – and found in its very oral sensationalism, in its very meaninglessness, it represented for him and his readers a satisfying return to infancy. This may or may not be linked with the man's alcoholism and his sexual promiscuity: but the baby-prattle has a tremendous disarming effect – the effect of involving all our weaknesses in a special plea for his. You don't smack a baby: and so every attitude to Dylan Thomas accepts the dangerous amorality of engaging the *enfant terrible*.[4]

Holbrook's analysis amounts to what is, in reality a very crude psychoanalytic appeal for adult normalcy. And, drawing almost exclusively on the wealth of sexual and pseudo-sexual imagery in the poetry,[5] in order to consolidate his theory that Thomas was the product of 'a regressive and infantile modernity which he simultaneously helped to create',[6] Holbrook soundly asserts that Thomas was a severely disturbed personality, desperately trying to come to terms with his problems *through* his writing. This contention has been particularly damaging, for it has given the impression that a psychoanalytic approach to Thomas could only ever be a negative one. For, even though in general terms that traditional, or classical, kind of psychoanalytic criticism which makes the author the object of analysis is nowadays apparently the most discredited, it is also perhaps the most difficult to extirpate.[7] Indeed, in both the field of Dylan Thomas studies and that corner of it that has concentrated on placing Thomas in his Welsh cultural context, the biographical continues to hold a perennial interest, and provides the grounds for the deployment of psychoanalytic approaches, from the professional to the most amateur.

But perhaps this needs some clarification and qualification. First, one cannot ignore – nor would one want to – the impact or scholarly value of the contributions made to the field of Thomas studies by such eminent figures as William York Tindall, William T. Moynihan, Ralph Maud and, in particular, Walford Davies, who continues to produce and publish quality research. These writers, who grew up under the auspices of New Criticism, focused their attention on detailed textual analysis, their work being instrumental in laying the foundations of the field of Dylan Thomas studies. And, certainly, the present study would not have been possible had it not been for their detailed exegeses of the early verse. Secondly, and with reference to David Holbrook, it should be noted that whilst the negative impact of his three-volume attack on Thomas cannot be denied, it is equally important to understand that this study was very much 'of its time', based, as it was, on a now very much dated, psycho-biographical approach. In short, and without wishing to discredit the serious body of criticism that already exists, my point is that despite his stature as a major twentieth-century literary figure, Thomas appears to have evaded the scrutiny of the theoretical gaze to which other canonical figures have been subjugated during the past three decades.

This said, more recently there has been a move away from the anecdotal and moralistic criticism that dominated in the past towards recognition of the opportunities offered by a newer, and arguably more sophisticated, form of criticism. This move was heralded by the 1997 Dylan Thomas

Conference at Swansea University, and by the subsequent publication of the *New Casebook*, which represents the first sustained attempt to read Thomas in light of current post-Freudian and post-structural theoretical trends. Yet despite these significant developments it is true to say that, for the moment, the spectre of psychobiography, as it survives in its various mutant forms, continues to haunt Thomas's critical reception.

A case in point would be Eynel Wardi's publication *Once Below a Time: Dylan Thomas, Julia Kristeva, and Other Speaking Subjects* (2000), which develops her doctoral thesis supervised by Kristeva herself. For, even though Wardi's 'psycho-semiological' interpretation is significant in so far as it registers the possibilities of a radically new way of reading Thomas, regrettably, and somewhat curiously, given her assertion that her study will be based on a dialogical principle that suggests the equal status of literature and psychoanalysis,[8] her account does appear to finally resolve itself into what might well be described as a kind of Holbrookian attempt to recover a latent text, a document that will somehow yield up the psychology of its author. Indeed, in the concluding chapter of her book, Wardi makes explicit, and lengthy, reference to Holbrook, asserting that 'Holbrook's analysis of Thomas in *The Code of Night* is perhaps one of the most pertinent that I have encountered', and acknowledging some kind of parallel gesture she admits:

> My interpretation of Thomas's letter is largely congruous with David Holbrook's analysis of the nature and the reception of his work in general. That analysis seems to coincide with the manifest content of the letter as well as with the critical judgement which colours it. Highly sensitive to the dissociative aspect of Thomas's work, Holbrook diagnoses what he generally deems to be its symbolic failure as symptomatic of the poet's suicidal 'schizoid predicament', namely, the predicament of a suspended psychic birth whose attempted achievement is doomed by hate-ridden, splitting ('paranoid schizoid') defensive strategies. Holbrook's purpose of investigating what he once defined as Thomas's 'not-poetry' is largely to explain its strong impact, as reflected in the 'immense industry' of Dylan Thomas criticism.
>
> Holbrook's analysis has been useful for me for a variety of reasons. In the first place, his psychoanalytic approach is very close to my own, and allows him to discern issues of textuality and intersubjectivity which will be the focus of this chapter.[9]

Wardi is however not alone, for it would seem that a whole range of contemporary interpretations have been applied which, on closer inspection, appear to mimic that 'recurring slide from author text to author' noted by Catherine Belsey as characteristic of the moralizing brand of criticism propounded and popularized by F. R. Leavis,[10] and which can be seen in Holbrook's condemnation of Thomas's 'lack of control and failure to organise deeply felt experience'; 'Leavisite categories whose moralistic animus', as Stewart Crehan observes, 'could take in the man, his public image and his working methods in one fell swipe':[11] 'Dylan Thomas's attitude to his work was a struck pose of carelessness, and frenzied spontaneity, *at least in public*'.[12]

Avoiding a biography-based approach, this volume will concentrate primarily on Thomas's early poetry with the aim of liberating it from the position of servitude to the discursive mastery of psychoanalysis, as established by the ad hominem readings of Holbrook et al., by placing the poetry and psychoanalysis together in a mutually illuminating dialogue.[13] As such, this study will attempt to demonstrate the ways in which the vital connection between psychoanalysis and Thomas's early poetry can be articulated without reductive simplification. To this end, it will replace the psychoanalytical models of Freud with those of Lacan and Kristeva, while also remaining alert to related developments in postmodern and poststructural modes of textual analysis.

'THE POETS WERE THERE BEFORE ME': THE INTERSECTIONS OF POETRY AND PSYCHOANALYSIS

> For, all mental systems, the Freudian psychology is the one which makes poetry indigenous to the very constitution of the mind. Indeed, the mind, as Freud sees it, is in the greater part of its tendency exactly a poetry making organ ... Freud has not merely naturalised poetry; he has discovered its status as a pioneer settler, and sees it as a method of thought.
>
> – Lodge (1972)[14]

Since its foundation, a little more than a century ago, psychoanalysis has always given a privileged place to literature. Freud himself was often noted as saying that the poets were there before him, the implication being that the findings of his psychoanalytic theory were anticipated by, and in, works of literature.[15] Not surprisingly then, Freud's most famous theory was inspired by a work of literature, the Sophoclean tragedy, *Oedipus Rex*; and indeed it could be argued that the whole tradition of psychoanalytic theory, that extends from Freud's earliest discoveries to Jacques Lacan's radical and innovative conception of psychoanalysis, consists of variations on the theme of Oedipus. Oedipus's exemplary status in psychoanalytic theory resides in the myth's illustration of the psychoanalytic claim that the human subject/psyche is constituted as a discontinuous riddle. Although it was only later in his career that Freud referred explicitly to the Oedipus complex, he made extensive use of the story as early as 1900, so that it soon became recognized as one of the key concepts of psychoanalysis. Taking his cue from the ancient Greek tragedy, where Sophocles' protagonist unwittingly kills his father and becomes king of Thebes by marrying his mother, Freud suggested that our deepest unconscious desire is to murder our father and thereby take sole possession of the maternal figure. As such, his theory of the Oedipus complex embodies Freud's attempt to map the child's ambivalent feelings towards its parents, and stresses the importance of the resolution of those feelings. Yet, perhaps most significantly, in terms of the relationship between psychoanalysis and literature, and the way in which they reflect on one another, as well as the patricidal and incestuous themes of *Oedipus*, Freud explicitly makes use of the dramatic form of the tragedy. For him the significance of the play rests on the process it unfolds, and Freud remained emphatic in his insistence that 'The action of the play consists in nothing other than the process of revealing', a process that he was adamant could 'be likened to the work of a psychoanalysis'.[16] Here, both drama and the work of psychoanalysis are presented by Freud as works of discovery, disclosure and interpretation. And, as such, it seems that for him literature and psychoanalysis almost instantly established a relation resembling family ties, or better still, perhaps, had formed some kind of glorious romantic union. For, as Steve Vine suggests, in his authoritative publication *Literature in Psychoanalysis: A Reader*, 'psychoanalysis could be said to be "in love with literature"':

> Freud's science is fascinated by literature's seductive games, artful ruses and knowing secrets, its tantalising hints that there is 'more' to be understood, 'more' to be found in what it says than is made explicit. Literature is a tease, literature tantalises; and psychoanalysis falls in love with what it seems both to offer and withhold. It is as if literature already knew what psychoanalysis was after, as if they had been made for each other: involved, 'implicated', sharing something to which psychoanalysis finally gives its own name.[17]

From the very start it seems that Freud had regarded literature – and poetry in particular – as essential to establishing and further developing his study of the human psyche. It is perhaps understandable, then, that, on the occasion of his seventieth birthday, when greeted by a well-wisher as the 'discoverer of the unconscious', he insisted 'The Poets and Philosophers before me discovered the unconscious.'[18] But, if Freud had been the first to uncover the happy, and untroubled, union between the two disciplines, it

INTRODUCTION

was, as Rainer Emig says, Jacques Lacan, his most audacious disciple, who would 'eventually g[o] all the way in relating psychoanalysis and literature by describing psychic phenomena in terms of textual ones':

> His claim that the unconscious is structured like a language marks the turning point, while his theory of desire as displacement on the chain of signifiers brings psychoanalysis's attachment to literature back to the basic element of language, the sign.[19]

As a clinical practice or as a theoretical model, psychoanalysis is clearly, as I have argued, an interpretive strategy, which concentrates particularly, as Sue Vice has pointed out, 'on the language which tries to render the body's experiences, the role of sexuality in defining the self, and the construction of subjectivity and gender':

> It might seem strange to use a therapeutic, medical practice (Freud, after all, trained initially as a neurologist) as the basis for a literary theory. However, in both the kind of practice where the patient (analysand) lies on the couch talking about his or her psychic life with the analyst who sits behind, and the kind where a literary critic uses the terminology and approach of psychoanalysis to investigate a text, the workings of language are clearly very important, and it is this fundamental fact which links the two practices. This is true of Freudian psychoanalysis, often called the 'talking cure', and even more so of post-structuralist, Lacanian psychoanalysis, which takes as its object the speaking human subject, and assumes that this adult, speaking subject, is constructed *in* language. Lacan's emphasis makes clearer the link between psychoanalysis as a therapy and as a critical practice: both are concerned with the workings of language and how the unconscious is expressed in it.[20]

Hence, Lacan's 'return to Freud', which involved a radical re-reading of the works of the great master in the light of Saussurian linguistics, had the important effect of offering a sophisticated alternative to traditional applied psychoanalysis, which uses literature to validate its own clinical findings.[21] In 1926, J. W. Krutch, in his influential study of Edgar Allan Poe, referred to the 'one distinctly new problem' facing the contemporary critic: 'He must, in a word,' declared Krutch, 'endeavour to find the relationship between psychology and aesthetics.'[22] Significantly, whilst Krutch himself never actually dealt with the question, three decades later the issue was addressed directly by Lacan in his methodologically unprecedented *Seminar on the Purloined Letter*. In 1956 Lacan made public his interpretation of Poe's short story which at once revealed his radical and innovative conception of psychoanalysis and challenged literary theorists. Using Poe's text as illustrative material for his theory of the genesis of the subject in relation to language, Lacan placed literature and psychoanalysis together, for the very first time, in a mutually illuminating dialogue. In suggesting that literature could be instructive for psychoanalysis, Lacan was effectively offering a radical inversion of the traditional approach, by liberating literature from its subordinate position of slave to the master discourse of psychoanalysis.[23] For his work calls into question both the theory and practice of applied psychoanalysis, by undertaking a thorough re-assessment of the role of language in the genesis and constitution of the speaking subject. Coming into being, Lacan suggested, was inseparable from a coming to language.

'TO SHADE AND KNIT ANEW THE PATCH OF WORDS': THE CASE FOR A POST-FREUDIAN RE-READING

In a paper entitled 'The function and field of speech and language in psychoanalysis' (1953), Lacan very forcefully declared, '[i]t is the world of words that creates the world of things – things originally confused in the *hic* and *nunc* of the all in the process of coming into being'.[24] The same might have been said by Dylan Thomas. For he, too, saw the *logos*, the word itself, as the great sculptor that created order from chaos, an idea that finds clear and explicit expression in his poem 'In the beginning' (1934):

> In the beginning was the word, the word
> That from the solid bases of the light
> Abstracted all the letters of the void;
> And from the cloudy bases of the breath
> The word flowed up, translating to the heart
> First characters of birth and death.[25]

A poem that is essentially quite different, but one that again begins with the idea of beginning with the word itself, is 'Once it was the colour of saying' (1938). This is one of Thomas's many poems on the subject of writing poetry and, in the first line, by stressing the very physicality of the signifier and giving as it were 'colour' and 'shape' to words – 'the colour of saying' – Thomas offers the reader some insight into the kind of radical linguistic materiality that governed his poetic practice. Of course, Thomas's ostensibly ungrammatical use of language has consistently been seen as the distinguishing feature of his work, and, as his own flamboyant response to an enquiry about his use of technical devices indicates, he was fully aware of what Goodby and Wigginton describe as 'its central even compulsive nature':[26]

I am a painstaking, conscientious, involved, and devious craftsman in words
... I use everything and anything to make my poems work and move in the
direction I want them to: old tricks, new tricks, puns, portmanteau-words,
paradox, allusion, paronomasia, paragram, catachresis, slang, assonantal
rhymes, vowel rhymes, sprung rhythm. Every device there is in language is
there to be used[27]

Highlighting the importance of verbal association in the construction of the poetry, Stewart Crehan notes how, from the outset, Thomas explicitly rejected the poetic model whereby 'rhyme and metre, image and metaphor are employed primarily as a means of shaping and "dressing" ... observations and reflections derived from ordinary experience'. For Thomas, whose poetic creed was to make poems out of words rather than to work towards words, instead of simply describing visual objects, the true poet treats words themselves as objects.[28] Implicit in this practice is the recognition of that Lacanian perception quoted above, that 'it is the world of words that creates the world of things'. Yet, curiously, despite the primacy that he grants to words, and his concomitant focus on the materiality of language, throughout the history of Thomas's critical reception, as I have already shown, psychoanalytic interpretations have been applied in which there has been a marked tendency, both implicitly and explicitly, to privilege the psychosexual over the psycho-linguistic elements of the work. His distinctive use of language has been treated as symptomatic of his (supposedly damaged, infantile or otherwise regressive) psychic state. The wealth of sexual and pseudo-sexual imagery that typifies the earlier poetry in particular has acquired a negative charge, and has been used to support the claim that Thomas the poet was, indeed, the epiphon of his own disturbed psyche. Holbrook's unreflective Freudian scenario is, of course, the apotheosis of this general reading that makes Thomas a victim of regression, reducing the poetry to the expression and recreation of the poet's schizoid neuroses.[29]

Yet, to say that his poetry functioned as a therapy, bringing up repressed material from the subconscious, and dealing with it in some kind of integrative manner, would be wrong. For, although it might be argued that there is an unconscious element at work in the Notebook Poems, the overt sexual motifs that characterize the poetry from 1934 on are in themselves sufficient evidence to suggest a very deliberate textual strategy on Thomas's part – a strategy that, I would argue, was central to the development of his highly original style. Thomas, in fact, very consciously makes (to quote Stewart Crehan) a 'Freudian exemplar' of himself, as both his controlled and artificial use of language and his verse form, which can be said to exemplify Freud's theory of psychic balance and the human personality, suggest, and as such blatantly manipulates a pervasive Freudian discourse to tease the reader into his poetry.[30] The explicit sexual charge of 'a candle in the thighs' is, for instance, indicative of the deliberate play with recurrent Freudian motifs, that has become a key feature of the writing. Yet, many of those who remain ignorant of his meticulous working methods have been deceived into believing that the poetry was a 'spontaneous and irrational outpouring', and as such, have failed to recognize the complexity of his challenge at the level of language that is, I believe, central to any serious discussion of the writing.[31]

Given that lifelong fascination with words that governed Thomas's poetic practice, it seems that a Lacanian reassessment is long overdue, for, in terms of their shared emphasis on the role of language, there are, it seems, a number of urgent and illuminating parallels to be drawn between the two writers. Thomas's use of language is certainly the feature of the writing that is most likely to capture the reader's imagination. Indeed, the characteristic richness and verbal density of the mesmeric lyrics, which arise from his controlled and artificial use of language, is widely recognized as the hallmark of his poetry. Indeed, I would argue that Thomas's bravura display of linguistic and psychic structures, and the way in which they bear upon the formation of the self, and hence all forms of authority, both demands and deserves a sustained post-Freudian re-reading. Throughout this study, then, emphasis will be placed on the psycho-linguistic elements of his early work, and correspondingly the jouissance, or the textual effect, of the writing.

Thomas's jouissance, it might be argued, arises from the power of the characteristic rhetorical innovations which jar the reader out of his everyday understanding of words, bringing his relation with language to a crisis. As such, I would suggest that, by removing words from their taxonomic restraints, Thomas wrests the familiar into the strange, and that, like the surrealists, he could further be said to adopt an aesthetic of the uncanny. The vision that the poetry articulates and embodies is one in which the authoritarian repressiveness of discursive language is, we might say, subverted by a radical linguistic materialism. This, then, exults in the multiplicity of sonorous meanings, which are often communicated before being understood. Thomas's liberal use of assonance, alliteration and heavy rhythm contribute to the sensory impact of the rich baroque writing, where the flavour, and colour, of words becomes an integral part of the way the language is being deployed. This principle creates a world that is physically exciting, sonorous and hypnotic in effect, intuitional as well as emotive and sensory in its communicative power.

It is my basic contention, then, that as body, mind and world overlap, in a way that normal modes of discourse find impossible to express, the writing becomes a vital articulation of the merging of human and natural forces, gesturing implicitly towards a pre-symbolic (and therefore effectively pre-verbal) stage of symbiotic unity, which Lacan theorized as the 'imaginary'. This is the time of absolute identification with the other – that precedes the castrating effects of the symbolic order, reaching back to that almost 'Edenic' bliss so powerfully evoked in Thomas's early poetry. From a post-Freudian perspective, it seems that the poetry, in its conscious articulation of those moments beyond language – death, sexual union and the embryonic – signifies an attempt to recover that lost state of bliss and plenitude, from which the speaking subject is irrevocably separated. As such, poetic discourse is very clearly for Thomas a means of restoring a nostalgic intimacy with the 'thing itself', since it is the fossilization of the signifier-signified bond that his writing subverts, attacking the repression of our own pre-moral delight in words. This, I would suggest, is indicative of the operation of the semiotic, as theorized by Julia Kristeva in her development of Lacanian thought, in Thomas's early poetry. Moreover, since the semiotic is associated explicitly with sonority and rhythm, with the stuff of speech, in which language coalesces with the body and the orchestration of the drives, I would suggest that there is, in fact, an explicit thematic correspondence with Thomas's poetry that would make Kristeva's theoretical contribution essential to any post-Freudian discussion of his work. For it is my contention that Kristeva's sophisticated revision of both Freud and Lacan has a specific relevance in terms of the early poetry, and can be used to shed a positive and new critical light on what David Holbrook dismissed as his 'babble language' which satisfied his readers' demands for some sort of perverse infantile regression.

The book is divided into three sections. Broadly speaking, the first section deals with the subject of Thomas's poetic development as a belated and marginal, but positive and critically engaged, modernist. Part two deals with Thomas's exuberant linguistic experimentation, which is widely recognized as being the defining feature of his work. And the final section of the book is devoted to Thomas's obsessive fascination with the body, 'the strong stressing of the physical' as he put it.

Part one – Dylan Thomas's jouissance of influence – will focus on Thomas's literary, social and historical contexts. The larger framework for this approach is my view of Thomas as a belated, but positive and critically engaged, marginal modernist, whose radical style is interpretable as a hybrid near-parody of high modernism, one which subjects the 'difficulty' of modernist poetry to the constraints of traditional verse-forms. Taking my initial cue from Harold Bloom's spectacularly daring theory of influence, which undertakes the mammoth task of re-writing literary history in terms of an 'oedipal agon' (a wrestling with the writer's most powerfully influential precursors/progenitors), I argue that it would be a mistake to read the complex nature of Thomas's relationship with his most immediate literary forebears (Eliot, the high priest of modernism, and Auden, the un-crowned but undisputed leader of the literary left) in terms of the Freudian family romance. There is, I propose, no evidence in the poetry to suggest any kind of agonistic struggle on Thomas's part. Indeed, rather than exhibiting any form of 'anxiety of influence', Thomas's richly inter-textual writing displays what might well be described as a 'jouissance of influence' – a heady, sensuous, exuberant delight in creative kinship – which allows us to liberate Bloom's own highly suggestive notion of a major author's creatively liberating 'misreading' of his/her predecessors from the Oedipal straitjacket to which he confined it. In order to provide some theoretical understanding of the psychic and psychological processes involved in shaping and establishing his poetic ego, Thomas is here interpreted in the light of the models of psychic and poetic development proposed not by Freud and Bloom but by Kristeva and Lacan.

Thomas's poetry, like the psychoanalytic theory of Lacan and, indeed, Kristeva, is much concerned with creation and origins, and hence with conception, birth and infancy. But if Lacan was concerned, exclusively, with the birth of the speaking subject, the multiplicity of twentieth-century births to which Thomas's poetry implicitly bears witness also entails a gesture towards sexual awareness and, perhaps most importantly, towards the process of formation of a poetic voice. Accordingly, his poetry invariably parallels the transitional state of infancy with that of adolescence. A case in point would be 'From love's first fever' (1934), which offers a thematic paradigm for Thomas's own poetic development. It stages the movement from a primary identification with the maternal, associated as it is in his experience with the materiality of language, through to his successful interpellation, via the paternal metaphor, into the symbolic order of tradition and genre that make possible for Thomas a poetic maturity and a position, albeit an ambivalent one, within the pantheon of English literature. This poetic summation of his own development is quite remarkable and since, in many ways, it actually seems to anticipate that post-Freudian synthesis of Lacanian and Kristevan thinking that informs this book, it is discussed in detail in this first chapter.

Chapter 2 charts the poet-self's journey from the specular moment of his primary identification with the literary other, to the achievement of authenticity and a mature style. Close attention is paid at this point to the four extant notebooks (1930–4) that chart Thomas's development in those crucial, formative years. The progression from the early experiments in *vers libre* that we see in the first two notebooks to poetic synthesis, and the inauguration of the hybrid 'process style', that is first heralded by an unexpected breakthrough in April 1933 (notebook three) with the composition of 'And death shall have no dominion', is understood (and here we encounter Lacanian terms that will be explained clearly) as involving a movement from the imaginary specular projection of the ideal ego (the infant's narcissistic perception of itself as/in a mirror) to the ego ideal as a symbolic introjection. This process has been glossed as follows by Slavoj Žižek:

> the 'ideal ego' stands for the idealized self-image of the subject (the way I would like to be, I would like others to see me); the Ego-Ideal is the agency whose gaze I try to impress with my ego image, the big Other who watches over me and propels me to give my best, the ideal I try to follow and actualize; and the superego is this same agency in its revengeful, sadistic, punishing, aspect. The underlying structuring principle of these three terms is clearly Lacan's triad Imaginary-Symbolic-Real: ideal ego is imaginary, what Lacan calls the 'small other', the idealized double-image of my ego; Ego-Ideal is symbolic, the point of my symbolic identification, the point in the big Other from which I observe (and judge) myself;[32]

In other words, the movement is one from primary to secondary identification, which is supported and facilitated by Kristeva's concept of the 'imaginary father', her version of a 'loving' third term. For Thomas is, it seems, propelled into the Symbolic of literary tradition, not through any Freudian, or Bloomian, fear of castration but rather through pleasure, or jouissance, and excess.

If chapter 2 charts the poet-self's journey, then chapter 3 focuses its subsequent interpellation within the Symbolic of literary tradition. Of course, as Lacan reminds us, however well adjusted a subject might be, he/she can never entirely escape the Imaginary, just as he/she can never truly rid him/herself of the pressures of the Real. And this certainly seems relevant to an understanding of Thomas's ambivalent position within the canon. For even though Thomas did undoubtedly always have his eye on London publication, he never really shared Eliot's reverence for tradition, or his desire to assume a position of true patriarchal authority within the pantheon of English literature. Chapter 3, then, highlights the playful and near parodic fusion of the contemporary and near contemporary that is the hallmark of Thomas's mature style. Detailed poetic analysis again confirms that his work bears no evidence of any kind of agonistic struggle such as Bloom proposes is inevitable for an aspiring young author. Rather, it exhibits a jubilant or festive excess, a jouissance of influence, as revealed in his extension of high modernist practice to include a playful and uncanny simulacrum of avant-garde style, that is at once a mockery of it and a tribute to it. One of a plethora of examples discussed here is that of the highly provocative 'Now' (1935). Although the text hints at Dada, *zaum* and nonsense poetry, its peculiarly shaped stanzas can, in fact, be disconcertingly resolved into perfectly traditional forms. the total syllabic-count of the first four lines (one, two, three, and four) adds up to that of an iambic pentameter, while the next three complete a symmetrical, quatrain pattern (ten and eleven alternately), pararhyming 'anchor' / 'anger', and highlights the difficulties involved in attempting to contextualise Thomas. In fact, it might be said that Thomas, like some kind of spectre, uncannily haunts the boundaries and borders of literary tradition. A destabilizing and disruptive force within the pantheon, he sits uneasily between Eliot and Auden. Rather like Hamlet, who wishes to identify with the Name-of-the-Father but is bound to the mother's desire, Thomas is, we might say, in this case a liminal, or mixed, character – what Lacan would wittily describe as an *hommelette* – and he seems quite happy to continue existing in this semi-transitional space.

The second section of the book, 'Presenting and Representing the Unpresentable', will take as its focus the concept of the Real (the realm that lies forever beyond the reach of conceptualization and verbalization), which by definition resists any form of verbalization or symbolization. Drawing on the idea of a postmodern sublime (as theorized by Jean François Lyotard) I will suggest that the festive radicalism of the signifier in Thomas's early work is his way of gesturing towards the un-presentable, and as such would seem to indicate the presence of a postmodern impulse in his writing which has hitherto been unexplored.

In a letter postmarked 21 March 1938, Thomas wrote to his close friend and fellow Swansea poet Vernon Watkins recommending that he introduce a 'destructive' element into his poem 'Call It All Names, But Do Not Call It Rest':

> A motive has been rarefied, it should be made common. I don't ask you for vulgarity, though I miss it; I think I ask you for a little creative destruction

destructive creation ... [a]ll the words are lovely, but they seem so *chosen*, not struck out. I can see the sensitive picking of words, but none of that strong inevitable pulling that makes a poem an event, a happening, an action perhaps, not a still-life or an experience *put down*, placed, regulated.

This passage illuminatingly complements what he was saying about his *own* method at this time. His lengthy critique rests on his objection that Watkins's poem appears to have been born 'out of the nostalgia of literature', so that it seems more 'literary' than 'living ... a poem so obviously written in words'. Of course, as a writer whose declared aim was that a poem should do more than merely appear to have been created, Thomas remained acutely aware of the fundamental limitations of language as a mode of artistic expression. Yet, without wishing to discount any obvious sense of the conventional, essentially Romantic, conflict between a poem's emotional impulse and its imprisonment in language, there are, I think, far greater issues at stake here for Thomas. Issues which, when taken in the broader context of his characteristically modernist, and paradigmatically 'poetic' practice, seem to extend beyond the Romantic dilemma of imaginative creation and into a radical questioning of both the internal limits and the status of language itself.

Using the idea, then, of a postmodern Thomas to furnish a starting point for my discussion, I will suggest in this chapter that Thomas's poetic of excess, with its playful materiality and valorization of plurality, enacts a postmodern awareness of difference and heterogeneity. As such, it inevitably critiques and destabilizes the closed forms and systems favoured by high modernism, partly in the interests of exploring the 'un-sayable', the 'invisible' and the 'incommunicable'. This latter concern of Thomas's will then be explained in terms of the third of Lacan's topological categories, the Real, which will provide the theoretical and conceptual framework for this section.

Thomas, like Lacan, sees the process of separation (from the Real) as being caused by language. And this accounts partially, at least, for his ambivalent attitude towards words. For, whilst Thomas was a self-declared and unashamed lover of words,[33] he nevertheless recognized the inherent inadequacy of the verbal medium as a mode of artistic expression. And whilst it is true to say that there is no real sense in his writings of his modernist precursors' scepticism towards language, Thomas did in fact foster what might now be characterized as a basic postmodern belief in its incommensurate qualities. Indeed, on occasion he found himself so consumed with frustration that not only did it become inscribed in the symbolic structures of the poetry itself but actually acquired a specific thematic significance. This point is developed clearly in chapter 4 through detailed analysis of 'The force that through the green fuse' (1933), which is read as a dramatization of the psychic conflict between the Symbolic and the Real. The speaker in that poem is ever reminded of his inability to communicate, so that he remains forever 'dumb to tell'. In like manner, 'How shall my animal?' (1938) offers a poetic summation of the conflict between the orders of the Real, the Imaginary and the Symbolic, re-enacted in Thomas's articulation of the self-contradictory nature of writing poetry.

Throughout his career Thomas displayed a concern to communicate a sense of those moments normally deemed to be beyond language – most notably birth, death, conception and sexual union. Although such moments are by no means limited to the 'process poetry' it is nevertheless there that this gesture towards the Real becomes most apparent. Chapter 5 therefore concentrates on this early group of texts (including 'A process in the weather of the heart' (1934), 'Light breaks where no sun shines' (1933) and 'Where once the waters of your face' (1934)) in order to investigate in detail the specific ways in which his poetry manages to communicate something of that vitality and physicality that Lacan calls the Real, and which is generally inaccessible to normative discourse.

The final section of the volume – 'Re-routing Abjection, from Pessimism to Parody' – returns to this subject of the Real, but here attention is specifically focused on the real of the body and of bodily discourse, which manifests itself as the affective materiality not only of flesh but of language in Thomas's writing. His early work is here shown to posit a concern to challenge the ways in which the body has traditionally been relegated to a subordinate position relative to the primacy of the mind. Yet, if Thomas's fascination with the physical, which also, importantly, includes the materiality of discourses, seems to concur with current theoretical trends, his privileging of the body, 'the strong stressing of the physical', as he put it, coupled with what might well be described as an excessive emphasis on the acoustic tissues of the word, placed him immediately at odds with both his contemporaries and near contemporaries. To illustrate this, the discussion makes use at this point of Julia Kristeva's theory of abjection, in support of the argument that Thomas's return to the body or, more precisely, to bodily signification (whereby language coalesces with the orchestration of the drives), can be read as a parodic 'outing', or carnivalesque re-inscription, of what Eliot's high modernism, with its aesthetic of abstraction, impersonality, intellectuality and emotional distance, had so desperately attempted to repress.

Between November 1933 and December 1936 Thomas wrote at least seven letters that referred specifically to his use of anatomical imagery. The first of these, dated early November 1933 and written to Pamela Hansford Johnson, is particularly significant, because it includes an early statement of the poetic principles associated with the body. I place this important piece of correspondence in dialogue with Kristeva's theory of abjection in order to provide the theoretical and conceptual framework for this final section. Chapter 7 accordingly argues that, through his poetry, Thomas reclaims the body, harnessing its energies and celebrating it as a site of subversive potentialities. The poems challengingly project the threat of an all too solid and 'fleshy' corporeality into what for male modernists and mid-century critics alike was a horrible and menacingly close proximity. This re-turn to the body by Thomas is performed most rigorously and most creatively in *18 Poems*. Hence, chapter 6 will concentrate on a selection of texts from this first volume – 'When once the twilight locks' (1934), 'A process in the weather of the heart' (1934), 'Before I knocked' (1933), 'Light breaks where no sun shines' (1934), 'I dreamed my genesis' (1934). These early works have come to be collectively known as Thomas's 'womb and tomb' poems, and reveal a grim biological reductionism which, importantly, is always offset by a playful excess of signification. It is perhaps here that we best see how Thomas differs so profoundly from the Eliot of *The Waste Land*. For, in its body-centredness, Thomas's writing might be said to stage the abject – not simply in its vital articulation of the 'abject mother', figured partly via the intra-uterine poetic locus of these works, but also in its more general foregrounding of a vivid and visceral panorama of corporeality. This immediately set Thomas in opposition to the agendas of an elitist and profoundly masculinist modernism with its narratives of absence, exclusion and concealment.

Chapter 7 draws on Lacan's later theorization of the *sinthome*, and Žižek's notion of 'the obscene object', to suggest that the hyper-visibility of flesh in the early poetry can be read as a parodic outing of Eliot's demonized and displaced body. That manoeuvre, it is then argued, established Thomas as the *sinthome* to Eliot's repressed symptom. Perhaps the most shocking and crudely spectacular manifestation of what Žižek might call Thomas's 'obscene object' is the blasphemous identification of Christ with the most literal symbol of phallic authority, the male member or penis. Through detailed reference to 'If I were tickled by the rub of love' (1934) and 'My hero bares his nerves' (1933), it is argued that the 'over-proximity' of both flesh and language that distinguishes Thomas's early work, and which seems to persist as a surplus to Eliot's own abject text, is pushed to its parodic limit in the blasphemous figure of Thomas's 'Jack of Christ'. Thus, the movement from symptom to *sinthome* might be said to re-route abjection from pessimism to parody.

Part One

'[M]aking deadly whoopee': Dylan Thomas's Jouissance of Influence

To proceed to a more intelligible exposition of the relation of the poet to the past: he can neither take the past as a lump, an indiscriminate bolus, nor can he form himself wholly on one or two private admirations, nor can he form himself wholly on one preferred period. The first course is inadmissible, the second is an important experience of youth, and the third is a pleasant and highly desirable supplement.

T. S. Eliot, 1919

he brings back into present time the origins of his own person. And he does this in a language that allows his discourse to be understood by his contemporaries, and which furthermore presupposes their present discourse.

Jacques Lacan, 1958

Am I not father too, and the ascending boy ...?

Dylan Thomas, October 1935

Chapter 1

'Every writer', as Jorge Luis Borges neatly puts it, 'creates his own precursors. His work modifies our conception of the past, as it will modify the future.'[1] And this is certainly true of Dylan Thomas: as the inheritor of a modernism rendered problematic at a time of formal re-entrenchment in British poetry his work illuminates and is illuminated by both his predecessors and contemporaries alike. Yet, when his first slim volume, the laconically titled *18 Poems*, appeared in 1934, a modernist lineage was anything but apparent to early reviewers. Indeed, for an audience whose readerly expectations had been nurtured largely on the modish propagandist verse of the preceding three to four years, the impression of sheer originality, created by his stylistically radical and rhetorically innovative writing, made the collection appear as if it were entirely without precedent. This said, however, the reception of *18 Poems* was not, as John Ackerman has remarked, unlike the 'baffled astonishment' that had greeted T. S. Eliot's iconic poem, *The Waste Land*, more than a decade earlier.[2] Different though their impact and message were, the shared insistence on complexity, innovation and an altogether explosive linguistic experimentation made the work of both these poets, particularly on first appearance, seem unparalleled and utterly unprepared for. And this, I would suggest, certainly goes some way to providing an explanation for the bewildering array of critical reactions to their work.

Although Eliot's 1917 volume, *The Love Song of J. Alfred Prufrock and Other Observations*, had won the attention of the London literary avant-garde, it was of course his longer poem, *The Waste Land*, that launched him as a public figure. Overnight he became known to a readership that extended far beyond the small bohemian coterie in London with which he had been associated since his arrival there in 1914. Yet, ever since its first appearance in 1922, *The Waste Land* has stimulated a range of amazingly diverse reactions: if some have hailed the poem as the finest example of modernist art, reflecting in its own difficulties the complexity of the modern world, others have been suspicious about a work in which so much remains unclear, and even unfathomable. Similarly, when Thomas first came to the attention of the London literati via journal publication and culminating in the publication of *18 Poems* in December 1934, his work stimulated a bewildering array of critical responses. Early publicists and defenders, like Edith Sitwell and Herbert Read, were inclined to statements such as Read's famous 'these poems cannot be reviewed; they can only be acclaimed'.[3] Though equally vehement in his response, Thomas's contemporary, Stephen Spender, on the other hand, could see 'just poetic stuff with no beginning or end, or intelligent or intelligible control'.[4] The more common and less extreme reactions that lay between these poles, although generally acknowledging the work to be powerful, original and astonishingly accomplished for a first volume, still tended to refer to the writing as 'obscure', 'incomprehensible' and 'baffling'. The parallels with the reception of Eliot's work are striking and, I would argue, more than merely coincidental to a properly contextualized understanding of Thomas, as a belated, but positive and critically engaged, modernist. However, whilst Eliot's modernist credentials were firmly established, those of Thomas were most certainly not. If anything, there was a stubborn and insistent inability on the part of early reviewers to conceive of him as anything other than a *sui generis* writer, 'a kind of literary naïf', as John Goodby puts it, 'who had emerged, Rimbaud-like, from a Welsh literary nowhere, [and] whose *hywl* [sic] and bardicism were an instinctual, "Celtic" revolt against the urbane, cerebral and socially discursive style of New Country'.[5]

Only one reviewer of *18 Poems*, Desmond Hawkins, appears to have grasped the significance of Thomas's unique hybrid fusion of Eliot and Auden:

> [T]he Audenesque convention is nearly ended; and I credit Dylan Thomas with being the first considerable poet to break through fashionable imitation and speak an unborrowed language, without excluding anything that has preceded him ... he is a grateful heir to Eliot's magical sense of the macabre and to Auden's textual firmness, but by inheritance rather than by imitation ... Airmen and pylons are no longer stewed to a smooth fluency ... [Thomas] is at present obsessed with the vocabulary of physiology in its more sinister aspect, and he is apt to repeat certain block-phases of a private code of thought.

These are minor faults, however, and they vanish in the achievement of fusing metaphysical poetry into sensuous terms.[6]

Hawkins's assertion that Thomas was not in fact, as the vast majority of early reviewers had suspected, a *sui generis* writer but the 'grateful heir' to both Auden and Eliot, will form the basic premise throughout the following discussion of what might well be described as Thomas's imploded simulacrum of modernism. It will become apparent that the writing must be seen in its proper context, as a positive response to the high modernist poetry of 1918–28. It would certainly be true to say that Thomas's hybrid tactics do indeed have much to do with his own hybrid identity, or sociocultural displacements, making it possible to read his poetry in a postcolonial way, and revealing hybridity to be transformed into a source of power. But this section of the book will concentrate more specifically on the way in which his unique fusion of the contemporary and the near contemporary is underwritten by an acute sense of belatedness. Distanced as he was from the literary epicentre, Thomas very consciously turned this 'belatedness' to his own aesthetic advantage.

That writers assimilate and then consciously or unconsciously affirm or deny the achievements of their predecessors is, of course, as Sandra M. Gilbert and Susan Gubar have remarked, a central fact of literary history:

> a fact whose aesthetic and metaphysical implications have been discussed in detail by theorists as diverse as T. S. Eliot, M. H. Abrahams, Erich Auerbach, and Frank Kermode. More recently, some literary theorists have begun to explore what we might call the psychology of literary history – the tensions and anxieties, hostilities and inadequacies writers feel when they confront not only the achievements of their predecessors but the tradition of genre, style, and metaphor that they inherit from such 'forefathers'. Increasingly, these critics study the way in which, as J. Hillis Miller has put it, a literary text 'is inhabited ... by a long chain of parasitical presences, echoes, allusions, guests, ghosts of previous texts'.[7]

The first and foremost student of what might be described as this kind of literary psychohistory has been Harold Bloom. Applying Freudian structures to literary genealogies, Bloom has postulated that the dynamics of literary history arise from the poet's 'anxiety of influence', that innate fear that he is not his own autonomous creator because the works of his predecessors assume some essential priority over his own works. The 'anxiety of influence' is thus Bloom's metaphor of literary paternity: his paradigm of the sequential historical relationship between poets (and poet-critics) is the relationship of father and son, specifically as defined by Freud. Thus in Bloom's account a 'strong poet' must engage in heroic warfare with his 'precursor', for involved as he is in a literary Oedipal struggle a man can only become a poet by somehow invalidating his poetic father.

When Thomas came of age as a poet in the early 1930s the poetic father was, of course, the premature patriarch W. H. Auden. Offering a viable alternative to the increasingly right-wing orientations of Eliot and Pound, Auden became so influential that critics named an entire generation of poets after him. But if the 'Auden gang' were busily engaged in slavish imitation of the exalted and newly appointed leader of the literary left, Thomas, who took no reputation for granted, was far more ambivalent in his response.

Bloom's theory of influence is certainly useful for exploring the psycho-literary history of Thomas's own poetic development, as long as one jettisons the central premise of a writer's struggle to the death with his/her most seminal literary ancestors. Thomas's relationship with his poetic 'elders' rather took the form of a sheer delight in ambivalent, exuberant play with their legacy. In this chapter, then, I will place Thomas in dialogue with Lacan and, also, with Julia Kristeva and attempt to read the enigma of his relationship with Auden and Eliot in terms of Kristeva's 'imaginary father', and the Lacanian Oedipal complex [*sic*], according to which the father, of the third stage of Freud's Oedipus complex, is transformed from the depriving and identificatory rival that he there is into the legal, symbolic father. He thus becomes enabling rather than disabling, empowering rather than emasculating. And this is what Lacan means by the term 'paternal metaphor':

> In place of the imaginary phallus (understood as the mother's illusory object of desire) there is a 'metaphoric' substitution of a symbolic identification with the phallus as a *signifier* of the mother's desire (that is, as the symbol she lacks). In a word, the child is asked to abandon its identification with the mother's phallus and to identify with the father who holds the phallus as a legal symbol.[8]

It would seem, then, that Lacan's *re*formulation of his predecessor's doctrine corresponds with a desire to find a solution to a problem; a problem that, as Mikkel Borch-Jacobsen insists, 'Freud was already obsessed with but that Lacan was undoubtedly the first to have deliberately confronted'.[9] That problem is the problem of identification: the alpha and omega, we might say, of the Oedipus complex – a problem that finds its origins in the mother/child dyad and culminates in the paternal metaphor.

'[F]ROM THE FIRST DECLENSION OF THE FLESH': INVENTING THE 'I'

Lacan's post-structuralist re-interpretation of the Freudian model of human psychological development is, by now, well known, but a brief and necessarily simplified overview will help establish the context of the present discussion. Lacan proposes a tri-partite schema, which involves the Real, the Symbolic and the Imaginary (RSI). These are the three 'orders' that constitute the psyche. The Imaginary is, as the term itself suggests, defined by pre-verbal images, and represents a state of symbiotic unity where the child's self-identity is wholly defined in terms of his/her biological dependence on the (m)other. The mirror stage, *stade du mirroir*, is a central feature of this order and highlights the origin of individuation, that is to say, the recognition, the understanding, that one is separate from the mother, and that *objets á* – sounds, human waste, the 'mother's touch', etc. – are also separate and distinct from the physical self. This discovery creates a sense of lack and, in turn, a desire to re-gain those things that are now felt to be 'missing'. A successful negotiation of the mirror stage precipitates the child's interpellation into the propositional and rule bound order of the Symbolic, which is characterized by an acute sense of fragmentation and division. Here the child becomes subject not only to social and cultural norms, but also, and most importantly for Lacan, to the laws of language, all of which are associated with the *nom du père*, the 'Law of the Father'. Finally, the Real belongs to that most remote part of the psyche that exists both before and beyond the specular existence of the Imaginary, and the linguistic experience of the Symbolic. A kind of primal, brute materiality, as it were, that contains those strong emotions we might associate with birth, death and sexuality, the Real remains largely inaccessible to the individual, and can be glimpsed only fleetingly in moments of joy and pain, known as jouissance. Importantly, however, it should be understood that Lacan's three orders are topological rather than chronological categories. In other words, while they are in one sense chronological, they are also, in another co-existent. The speaking subject can never, even after entering the Symbolic stage, truly rid him/herself of the Imaginary, just as he can never entirely escape the pressures of the Real. Thus, for Lacan, self-identity is entirely predicated upon the lifelong conflict between isolation and fragmentation and that innate desire for 'wholeness' and unity with the unattainable other.

Thomas's poetry, like the writings of Lacan and, indeed, Kristeva's post-Freudian psychoanalytic theory, is much concerned with creation and origins, and hence with conception, birth and infancy. But if Lacan was concerned, exclusively, with the birth of the speaking subject, the multiplicity of twentieth-century births to which Thomas's poetry implicitly bears witness also entail a gesture towards sexual awareness and, perhaps, most importantly, towards poetic voice; since the poetry invariably uses terms that are interchangeable for adolescence and infancy. This merging of the ostensibly quite disparate processes of physical and poetic development is most clearly apparent in 'From love's first fever' (1934). It is a poem that enacts the progress from a fascination with the stuff of words to awareness of their social and literary provenance and simultaneously tracks the progress from physical self-obsession to mature self-awareness.

One of the many miniature portraits of the artist that he composed in both verse and prose, this poem, by Thomas's standards at least, is a fairly simple one, and pursues the poet's life 'from creation to creation, from conception to art'.[10] It is composed in irregular blank verse, and the narrative impulse traces the chronological stages of development from conception ('the soft second' of the parents' love-fever, which resulted in a child, the 'plague' of calamitous reproduction) on to weaning, walking and talking: 'the miracle of the first rounded word' (l. 12).[11] The various stages, which broadly speaking correspond to a psychoanalytic model of psycho-sexual/psycho-linguistic development, are registered numerically: infancy with a 'one' (ll. 8–9), the beginnings of self-awareness 'two' (l. 16), puberty and adolescence 'four' (l. 20), and thence 'multiplying' with the onset of adult maturity (l. 23), in what Ralph Maud describes as 'a nice biological image of growth': 'Each golden grain spat life into its fellow' (l. 24). As the lyric narrative progresses so we are able to discern something of that characteristic overlapping of body, mind and world which has become recognized as a defining feature of Thomas's 'process' poetic. In this sense, the writing becomes a vital articulation of the merging of human and natural forces – a fusion, perhaps, that normal modes of discourse would find virtually impossible to express – and gestures both implicitly and explicitly towards a pre-Symbolic stage of primal and uninterrupted unity. This is the time of absolute identification with the (m)other: '[t]he time for breast and the green apron age', that in Lacanian parlance precedes the castrating effects of the Symbolic order, reaching back to that archaic moment of undifferentiated pre-Oedipal bliss, so powerfully evoked in the poem's opening stanza, when

> All world was one, one windy nothing,
> My world was christened in a stream of milk

> And earth and sky were as one airy hill,
> The sun and moon shed one white light.[12]

Without wishing to over-inflate the thematic correspondence with Lacan, a comparison here seems unavoidable. For Lacan's psychoanalytic configuration of the genesis of the speaking subject does seem to resonate quite remarkably with Thomas's poeticized staging of linguistic/poetic subjectivity. This begins with a primal un-gendered unity, reminiscent of the Imaginary, and moves to the first signs of identity and individuation, registered by the use of the first person singular pronoun 'my' in line seven. It progresses, in stanzas two and three, through the 'miracle of the first rounded word', to an infantile acquisition of speech. And, perhaps most importantly, since this is, after all, a narrative of the genesis of a *poet* 'self', to poetic voice also:

> From the first print of the unshodden foot, the lifting
> Hand, the breaking of the hair,
> And to the miracle of the first rounded word,
> From the secret of the heart, the warning ghost,
> And to the first dumb wonder of the flesh,
> The sun was red, the moon was grey,
> The earth and sky were as two mountains meeting.[13]

In the first stanza, through the use of the first person pronoun, we witness the very first instance of the development of an ego, of an integrated self-image: 'My world was christened in a stream of milk'. Crucially, however, and because the speaker has only just begun the process of constructing a centre of self, at this point, a blurring of subject and object still obtains: 'earth and sky were as *one* airy hill, / The sun and moon shed *one* white light' (my own emphasis). No gap has yet opened up between subject and world, or between the signifier and signified. And, so far, the speaker of Thomas's poem remains (to borrow a phrase from Terry Eagleton) 'happily un-plagued by the problems of post-structuralism'.[14] But, as Lacan has taught us, the relationship between language and reality can never be as smoothly synchronized as this situation would suggest. And this is a point that is certainly borne out by Thomas in stanzas two and three. Here, prompted by the inception of language, figured as 'the miracle of the first rounded word', the speaker is plunged into the initial awareness that identity depends upon difference, as the 'illusions' of wholeness, synthesis and, above all, similarity, give way to division, differentiation and plurality: 'sun' and 'moon', which, previously, had 'shed one white light', are now 'red' and 'grey', whilst earth and sky are distinguished from one another becoming as 'two mountains meeting'.

But if, for Lacan, the recognition of plurality and difference entails a profound sense of loss, that plunges the Lacanian subject headlong into post-structuralist anxiety, this is certainly not the case for the nascent self of Thomas's poem,[15] who jubilantly recounts how,

> the four winds, that had long blown as one,
> Shone in my ears the light of sound,
> Called in my eyes the sound of light.
> And yellow was the multiplying sand,
> Each golden grain spat life into its fellow[16]

Here, it would seem that multiplicity and division evoke not a sense of loss but a deep delight – a point endorsed by Harri Garrod Roberts who adds that '[t]his is partly to do with the construction, through language's endless proliferation, of an ever more wondrously complex and differentiated world'. But, what is perhaps even more significant for Roberts is the way in which 'this world', as he puts it, 'refuses to maintain any discrete, ordered identity': 'the poem implies that it is within the *mixing* of categories and identities that delight in life is to be found ... [t]he emphasis is thus on language's creative potential'.[17] Certainly, for a poet like Thomas, the mockingly self-styled 'Rimbaud of Cwmdonkin Drive', the complications of synaesthesia held obvious appeal. And, whilst Roberts is quite right to stress the emphasis on the creative potentialities of language, his assertion that the poem implies that it is 'within the *mixing* of categories and identities that delight in life is to be found' is simply a fallacy of logic. For even though the poetry does reject the bourgeois concept of a coherent, autonomous 'I', this is not to say that it embraces or celebrates the divided, fragmented self. What the early poetry does, in fact, is to chart the impossibility of even achieving, let alone maintaining, any unitary identity: the 'split subject' is a fact of the writing rather than a cause for celebration. Moreover, within the broader context of the early poems there are instances when the failure to achieve a coherent identity becomes something of a horrified and terrifying realization.[18] Plurality and multiplicity at the level of language are, as Roberts suggests, an entirely different matter. The slippery instabilities of the signifier are precisely what provide the energies, the driving force, of these early poems. In fact we might even go so far as to say that the writing is, above all, an assertion, a celebration even, of the aesthetic opportunities made available by language's endless proliferation into an infinite chain of signifiers.

It is hardly surprising then that the speaker of this miniature 'portrait of the artist' should share something of Thomas's own verbal infatuation. And as such it would seem that the renunciation of pre-Oedipal jouissance, that Symbolic castration normally and necessarily entails, is hugely overshadowed, for our nascent poet, by the promise of a wealth of linguistic plenitude. But things are rarely as straightforward as they might seem with Thomas. His figuration of this linguistic legacy as the 'stony idiom' does perhaps hint at something of that frustration with language, as an alienating system of signs, which seemed, at times, to temper his love affair with words.[19] This said, the overall impression that we get from the final stanzas is not, however, one of regret: Thomas clearly does not mourn this fall into the Symbolic. Rather, he embraces what might be described as a kind of Blakean fall into consciousness although, of course, transposed here into explicitly linguistic register and, as such, actually celebrates the liberation of the self cast in language. And so it is with the utopian vision of pre-Oedipal bliss having faded into little more than a distant memory, that the writing finally registers the subject's induction into the social order.

> And from the first declension of the flesh
> I learnt man's tongue, to twist the shapes of thoughts
> Into the stony idiom of the brain,
> To shade and knit anew the patch of words
> Left by the dead who, in their moonless acre,
> Need no word's warmth.[20]

Body and language are conflated here in a metaphor of grammar, 'first declension of the flesh', which like that of Latin is, of course feminine, and, significantly, in its adjectival sense acquires connotations of decline and decay, specifically denoting a kind of descent, which in this instance surely anticipates the speaker's inevitable fall into the patriarchal realm of the Symbolic, particularly as regards literary tradition. As the linguistic analogy spills seamlessly into the next strophe, decline is, however, rapidly superseded by conjugation, as the oscillation of the child/poet's vowels into intelligible speech, or the genre of poetry, figured in terms of his education in 'the verbs of will', marks his interpellation into the propositional and rule-bound system of signs. And so it is that the newly defined poet subject finally takes his place, albeit an ambivalent one, as a signifier in the structure of literary tradition. It is at this point then, according to Lacan, that the *parle-être*, the speaking being, must resign himself to the fact that he can never again have any direct access to reality, in particular to the now prohibited body of the mother:

> It has been banished from this full, imaginary possession into the empty world of language. Language is empty because it is just an endless process of difference and absence: instead of being able to possess anything in its fullness, the

child will now simply move from one signifier to another, along a linguistic chain which is potentially infinite. One signifier simply implies another, and that another, and so on ad infinitum: the metaphorical world of the mirror has yielded ground to the metonymic world of language. Along this metonymic chain of signifiers, meanings, or signifieds will be produced; but no object or person can ever be fully 'present' in this chain, because ... its effect is to divide and differentiate all identities.[21]

But for the speaker of Thomas's poem this knowledge comes as a blessing and a curse. For even though the *parle-être* can never escape the fact of his being as a creature of difference, it is precisely the conceptual and phonic differences that issue from the signifying chain that generate his poetic enterprise. Increasingly aware of words, and alert to the plural possibilities of the signifier, he is now able to 'shade and knit anew the patch of words' bequeathed to him by the great poets of the past, to refashion their linguistic legacy into the new and original shape of his own idiom.

It would seem, then, that, within the context of the poem, literary tradition is likened to the material in the individual unconscious, and relations between the generations compared to a form of transference. But, even if Thomas's speaker does appear to stand in some kind of filial relation to his forebears, this is a far more complex staging of poetic development than the Bloomian account of influence would allow. Moreover (and as will become even more apparent in the poem's final stanza), the continued insistence on plurality and difference, and the obvious sense of delight that this arouses in the speaker, seriously problematizes and calls into question the neat orderings of Blooms's quasi-Oedipal, poeticized version of the Freudian family romance.[22]

Broadly speaking, the final section of the poem as published is a recapitulation of the movement from unity to diversity.[23] Once again we see the father, figured appropriately as 'the divorcing sky', intervene, as the 'third term', in the mother/child dyad to disrupt that primary and all-encompassing relationship. But this figure of paternal authority is certainly not the castrating precursor of Bloom's Oedipal scenario, the signifier of the poet's nightmare predicament of belatedness, of having come 'too late' as it were, or after the event. Transposed into a 'million minds' that 'gave suck' he is both the social, cultural and ideological forces that intersect in the Name-of-the-Father to mediate the Imaginary dual relationship between mother and child to introduce a necessary Symbolic distance between them, *and* the Imaginary 'ideal' father as the prototype of the God-figure in all religions, the all-powerful protector.[24] Radically suspended between Symbolic and Imaginary modes, this uneasy composite bears little relation, however, to the father as he is in reality. An enabling presence, as much as the source of division and dissemination, in Thomas's poem, this powerful but radically unstable symbol of literary paternity is curiously linked to the maternal via the repetition of the verb phrase 'gave suck', and calls to mind, perhaps, Kristeva's re-configuration of a loving third term, the pre-Oedipal father, who is, amongst other things, a conglomerate of both sexes.[25]

Chapter 2

Hitherto, the Notebooks have received only scant critical attention, and have been relegated to a purely minor role.[1] The poems have been treated as significant in terms of Thomas's poetic development only in so far as they can be seen to provide the original templates for much of the material in his first three volumes.[2] They need, however, to be urgently re-visited and re-evaluated, because the text of these four manuscript exercise books, in which Dylan Thomas fair copied approximately two hundred poems as he completed them during the crucial period of his youth, 1930 to 1934, provides us with a highly significant and revealing document. For the text very clearly charts the progress of the newcomer (or '*ephebe*' to use the term Harold Bloom adopted from Wallace Stevens) from admiration and initial imitation of his poetic forebears to rejection, displacement and, finally, to a crucial 'misprision' or misreading by which the newcomer, Thomas, radically deforms and re-casts the work of his precursors to make something quite new.

Paying close attention to the first of the four extant notebooks (1930)[3] and its very early experiments in *vers libre*, this chapter seeks to explain the origins of the poet-self's journey from its inauguration in what Lacan would term the specular moment of his primary identification with the literary other. This first attachment resembles something of the symbiotic unity of the Lacanian Imaginary whereby images, themes, allusions, etc. are first fed to Thomas not by a castrating precursor but by a nourishing literary mother, since there is no evidence in the writing to suggest any kind of Oedipal anxiety on Thomas's part. Furthermore, as will be shown in the next chapter, Thomas is, it seems, propelled into the Symbolic of literary tradition, not through fear of castration but through pleasure, or jouissance and excess. In the asemantic manoeuvres and detours of Thomas's radical signifying practice this trace of maternal love is writ large, and repeatedly overflows its symbolic containment, so that, to cite the Lacanian model, the Semiotic is allowed to gain the upper hand over the Symbolic, as it were.

Of course, in a sense we might say that the Semiotic always had the upper hand with a Thomas who captured and was captured by its spell, possessed and obsessed with what, in a dangerously memorable phrase, he would elsewhere call 'the colour of saying'. In fact, this personal recollection of his early infatuation with the physical, material basis of language, with the 'colour' and the 'shapes' that the words suggested to him, and the way in which those rhythms first aroused and excited him, could not be bettered as an account of the lure of the Semiotic, as conceived of in the maternal terms of Julia Kristeva:

> I wanted to write poetry in the beginning because I had fallen in love with words. The first poems I knew were nursery rhymes, and before I could read them for myself I had come to love just the words of them, the words alone. What words stood for, symbolised, or meant, was of very secondary importance. What mattered was the sound of them as I heard them for the first time on the lips of those remote and incomprehensible grown-ups who seemed, for some reason, to be living in my world. And these words were, to me, as the notes of bells, the sounds of musical instruments, the noises of wind, and sea, and rain, the rattle of milk carts, the clopping of hooves on cobbles, the fingering of branches on a window pane, might be to someone, deaf from birth, who has miraculously found his hearing. I did not care what the words said, overmuch, nor what happened to Jack and Jill ... I cared for the shape of sound that their names and the words describing their actions, made in my ears; I cared for the colours the words cast on my eyes ... I fell in love with – that is the only expression I can think of – at once, and am still at the mercy of words, though sometimes now, knowing a little of their behaviour very well, I can influence slightly and have even learnt to beat them now and again, which they appear to enjoy. I tumbled for words at once. And, when I began to read ... I knew I had discovered the most important of things, to me, that could be ever ... My love for the real life of words increased until I knew that I must live with them and in them always. I knew, in fact, that I must be a writer of words, and nothing else. The first thing was to feel and know their sound and substance; what I was going to do with those words, what use I was going to make of them, what I was going to say through them, would come later.[4]

From what could be described as possibly the best account of Thomas's jouissance, it would seem that his apprenticeship to nursery rhymes like 'Mother Goose' was crucial in fostering that remarkable sensitivity to the textures and 'taste' of language that would in time become recognized as the mark of his lyric genius. But, more importantly still, Thomas's uniquely personal recollection stands as testimony to that lifelong infatuation with the sensuous material 'substance' of words – the 'shape of sound', as he cleverly called it – to which he clearly, and without hesitation, attributed his genesis as a poet.

In keeping with post-Freudian psychoanalytic theory, Thomas's primary identification – his first attachment, we might say, as a poet subject – was with the maternal as the material basis both of language and of his Semiotic signifying practice. Indeed, the idea of maternal continuity as a pre-requisite for subjectivity and for poetic identity, since Thomas's poems are always at some level about the act of writing itself, finds thematic significance in the penultimate poem of his first collection 'My world is pyramid' (*CPDT*, pp. 27, 28).

> Half of the fellow father as he doubles
> His sea-sucked Adam in the hollow hulk,
> Half of the fellow mother as she dabbles
> Tomorrow's diver in her horny milk,

Written in two parts, the poem was first published in *New Verse*, December 1934, and was, it seems, originally submitted as two separate poems.[5] In conventional terms the subject matter of this dark and mysterious poem is generally regarded as being that of human genesis: part I is a meditation on the mystery of division, whilst part II is a meditation on the divided or 'bisected' embryo. As if to reinforce the idea of division, parts I and II are more or less parallel and structured around a consistent a, b, a, b, c, c, rhyme scheme, whilst a fairly simple but effective lexis of doubling and multiplication is evident throughout: 'fellow' (ll. 1, 3), 'halves' (l. 13), 'cloven' (l. 19), 'bisected' (l. 5). Here, as in Thomas's other 'womb and tomb' poems, the intrauterine *poetic locus* and pre-natal voice of the first-person narrator serve to accentuate the central role of the maternal in the drama of human genesis and identity formation, whilst repeated references to the word 'milk' (ll. 4, 10) would seem to suggest that this continuing female presence is both nourishing and nurturing. In the broadest psycho-analytic terms, the poem, whose title seems to announce the ternary structure of the Freudian family romance, can be read as a dramatization of the fragmented, or as Thomas would have it, 'patchwork' (l. 19) identity that emerges as a consequence of the individual's successful negotiation of the Oedipus complex. Of course, from a more specifically post-Freudian perspective where attention is focused explicitly on the role of language, the 'swing of milk' (l. 10) might be read as a reference to the aural and oral pleasures of the word that in this instance can be discerned in the multiplicity of slant rhymes (rhymes in which the stressed syllables of ending consonants match, but where the preceding vowel sounds do not match) that structure the text. This use of half or slant rhyme is sometimes as explicit as 'doubles' (l. 1)/'dabbles' (l. 3) and 'bubbles' (l. 7)/'babbles' (l. 9), but often more subtle as in 'scudded' (l. 19)/'cyanide' (l. 21) or 'drill' (l. 23)/'angel' (l. 24). This use of half or slant rhyme, which is consistent in at least half of the poems in Thomas's first two collections, allows for endless variations and includes all types of cognate alliteration and assonance thus inscribing the maternal into the linguistic textures of his verse and can be seen as further confirmation of Thomas's commitment to a Semiotic signifying practice.

Yet whereas Thomas's literary identity can be seen as predicated upon the idea of a maternal continuity, in the drama of psychic splendour that surrounds Harold Bloom's epic battles of poetic giants the figure of the mother remains a curious, and unaccountable, absence. For, even though the Oedipus complex is, indeed, the basis of Bloom's theory of a young writer's inevitable struggle to the death with the main literary antecedent that threatens to stifle his talent, the ternary structure of the original Oedipus story is entirely abandoned by Bloom, since he never makes any attempt to explain or to demonstrate just how it is that the central figure of the Freudian mother fits in to his *agon* of intertextual rivalries.

But whilst Bloom would undoubtedly see this omission as a legitimate and creative malformation of the founding myth of psychoanalysis, since it involves a very consciously constructed misreading of his *own* literary forefather (Freud) which embodies 'the spirit of revenge' upon which his poetics of conflict is constructed, the erasure of the maternal remains nonetheless a stumbling block. Bloom asserts that every poet – at least since Milton – is, in a sense, belated: having grown up in the shadow of the great poets of tradition, every young writer suffers from some form of Oedipal anxiety with regards to the priority and superiority of his predecessors. Developing the Freudian theme still further, Bloom insists that the poet son, the novice or *'ephebe'*, becomes locked in Oedipal rivalry with the powerfully established poetic father who functions as a 'castrating precursor'. Deeply influenced by a 'parent poem' of the literary father, the *ephebe* experiences ambivalent feelings, compounded not only of admiration and love but also of envy, fear, aggression and even hatred. This literary version of Oedipal resentment is, of course, a consequence of the *ephebe*'s fundamental need to rebel against paternal authority in order to become autonomous and 'original' and thus to 'find his *own* voice'. As a result, for Bloom the entire history of the Western canon becomes a continuous series of 'misreadings' or 'misprisions' of earlier texts, as young, emergent, authentic or 'strong' poets attempt to first undermine and then overcome their literary fathers' position of priority (and superiority). Bloom summarizes his own theory as follows:

> Poetic Influence – when it involves two strong, authentic poets – always proceeds by a misreading of the prior poet, an act of creative correction that is actually and necessarily a misinterpretation. The history of fruitful poetic influence, which is to say the main tradition of Western Poetry since the Renaissance, is a history of anxiety and self-saving caricature, of distortion, of perverse, wilful revisionism without which modern poetry as such could not exist.[6]

According to this quasi-Oedipal scenario, Bloom's nascent poet stands in a filial relation to the figure of the literary *pater* who represents – and who, in the agon of intertextual rivalries and aliases that constitute Bloom's theory of influence, can only ever represent – the 'castrating precursor' as the punitive and legislative patriarch of Freud's nuclear complex. As such, and since any young poet inescapably identifies with a literary father who is both model and rival and wrestles with him through a precocious misprision of his work, it would seem that Bloom's *ephebe* is already inscribed within the Symbolic. But this is where I depart from Bloom, because, following Jacob Blevins, I would instead suggest that young writers – in their initial capacity as readers – are first joined to their literary forebears not in the manner decreed by Bloom, but rather in a manner which bears some resemblance to the Lacanian Imaginary and the prototypical dual relation that it entails.[7]

For Lacan, as for Freud, the process of self-identification is crucial to the formation of the 'I'. It is the 'hinge-pin' of the psychical apparatus, as both 'the source of its dynamism and the trigger for the ceaseless dramatic interplay between the individual and others'.[8] But, as Malcolm Bowie has been keen to point out, Lacan differs radically from Freud in his assertion that this process needs to be observed in its very earliest prototypical (and therefore pre-Oedipal) form if it is to have any true or 'compelling explanatory force':

> By the onset of the Oedipus complex, the infant is already too old, and the range of his or her possible identificatory manoeuvres too wide, for explanations based solely upon the principle of identification to be other than cumbersome or obscure. [And so] Lacan invites us to look back beyond the play of rivalries and aliases that the Oedipal phase initiates, and to behold an

anterior world in which the individual has only *one* object of desire and *one* alias – himself.⁹

This anterior world, that Thomas might well have described as that of being '[o]nce below a time', is of course the Imaginary, that realm of undifferentiated pre-Oedipal plenitude which, as was shown in chapter 1, knows neither difference nor division.¹⁰ It is structured solely in terms of the unificatory mother/child dyad and the absolute merging of self and other that that entails. It is here, according to Lacan, in this condition which precedes and pre-dates the emergent self's claim to subjectivity, that the recognition of oneself as 'I' first occurs. According to Lacan's theorization of the mirror stage (also translated in English as the 'looking glass phase') – the paradigm of his Imaginary – the ego is, above all, the result of identifying with one's own specular (i.e. reflected) image. The key to this phenomenon, as Dylan Evans has pointed out, lies in the prematurity of the human baby:

> [A]t six months the baby still lacks coordination. However, its visual system is relatively advanced which means it can recognize itself in the mirror before attaining control over its bodily movements. The baby sees its image as a whole [or gestalt], and the synthesis of this image produces a sense of contrast with the uncoordination [*sic*] of the body, which is experienced as a *fragmented body*; this contrast is first felt by the infant as a rivalry with its *own* image, because the wholeness of the image threatens the subject with fragmentation, and the mirror stage thereby gives rise to an aggressive tension between the subject and the image.¹¹

In an attempt to resolve this tension, the nascent self identifies with its specular (or reflected) image; and it is this primary identification with the counterpart that forms the basis of the ego. This specular moment, the moment of identification when the uncoordinated subject first identifies with its attractively holistic visible image and thereby comes to self-recognition, is described by Lacan as being accompanied by a sense of jubilation. This is because the experience is accompanied by an imaginary sense of mastery and autonomy, of synthesis and wholeness: '[the infant's] joy is due to his imaginary triumph in anticipating a degree of muscular coordination that he has not yet actually achieved'.¹²

Of course the mirror mentioned by Lacan does not necessarily need to be a literal looking glass. What is important at this stage is that the infant identifies with its projective reflection, whether that be the mirror image that it first beholds in the looking glass, or the imitative gestures that it sees reflected in the behaviour of the mother, of another child, or indeed of any significant other. The equivalent of this mirror stage in the case of the nascent poet is the point at which he equates with the projective reflection that he first beholds in the work of the great chosen precursor he regards as his literary other. The image that the infant (or emergent poet) sees is him/herself. And this identification is crucial. For, in so far as the mirror image is a 'paraphrase of the nascent ego', it does more than merely allow the infant to formulate, however hazily, the propositions 'I am that', 'that is me'.[13] Without the anticipation of mastery and autonomy that the specular moment provides, the infant could never hope to progress to the point of perceiving him/herself in terms of a gestalt, as a total form, a complete or whole being. The same could be said of the young emergent poet because, as Lacan steadily developed his concept of the mirror stage, his stress fell less on its historical value as an account of a specific stage in early infant development, and more on its representing a permanent structure of subjectivity. It came, for the mature Lacan, to represent a *stade* (state/stadium) in which the subject is permanently captured and captivated by its own image.

This idea of the later Lacan that one's self-image is, from its very earliest beginning and therefore constitutionally, caught in a continuous cycle of creation and re-creation certainly seems relevant to an understanding of the way in which poetic style is very often a matter of permanent evolution and goes some way to explaining why it is that poets, even after consolidating a mature style, continue to be such inveterate magpies, always on the lookout for materials that can augment their own creative being. And this is very much at odds with the limited temporal logic of the crude developmental model that underpins Bloom's 'Theory of Influence', according to which a nascent poet must overcome the pressures of his first imitative gestures in order to accede to a fixed and final position of priority.[14] Instead, the Lacanian ego is, like a modernist text, a schismatic, or conflictual, rather than a stabilizing force.[15] However, whereas the ego bears the impress of the Imaginary and is 'the seat of illusions' (or delusions even) and is, we might say, a *méconnaissance*, or misrecognition (of the symbolic writ large), the imitative gestures of modernist verse, by contrast, operate at a level of textual consciousness so that the incorporation of foreign material becomes an advertised feature of the writing that is inscribed with a kind of wilful knowingness. Think, for instance, of the various personae that are assumed in Pound's *Cantos*, or the multiplicity of intertextual references that create a kind of metatext beneath the distorted surfaces of Eliot's *The Waste Land* – a poem that Maud Ellmann has described as central to the authoritative modern canon of Western civilization.[16]

Whilst Thomas's mature work in some ways belongs to this same context, he is far more recalcitrant in his response to the classic Modernist 'tradition of the new' than either Eliot or Pound. For Thomas, in a general sense, always remains resistant to system, and never entirely succumbs to either tradition or the avant-garde. He is thus perhaps best described as a saboteur of inherited systems who pays mock homage to both his contemporaries and precursors alike. But the need to qualify almost every statement that one makes about his work is something of an occupational hazard when writing about Thomas. And if the extension of Modernist practice that evolves in his first three volumes – *18 Poems*, *Twenty-five Poems* and *The Map of Love* – would seem to suggest a remarkable degree of conscious control, then this, as Thomas himself would have been the first to agree, had not always been the case. Indeed, when asked by a research student in 1951 how and why he first began to write poetry, and which poets or kind of poetry he was first moved and influenced by, Thomas made no secret of the fact that his earliest works were naively derivative, and admitted that he 'wrote endless imitations'. In a remarkable echo of Lacan's mirror-bemused infant, whose 'joy is due to his imaginary triumph in anticipating a degree of ... coordination that he has not yet actually achieved',[17] Thomas declared that he 'never thought them to be imitations, but, rather, wonderfully original things, like eggs laid by tigers. They were,' he said, 'imitations of anything I happened to be reading at the time: Sir Thomas Browne, de Quincey, Henry Newbolt, the Ballads, Blake, Baroness Orczy, Marlowe, Chums, the Imagists, the Bible, Poe, Keats, Lawrence, Anon., and Shakespeare.'[18]

Since Thomas, quite clearly, tried his callow hand at almost every poetic form he had encountered between the ages of seven and fifteen, his dialogue with literature was an integral feature of his early attempts to construct some sense of a poetic-self. However, the spurious imitations he produced during those formative years point to an identity that is unmistakably 'other' to what turned out to be his own authentic gifts: one entirely predicated upon Thomas's own readerly engagement with literature. For in its simplest form imitation recognizes no difference between the self and other, effectively mistaking the latter for the former. It involves a blurring of subject and object, and the borrowed 'identity' (if identity is the right word) that emerges from those first imitative gestures is an identity that is entirely pre-Symbolic. Heavily freighted with what are no more than illusions of wholeness, synthesis and autonomy that characterize the Imaginary state, these primary identifications reveal the nascent poet-self, to some extent at least, still caught in a state of symbiotic unity with the literary other. Reminiscent in many ways of the Lacanian *l'hommelette*,[19] this amorphous being is a being without borders; a kind of indiscriminate bolus, who lacks distinction and who bears the impress of the primal archaic unity in so far as his apparent inability to distinguish or to separate himself from the other actually re-inscribes the very earliest prototypical relation of the mother/child dyad. In fact we might even go so far as to say that Thomas's first experiments in poetry, like a child's first sounds, actually mimic the bodily relationship of the maternal dyad, and as such involve a transference of the discourse of the other. Importantly, according to post-Freudian interpretations such as those instanced by Lacan and Kristeva, this mimicry or reduplication is central to the maturing ego's subsequent identity-laden negotiations of self-construction, which goes some way at least to explaining Thomas's happily promiscuous intertextuality.

In Lacan's psychic *schema* imitation plays a key role in the construction of an incipient poetic ego, because it is through an ability to assimilate, repeat and reproduce words that the infant develops into a subject, like the other with which it begins by identifying. But whereas both Kristeva and Lacan regard mimicry and imitation as laying the crucial foundations for subjectivity, Thomas discounted the work that he produced in early adolescence, dismissing it simply as 'my very first and forever unpublishable juvenilia'.[20] Of course, as Maud points out, from some perspectives it might be seen as a blessing that these earliest drafts ceased to exist, and that when Thomas chose to relinquish the Notebooks in 1941 he chose to retain only the four which might be 'not forever unpublishable'. For by the time he had reached the age of fifteen, in 1930, a 'far more serious apprenticeship' was underway.[21]

Maud has been keen to assert that the clue to the new development in Thomas's writing can be seen in the heading of the first of the notebooks that were available until 2014: 'Mainly Free Verse Poems' (a heading repeated, incidentally, on the notebook covering the period from 1930 to 1932). His argument is that up to this point indications suggest that Thomas's work had been wholly derivative, and that his early compositions had been essentially 'artificial', in so far as the imitative or 'borrowed' forms that he had adopted had tended to dictate the subject. The first notebook of April to December 1930, however, marks a break with the conservative verse forms that Thomas had, by then, already mastered, and the forty-two poems written mainly in *vers libre* pay homage to high modernism's break with the iambic pentameter. But if the formal looseness (so highly valued by Maud) that typifies the first, and indeed also the second, of the extant notebooks, would suggest Thomas's initial attempt to establish or construct a secure centre of self, then it should be remembered that this is only the very first stage in what will prove to be an ongoing process of separation, and to some extent at least a blurring of self and other, of subject and object still obtains. For, even though the free verse that he began to write marked a significant departure from the simple lyricism that had preceded it, it was certainly not without precedent and therefore far from representing a breakthrough to 'originality'.

Taking its cue from the ancient Egyptian myth of Isis and Osiris, the first notebook opens with a serious poem, dated 27 April 1930, that is quite obviously written in the early Yeatsian manner, 'Osiris, come to Isis':

> He stands at the steaming river's edge
> With his soft arms in the air,
> And snares the sun among his tangled hair.[22]

Satisfied with this that he had now proved himself to be a confident exponent of the Yeatsian Celtic twilight style, Thomas abandoned the Osin style, seemingly regarding it as an apprentice task now accomplished, and continued to forge ahead with the early experiments in free verse that constitute the greater part of the first two notebooks. This, for instance, is how poem number 8 opens:

> The lion, lapping the water,
> Moistening his gums
> [And restoring his vitality,]
> Is a balanced creature
> Who lives because he must,
> [And eats to live,
> And takes, and fights, and loves
> The lioness with a hard bestial love;][23]

Written sometime between mid-May and early June 1930 this is quite clearly a Lawrentian lion poem in the style, for instance, of those to be found in *Birds, Beasts and Flowers* that also feature poems in which animals are infused with qualities that Lawrence believed needed to be recovered by humans. Along with the Georgians, the Elizabethans, Tennyson, the later Beddoes, Webster, Flecker and Clare, Thomas did of course list D. H. Lawrence's animal imagery as one of the main influences on his work during this period. However the overriding model for the free verse composition of the April to December notebook is Imagism. Significantly, in an essay that he had written for the *Swansea Grammar School Magazine* only months earlier Thomas had singled out the

American poet and leading Imagist Richard Aldington for praise alongside Sachervell Sitwell. Aldington was admired for 'adopt[ing] the original method of accentuating the image and making it the first importance in the poem', while Sitwell was commended on his attractive and altogether intriguing obscurity: 'His difficulty is genuine, the strangeness of the picture he sees and wishes to explain, justifying the strangeness of the image he employs.'[24] This last remark is, as Maud has pointed out in his introduction to the Notebooks, exactly what one might say of Thomas's verse and, perhaps, even more importantly, 'probably what Thomas himself wanted to have said of it'.[25] In any event, the following examples will reveal just how difficult it is to distinguish Thomas's writing from that of either Aldington or Sitwell at this early juncture:

(1) At last, after fifty years, I am saturated
With pity and agony and tears;
At last I have reached indifference;
Now I am almost free–
A gold pellet of sunlight
Dropped, curdling, into green water.

(2) My love is deep night
Caught from the tops of towers,
A pomp of delicious light
Snared under the tips of each stalk,
Dew balanced to perfection
On the grass delicate beyond water.

(3) Grant peace;
For a space let there be no roar
Of wheels and voices, no din
Of steel and stone and fire.
Let us cleanse ourselves from sweat and dirt,
Let us be hushed, let us breathe
The cold sterile wind from colourless space.

(4) Let me escape,
Be free, (wind for my tree and water for my flower),
Live self for self,
And drown the gods in me,
Or crush viper heads beneath my foot.

(5) A wall of cactus guards their virgin sound–
Dripping through the sword-edged leaves
The wayward milking
Of your mental stalactites

>   On the strung bells of music,
>   Arrests the moment,
>   Petrifies the air
>
> (6) Each silver moment chimes
>   in steps of sound,
>   And I, caught in mid-air perhaps,
>   Hear and am still the little bird.[26]

The first and third are Aldington; the fifth is Sachervell Sitwell; and the second, fourth and sixth are taken from Thomas's 1930 notebook.[27] Although this early verse is accomplished and confident, it would be difficult to recognize it as an antecedent to the stylistically radical material that Thomas was to publish just four years later in his debut volume *18 Poems*. Set apart from the later work by a stylistic ethereality that in many ways appears entirely at odds with the brilliance and density of the richly textured and rhetorically innovative writing that first launched Thomas onto the London literary scene,[28] these early notebook poems might be thought of as a kind of *méconnaissance*. In other words, they represent the beginning, as it were, of a dialectic in which recognition, of one's self and of one's significant predecessors and models, is simultaneously a form of misrecognition. Like Lacan's mirror-bemused infant, who embarks upon a career of self-delusional ego-building, it seems that the early Thomas perceives, or identifies, in the work of Aldington and Sitwell a mirror-image that both is and is not himself, an image that is endowed with a coherence and autonomy that he desires, but which, at this stage, his 'own' work lacks. In other words, what we are actually witnessing here is the formation of the poetic ego via the process of identification with the literary other.

But, it should be remembered that the redoubling effect of Lacan's mirror manifests a 'split' in the subject, and if the external image it perceives seems to offer the promise of a coherent or stable self, then, at the same time, that image is actually alienating in so far as it becomes enmeshed or confused with the self. It is, we might say, as if the image comes to occupy the very place of the self, as the self is transformed into its counterpart. Therefore, as we saw in the three examples of Thomas's derivative juvenilia quoted above, it would seem that 'the sense of a unified self is only ever acquired at the cost of this self being an-other, that is our mirror image'.[29] The point that should be emphasized here, then, is that the ego is founded on an illusion, on a 'misrecognition', or *méconnaissance*, of the self as other. It is, we might say, the seat of illusions, and also the model for all subsequent misrecognized and fictive self-definitions that the forever alienated subject will endeavour to erect, in so far as Lacan's schismatic ego is '*both formed by and takes its form from the constituting properties of the image*'.[30] But if the ego is born in the specular moment of fascination with the subject's 'own image', then its birth is inscribed with a tension that arises from the frustrated realization that it is always, and already, a subject that is subjugated to and motivated by lack: the struggle begins when the mirror-bemused infant is forced to concede that its image is other and therefore alien and out of its control and yet, at the same time strangely constitutive of its own identity.[31] Interestingly, Lacan explicates this phenomenon in terms of desire: the desire of the child or of the nascent self is seen as being desire *of* the other:

> The subject originally locates and recognizes desire through the intermediary not only of his own image, but of the body of his fellow being. ... [It] is in so far as he recognizes his desire in the body of the other that the exchange takes place. It is in so far as his desire has gone over to the other side that he assimilates himself to the body of the other and recognizes himself as a body.[32]

Lacan sees this as a demand, a struggle for recognition that results in an absolute rivalry with the other. Prior to the subject's Symbolic interpellation, and entrance into the system of signs whereby the symbol will come to represent or stand in for its desire, 'desire is seen solely in the other'.[33] And, according to Lacan, it is this specular relation, whereby the subject perceives the self only in terms of the projective reflection of the other, that precipitates an absolute rivalry with the counterpart. It is almost as if 'the subject wants to annihilate the other so that it might exist'.[34]

Lacan's theorization of the specular moment certainly seems relevant to an understanding of the process of self-definition that is chronicled in the four notebooks under consideration. For, like the speaker of his 1935 poem 'Do you not father me?', the Thomas of the Notebooks is a 'wanton starer', an insatiable voyeur in a hall of mirrors where images endorse and oppose, compete and confirm, as his scopophilic gaze produces and *re*produces a multiplicity of often divergent and illusory identifications.[35] Written in the form of four irregularly rhymed eight-line stanzas, this obscure and difficult poem begins with a speaker who has the identity of a tall tower – a symbol of both youthful solipsism and of phallocentric creativity for Thomas – and who demands confirmation from his parents for their responsibility for his conception and birth. It is, however, worth noting at this point the curious gendering of the tower as 'her' (line 2) – a poetic and parodic manipulation of the standard Freudian as an image of the male organ. As the lyric narrative unfolds this complication increases in a series of questions posed by the speaker: did his parents not also 'sister me' and 'brother me', he asks? Further complications arise when the lyric 'I' claims both parental and sibling identities so that the various conjugations of consanguinity that emerge seem to indicate a deliberate meditation on the dilemma of Oedipus, at once sire and sibling to his own offspring. This is how the poem's second stanza opens:

> Am I not father, too, and the ascending boy,
> The boy of woman and the wanton starer
> Marking the flesh and summer in the bay?[36]

The ascending boy, who is by definition 'all of you', seems an appropriate metaphor for communicating a sense of the plural incarnations in which Thomas exists, not just in the first notebook of June to December 1930, but in all four notebooks, which span the years between 1930 and 1934. However, whereas Lacan would see the dual relation between the nascent ego and the specular image, which, as we've already seen, is crucially both constitutive of the self and at the same time alien and other to the self, as being essentially narcissistic and therefore always accompanied by a certain 'aggression',[37] the series of imaginary identifications that Thomas would endeavour to erect during those formative years are distinguished by the absence of any real sense of rivalry or struggle with the counterpart, that occupies the position of the Lacanian other. In fact, we might even go so far as to say that Thomas actually embraces certain aspects of the literary other which combine to form a kind of ideal ego, in the juvenilia.[38]

The genesis of the poetic ego in Thomas's work is, it would seem, founded not so much upon desire, which necessitates struggle and lack, as upon what Kristeva would see as an ultimately Freudian notion of *eros* and identification, which she has interestingly described as a kind of excess towards the other. Taking us behind and beyond the specular fascination of Lacan's mirror, and emphasizing the role of the (maternal) body in the ongoing process of self-identification, Kristeva argues that the libidinal drives are in operation prior to the onset of the desire. Her point is that desire emphasizes lack, whereas affect, while acknowledging the latter, gives greater importance to the movement toward the other and to mutual attraction. Since there is no textual evidence in Thomas's writing to support the idea of any kind of agonistic struggle or rivalry with the literary other it would seem inappropriate to read his relationship with his chosen models as characterized by desire, as outlined in the Bloomian model. Instead, his relationship with Aldington and Sitwell is best understood as motivated by what Kristeva would call an 'affect': it is an attraction or movement towards the (literary), to be discerned in a passion for the obscure un-glossed image that he had inherited from his post-Imagist forebears and which he was keen to absorb within the textures of his own verse. As early as December 1930, the Notebook Poems begin to offer resulting instances of the kind of assertion entirely through imagery for which the mature Thomas was to become renowned:

> How shall the animal
> Whose way I trace
> Into the dark recesses,
> Be durable
> Under such weight as blows me down,
> The bitter certainty of waste,
> The knowing that I hatch a thought
> To see it crushed
> Beneath your foot, my bantering philistine.[39]

However imperfectly and incompletely, this passage adumbrates Thomas's later, mature style, in that here for the most part images do not illustrate, augment or enrich thought, they actually aspire to constitute it and thus incarnate meaning. This final poem of 1930, that Thomas fair copied into the first of the extant notebooks on 9 December, is, in fact, a 'remote ancestor' of his magnificent opus 'How shall my animal?' that was first published in the *New Directions* annual of 1938, and also in *Criterion* in October of the same year. Even though it is far removed from the density and brilliance of the final and elaborately re-worked version that appeared in *Criterion* almost a decade later, and which would subsequently be published in Thomas's third volume, *The Map of Love*,[40] we do, at this early stage, already see something of that propensity for accentuating and intensifying the image which would, in time, become recognized as the hallmark of the writing. For, although Maud is certainly right in saying that the poem does seem to fall into 'mere exposition' with the 'bitter certainty of waste', for the most part the metaphorical image of the animal does appear to move through the poem evoking rather than describing or explaining its meaning, as images are substituted for rational statements. Thomas's later revisions of such early adolescent material were rigorously compressed, and invariably involved an even further 'imagification' of such explanatory statements as had been left showing. In this instance a bare, or 'straight' statement about waste became intensified, and reworked into what might well be described as a kind of crude Freudian scissor image: 'Sly scissors ground in frost / Clack through the thicket of strength.'[41]

Throughout his career Thomas would continue to stress the singular importance of the image to the construction of his poetics.[42] When asked in 1935 about his theory of poetry he responded by saying '[r]eally, I haven't got one. I like things that are difficult to write and difficult to understand; I like redeeming contraries with secretive images; I like contradicting my images, saying two things at once in one word, four in two words and one in six.'[43] Similarly, and again underlining his need to give the image precedence in his poetry, he stated emphatically in a letter to Henry Treece of 23 March 1938 that '[a] poem by myself needs a host of images, because its centre is a host of images'.[44] Of course, the recognition of the primacy of the image in Thomas's work is a commonplace of Thomas scholarship, and is generally deemed to be a neo-Romantic modernist practice that can be traced back via Yeats and the Symbolists. What is of importance, however, in terms of the present discussion of Thomas's poetic development, is that his internalization of the basic tenets of Imagism point to the introjection of an *ideal* ego, which, as Lacan has reminded us, 'always accompanies the ego' in the drama of human subjectivity, 'as an ever present attempt to regain the omnipotence of the pre-Oedipal situation'.[45] For, even though it is formed in *primary identification*, the ideal ego continues to play a role as a source of *all secondary identifications*, a point that will become clear in the following chapter, and goes some way at least to explaining the enduring quality of the image in Thomas's work.

Chapter 3

The first and second notebooks form a kind of continuum or medley, and, for the most part, the second notebook seems to repeat the primary identification of the prototypical dual, or dyadic, relation that we saw in the poems of April to December 1930. Composed in the same ethereal style and with the same formal looseness as its predecessor, the second notebook, whose seventy-two poems span the period between 1930 and 1 July 1932, opens with a short free-verse poem, based once again upon the lovelorn musings of an adolescent self:

> This love – perhaps I over-rate it,
> And make my god an [*sic*] any woman
> With lovely hair and teeth,
> Praising an empty gesture as a world of meaning,
> Thinking a smile meant faith,
> And a word so lightly uttered
> Immortality.[1]

By March 1931, however, the imaginary love affairs and mythological themes that had tended to dominate the pages of the Notebooks were about to give way to an altogether darker subject matter, as 'religion, suicide, madness, illness, sex and death' began to provide Thomas with 'new sources of imagery'. Often presented in 'a gothic and glowering register', they mix what John Goodby describes as 'late-Victorian lushness with the lugubrious excitement of Expressionism'.[2] Poem XLIX (26 October 1931) provides us with an impressive and striking example:

> No use to run your head against the wall
> To find a sweet blankness in the blood and shell,
> This pus runs deep.

> There's poison in your red wine, drinker,
> Which spreads down to the dregs
> Leaving a corrupted vein of colour,
> Sawdust beneath the skirts;
> On every hand the evil's positive[3]

The fact that Thomas had, in the months before he fair copied this poem into the second of the notebooks, already started to assemble a lexis of visceral and grotesquely inflected terms such as 'scabrous', 'cankered', 'pollution', 'lipless', 'itch', 'spewing', 'emetic', 'cancer', 'weariness', 'poison', 'nightmare' and 'vermin', seems to suggest that some of the definitive themes, and even the verbal structures, of the poetic process emerged at a relatively early stage of the writing. Although generally seen in a more purely Freudian or surrealist guise, Thomas's use of grotesque style and the Gothic can be linked, according to Chris Wigginton, to the poet's own 'displaced, hybrid location'. Traditionally associated with impropriety and the transgression of social and aesthetic limits, the Gothic/grotesque has affinities with the south Walian black humour and brutal sexuality of Caradoc Evans and also, importantly, with broader literary trends.[4] For the grotesque, as Tony Conran has argued, has always played a central role in the construction of a Welsh Modernism:

> Modernism in Wales is most at home with the grotesque. It is there that modernism characteristically shows itself, in Saunders Lewis as much as in Caradoc Evans and Dylan Thomas. The nightmare of monstrosity underlies the middle-class rejection of the *buchedd* [the pious Nonconformist way of life], the sense of being suffocated by its hypocrisy and narrowness.[5]

It would seem then that Thomas's move to incorporate the grotesque has a wider socio-literary and cultural significance, and can thus be read as the first stirrings of his identification with, or internalization of, an Anglo-Welsh or South Walian cultural consciousness. One of the glaring problems with Bloom's agonistic theory of influence is the tendency to reduce literary history, imitation and influence to a single psychological structure. But, as Blevins acutely observes, Lacan hardly allows for such reductionism, since he fully recognizes that the process of self-formation is also a process of socialization. For the nascent self to mature towards fully conscious being inescapably involves its entry into the realm of endless derivativeness and pre-existent convention. The 'entire notion of the self *in* the Symbolic is illusory, [and] dictated by a conception of self based on *difference* and signifiers leading endlessly to other signifiers' – a fact that also illustrates and underlines the subject's continuing presence in the

Imaginary.[6] Although the Symbolic is essentially a linguistic dimension, it is not limited to the system of language. It is the order of the law that cannot be reduced to a single system of signifiers for it embodies a matrix of already fully established cultural, social and ideological positions, all of which must be negotiated by the subject in his/her attempt at self-construction. Though Blevins's assertion that the Symbolic is where the 'strong' poet '*must* exist' is questionable,[7] his basic assumption that any theory of influence demands a consideration of the wider cultural and ideological forces that intersect within the Symbolic is certainly valid. Unlike Bloom's reading of Freud, the current reading of Thomas's poetic development necessitates some consideration of the role that a wider cultural consciousness plays in the construction of the poetic ego.[8] For the poet does not, as Thomas would certainly have agreed, exist, or indeed write, within a vacuum. And, like the rest of us, the poet-self is subject to an entire network of discursive systems since his/her Symbolic inscription involves and even demands participation in a matrix of broader social, cultural, ideological and discursive patterns. Introducing one of his American poetry readings in 1952, Thomas humorously evoked his Swansea childhood and its formative influences on him:

> I first saw the light and screamed at it in a loud lump of Wales ... and of course my writing would not be what it is ... if it had not been for the immortal fry of the town in which I simmered up. Naturally, my early poems and stories, two sides of an unresolved argument, came out of a person who came willy-nilly out of one particular atmosphere and environment, and are part and parcel, park and castle, lark and sea shell, dark and school bell, muck and entrail, cock, rock and bubble, accent and sea-lap, root and rhythm of them.

Confirming the importance of Wales as a principal determinant of his emergence as a writer he declared: 'If I had been born and brought up in an igloo and lived on whales not in it, the same would be true except that then it would have been extremely unlikely had I become a writer.'[9] Explorations of Thomas's 'Welshness' and his positioning as an Anglo-Welsh writer are of course common in the established body of Thomas criticism and have been undertaken in significant detail and with remarkable lucidity by such critics as Walford Davies, M. Wynn Thomas, James A. Davies and John Ackerman. Interestingly, Ackerman, commenting on the instinctive rhythms and sensuous, affective use of language that were to become the hallmark of Thomas's mature work and which, as the present chapter will show, would become clearly discernible in the third and fourth of the notebooks, suggests that those features of style owe little to English poetry in the 1930s:

Rather do they derive from his Welsh background with its living tradition of exuberance in language – though allied to strict formal control in poetry. Anglo-Welsh writing exhibits a craftsmanlike delight in the sound and sensuous quality of words; a rejection of the English addiction to meiosis in favour of a more vivid, emotional, dramatized response to experience – and particularly is this true of the South Wales temperament and character.[10]

This apparent move to subsume some of the key features of his Welsh cultural and literary heritage seems to signify an attempt, on Thomas's part, to symbolize, or to harness, some form of Symbolic consistency. This can further be seen in the pounding pulpit rhythms of 'And death shall have no dominion', which will be discussed in detail in the present chapter, and shows Thomas drawing on a Welsh nonconformist sub-stratum. Clearly, then, the presence of a cultural consciousness operated as an important determinant in Thomas's negotiations of self-construction. For it is, as Lacan reminds us, through the internalization of the social rules and 'laws' that are inscribed therein that the individual is first interpellated, as a subject, within the wider cultural system of the Symbolic universe. As such, it might be said that Thomas's engagement with the distinctive cultural consciousness of his native south Wales signifies a movement from his primary identification with the 'Small Other' – those powerful precursors whom he had tried to emulate in his early imitations – to a secondary identification with Lacan's 'Big Other' of a wider social matrix.

Though no notebook exists for the period July 1932–January 1933, eight typescript poems dating from that time do survive and importantly show that Thomas had not only read Michael Roberts's anthology *New Signatures*,[11] published in February 1932, but that he was also exploring, and tentatively testing out, the 'New Country' poets' social concerns in his own writing – though never entirely abandoning his own gloomier inclinations.[12] Crucially, the last of these typescript poems, a not too remote ancestor of 'Especially when the October wind',[13] shows Thomas departing from *vers libre*, and opting, instead, for free irregularly rhymed verse, as is evident from the following sample:

> Especially when the November wind
> With frosty fingers punishes my hair,
> Or, beaten on by the straight beams of the sun,
> I walk abroad, feeling my youth like fire
> Burning the weak blood and body up,

> Does the brain reel, drunk on the raw
> Spirits of words, and the heart sicken
> Of Newarid syllables groped and regrouped with care,
> Of the chosen task that lies upon
> My cold belly like a stone.[14]

Taking the form of three eight-line, rhymed stanzas before lapsing back into irregularity, this poem offers some illustration of Goodby's assertion that '[d]abbling in New Country subjects seems to have suggested to Thomas that he try out the traditional rhyme-schemes, metres, and stanza forms which these poets were using'.[15]

The third notebook (1 February–16 August 1933), which is generally referred to as The February 1933 Notebook, contains fifty-two poems and shows Thomas tentatively experimenting with the themes and strategies that we now associate with his process poetic. The *vers libre* style adopted in 1930 gradually gave way to rhyme and more conservative verse forms heralding an unexpected breakthrough in April 1933 with the composition of 'And death shall have no dominion', an altogether remarkable anticipation of what was to come:

> And death shall have no dominion.
> Dead men naked they shall be one
> With the man in the wind and the west moon;
> When their bones are picked clean and the clean bones gone,
> They shall have stars at elbow and foot;
> Though they go mad they shall be sane,
> Though they sink through the sea they shall rise again;
> Though lovers be lost love shall not;
> And death shall have no dominion.[16]

The very first of Thomas's famous rhetorical challenges to death and conventional ways of mourning,[17] the poem embodies his initial attempt to use a near-regular metre and rhyme scheme, and to maintain a regular stanza form throughout. Its title and the first and last lines of each of the four stanzas are taken from Romans 6:9: 'Christ being raised from the dead dieth no more; death hath no dominion over him', and suggests an implicit Christian orthodoxy that promises religious consolation in the form of spiritual resurrection. Paradoxically, however, in becoming one with the moon, wind and stars the 'dead men naked' (l. 2) seem to have attained an entirely secularized immortality. Moreover, even though the lyric narrative of the first stanza describes how on the Day of Judgement the dead men, their bones 'picked clean', will reassemble their fragmented bodies and be reunited with nature, this is entirely undermined at a linguistic level by Thomas's use of refurbished cliché, 'the man in the wind and the west moon' (l. 3), scrambling elements that resurrection would otherwise unite as the 'man in the moon' acquires a distinctly Shelleyan or Daliesque hue. Hence it might be said that the text stages, and embodies within its own linguistic textures, something of the fundamental conflict between the material and the spiritual, and is perhaps best described as a highly imaginative statement of the scientific fact of the indestructibility of matter that goes beyond any simple pantheism. This said, it cannot be denied that the poem does appear to communicate a remarkably strong defiance of death and mortality. However, it is fair to say that this is achieved through the reiteration of a strong rhythmical biblical phrase ('And death shall have no dominion' is repeated six times within the space of twenty-seven lines) which acquires an incantatory resonance rather than at the level of theme.

Importantly, it is the first poem that seems to gesture towards the fusion of philosophical, religious, linguistic and bodily aspects of the writing that David Aivaz, Ralph Maud and other eminent critics have called Thomas's 'process poetic' or 'process metaphysic'.[18] The key word here is fusion, and when discussing the early writing one should always bear in mind the fact that this 'fusion' is itself part of the meaning of the poetry. Whilst, to some extent, for the purposes of analysing Thomas these aspects of the work must be examined as discrete fields, the governing principle of interconnection that leads to a blurring of 'inner' and 'outer' worlds makes it virtually impossible to wholly distinguish between the metaphysical, religious, linguistic and the material, or bodily, elements that combine and collide within Thomas's vision of micro-macro cosmic identification. Developing this line of thought, and keen to emphasize the fact that 'process' exists not simply as a philosophy behind the text but is actually constitutive of the text, in so far as it acquires a certain thematic and structural importance, Jacob Korg has described this central organizing concept in the following terms:

> The universe which is both the subject and the setting for Thomas' early poems and short stories ... is an arena of conflict between the forces of creation and destruction embodied in the processes of nature. Fertility, birth, death, growth, decay, and in fact, all events are episodes of a war of processes which rages in every organism and in every living cell. The energy driving these [systems] ... manifests itself in the sexual urge, in the fertility of the soil, and in the life-giving elements of water and sunlight. The seasons of the year, the unfolding of generations, and the alternations of life and death are stages in the dialectic drama of existence. This schematisation of the biological

processes yields the accurate, if elementary, insight that all things participate in all others because the natural changes involve the constant shifting of particles of matter from one form of life to another ... the unity of matter is paralleled by a unity of spiritual life. All nature is joined in one great brotherhood, so that the separateness and even the antagonism of individual creatures is merely a transient aspect of their essential unity with each other.[19]

This view of the universe as a 'seamless fabric' is typical of the myth-making imagination that underwrites the conception of life and death as being merely stages within the continuum of cosmic process that is expressed in 'And death shall have no dominion'. Here, human immortality is presented as being nothing more than a spiritual consequence of the unity of matter. For each and every state of life contains its opposite in the thoroughly relativistic dynamic universe of the poem. Contrary to Maud's assertion, therefore, this was Thomas's first process lyric. The intensity of the presentation of the universal flux and the cyclical process of death and rebirth is far in excess of any straightforward or simple Romantic pantheism, whilst the biblical source of the refrain and the measured pulpit rhythms show Thomas discovering 'a richly suggestive way of tapping into his Nonconformist Welsh cultural substratum', making the poem far more impressive than anything he had written to date.[20] But this, as Goodby says, is of course the problem: 'for it was written in a form and style (refrain, regular rhythm and stanza-form, rhyme) at odds with the free verse that largely preceded it, and which Thomas associated with being a contemporary poet'.[21] In other words, Thomas failed to recognize the massive implications of this chance breakthrough because, thematically, formally and structurally, the poem was in conflict with, and entirely opposed to, the ideal ego and its promise of future synthesis.

The 'ideal ego' is a powerful determinant in the subject's identity-laden negotiations of self-construction. It is born in the almost hypnotic moment of the specular image, continues to accompany the individual in his career of self-delusional ego-building, and is the source of all subsequent secondary identifications. As has already been shown, the formation of identity occupies an important place in Lacan's work, and he places a special emphasis on the role of the image in defining the process as 'the transformation that takes place in the subject when he assumes an image'. For, to assume an image is to recognize oneself in that image, and to appropriate the image as oneself. However, as Lacan reminds us, this identification with something outside the self, or even in some cases opposed to it, is precisely also 'what structures the subject as a rival with himself' and thus involves alienation and 'aggressivity' [*sic*].[22]

This early version of 'And death shall have no dominion', then, proved a problem for Thomas because it failed to correspond to the image of the other that he had hitherto assumed and mistakenly appropriated as himself through his imitations of Sachervell Sitwell and Richard Aldington.[23] He had assumed that it was in and through their example that he had found his true poetic self. But this poem was a radically different kind from any he had hitherto written under their influence. Its regular nine-line stanzas and near regular rhyme scheme (stanza one is a, b, a, b, c, d, d, c, a; two is a, b, b, c, d, e, e, d, a; three is a, b, c, c, d, e, b, d, a) placed it immediately at odds with that freedom from the constraints of regular metre and fixed forms that Thomas had formerly admired and adopted as his own supposedly signature practice. Thematically, too, its metaphysical theme of resurrection set it apart from the overt social agendas of the New Country poets who, during this period of formal re-entrenchment in British poetry, were swiftly becoming established as the vanguard of a politically left poetic movement, and whose concerns he had also begun to echo, albeit rather tentatively, within the body of his own writing.[24] Still inextricably bound to an image of self that was almost wholly predicated upon an imaginary identification with the literary other exemplified by certain contemporary free-metre poets, Thomas failed to grasp the significance of this chance breakthrough as a major step towards achieving the poetic authenticity that he craved. This is perhaps hardly surprising given that the early version of 'And death shall have no dominion' established Thomas in an 'alienated' subject position in which, according to Lacan, the individual exists, first and foremost, as a rival to himself, through identification with a 'model' unsuited to his own distinctive potentialities.

This goes some way at least to explaining just why it was that Thomas should initially have been reluctant to see 'And death' as anything other than an occasional poem on the subject of immortality, and why, after such an apparently striking anticipation of true originality, he would continue to write and even to publish works in the brooding, social realist and metrically irregular style of 'That sanity be kept'.[25] Written sometime between April 1933, when 'And death' was composed, and 6 September, when the first process lyric of *18 Poems*, 'Before I knocked and flesh let enter', was fair copied into the fourth notebook, this was Thomas's first major published poem, and when it appeared in the *Sunday Referee* on 3 September 1933 the then editor Victor Neuberg commented that it was 'perhaps the best modernist poem that I've yet received'.[26] It opens as follows:

> That sanity be kept I sit at open windows,
> Regard the sky, make unobtrusive comment on the moon,
> Sit at open windows in my shirt,
> And let the traffic pass, the signals shine,
> The engines run, the brass bands keep in tune,
> For sanity must be preserved.

Yet, despite the fact that in Neuberg's opinion this was a poem clearly worthy of note, even the most cursory reading of the text reveals this early published work as lacking the striking originality of the emergent process style. Set within a recognizable social scene, as opposed to the indeterminate poetic loci of *18 Poems*, and lacking the linguistic density, verbal invention and rhythmic energy that we now associate with the 'process' lyric, the poem is a very consciously crafted parody of the style of the 'Auden generation' of poets, who 'mow and mow': hence the assumed role of an easily identifiable speaker as dispassionate observer, rather than the fluid womb voices; the use of 'everyday' language of social discourse in stanza one ('let the traffic pass, the signals shine, / The engines run, the brass bands keep in tune,'); the social façade, and so on.

But, in spite of obvious differences it would be a mistake to assume that this 'Audenesque', or New Country style poem was entirely at odds with either 'And death shall have no dominion' or 'Before I knocked'. For, although its flaccid structure and movement sets it apart from the mesmeric lyrics that have come to define Thomas's first volume, *18 Poems*, it can nevertheless be seen as containing, or embodying, the major process themes – 'appearance versus reality, sexual angst, fear of death and madness'. In other words, as John Goodby has suggested, 'it contains the basic ingredients of the process poems, but arranged inertly. As in Thomas' other poems of this kind, it presents the ingredients-to-be of the process poetic hybrid in juxtaposition only; their fusion has yet to take place.'[27]

'[M]Y INTRICATE IMAGE': THE HYBRID POETIC AS 'EGO IDEAL'

Following the composition of 'And death' in April 1933, the social-realist elements of the third notebook started to fade as Thomas gradually began to realize that the impact of the breakthrough that he had made was directly connected to the use of regular stanza form and rhyme. These were the very features that he had hitherto dismissed as incompatible with his vision of avant-garde practice, as he had regarded it as inextricably linked to free-verse composition. But, in grasping the significance of his achievement, Thomas was faced with a dilemma: he now had to modify and expand his conception of contemporary verse, or else risk shattering the ideal ego – the vision of poetic 'perfection' that he had believed he had discovered in the work of the Imagists, and which he had tried to emulate in his own verse – and its promise of future (poetic) synthesis.[28] However, given Lacan's assertion that this imaginary projection continues as an ever-present accompaniment to the ego, in so far as it is the source of all secondary identifications, the latter option of total rejection of 'ideal' Imagist practice could never be a viable one. Hence, Thomas's newly established mastery of traditional verse form, which led to repeated success with 'Find meat on bones' (15 September) and 'Ears in turrets hear' (17 July), can be read in terms of a recognition of the enhanced aesthetic opportunities made available by a broader, yet arguably more sophisticated, re-imagining of the contemporary lyric.

'Ears in the turrets hear' (*CP*, pp. 48, 49) is, by Thomas's standards, a fairly simple poem, although it is fair to say that it lacks something of the verbal brio of 'And death' and, in comparison, seems somewhat slack. Indeed, Thomas himself referred to it in a letter dated 9 May 1934 to Pamela Hansford Johnson as 'a terribly weak, watery little thing'.[29] Yet, this was the first poem that he read to Vernon Watkins on opening, at Cwmdonkin Drive, 'a large file, marked in block letters POEMS': and he later sent it to Thomas Taig as one of the two poems of his 'most suitable for dramatic presentation' – that is recitation.[30] Composed in the form of a monologue, the poem comprises four stanzas and a coda. Rooted in epistemological pessimism, it can be read either as the meditation of a virgin on the subject of sexuality or as a pondering by any individual as to whether or not to trust others and indeed life itself. In either case the question that pertains, and which is stated in lines 9 and 25 and finally reiterated in the coda is: 'Hold you poison or grapes?' Reminiscent of Donne perhaps, the controlling metaphor, which is established in the poem's second stanza, is that of the human body as an island 'bound / [b]y a thin sea of flesh / [a]nd a bone coast' (ll. 10, 11, 12). However, this bears little resemblance to the grotesque corporeality of *18 Poems*. And the obvious weakness of lines such as '[h]ands grumble on the door' (l. 26), coupled with the somewhat tired cliché 'till the day I die' in the poem's final stanza, does very little to suggest the kind of radical linguistic experimentation that was to come. This said, the conservatively shaped stanzas and use of both internal rhyme ('grumble'/'gables') and para-rhyme ('hear'/'door', 'fire'/'hair', 'stranger'/'sailor', 'sound'/'mind', 'ships'/'grapes') make the poem significant in so far as it registers Thomas's commitment to the formal and stylistic breakthrough of 'And death shall have no dominion'.

Yet, as he continued to develop his poetic of universal flux, it seems that Thomas became somewhat dissatisfied with 'And death', which, like 'Ears in the turrets', was excluded from the paradigmatic nexus of poems in the process style that would constitute the main body of his first volume *18 Poems*. Moreover, it was only with some reluctance that he eventually agreed to include it in his subsequent publication, *Twenty-five Poems*, and even then he chose to omit the final stanza, which reads as follows:

> And death shall have no dominion.
> Under the sea or snow at last
> Man shall discover all he thought lost,
> And hold his little soul within the fist;
> Knowing that now he can never be dust,
> He waits in the sun till the sun goes out;
> Now he knows what he had but guessed
> Of living and dying and all the rest;
> He knows his soul. There is no doubt.
> And death shall have no dominion.

Part of the problem was the fact that whilst the poem expresses the notion of process through its pantheistic imagery, it seems unable to embody this idea of universal flux at the level of its own linguistic textures.[31] But even if it did thus fail to fully live up to the modernist ideal whereby 'the medium is the message', 'And death' remained 'a powerful demonstration ... that traditional form could give meaningful structure to the inchoate material that had otherwise resisted shaping in Modernist form'.[32]

The August 1933 notebook begins with an epigraph that reads:

> To others caught
> Between black and white.[33]

But though Maud is certainly correct in saying that the parameters of the August 1933 notebook can be thought of as the polarities between which Thomas trapped 'the forces of light and darkness, life and death, "the green fuse" and "the crooked worm"', to read Thomas's incisive epigraph simply in terms of its thematic significance would be a mistake.[34] His maxim carries a wider significance that reflects interestingly on the status of the 'process' poetic, representing it as a form of writing that is radically suspended between realist and experimental modes. Hovering jubilantly, though unstably, as it does between these two alternatives, the poetry exists in a state of tension, as an 'other', in the Lacanian sense. In other words, it is caught between the black and white of Eliot and Auden – the one being the high priest of literary modernism and the other un-crowned, but undisputed, leader of the new literary left. The forty-one poems of the fourth notebook, which were written between 17 August 1933 and 30 April 1934, show Thomas consolidating the hybrid 'process style'.[35] And it is significant that thirteen out of the eighteen poems in his first collection first appeared here.[36] The following, for instance, are the first two stanzas of poem number seven, the now familiar 'Before I knocked and flesh let enter', which was fair copied into the fourth of the notebooks on 6 September 1933:

> Before I knocked and flesh let enter,
> With liquid hands tapped on the womb
> I who was shapeless as the water
> That shaped the Jordan near my home
> Was brother to Mnetha's daughter
> And sister to the fathering worm.
>
> I who was deaf to spring and summer,
> Who knew not sun nor moon by name,
> Felt thud beneath my flesh's armour
> As yet was in a molten form,
> The leaden stars, the rainy hammer
> Swung by my father from his dome.

This is an obscure and difficult poem, even by Thomas's standards. He himself declared it to be 'distinctly unfashionable' but, at the same time, to be one of his 'very best'.[37] In fact, it seems that Thomas actually valued this poem more than any of the others he was writing at the time.[38] The voice here is a wholly mature one, and the poem certainly succeeds where 'And death' had 'failed', since unlike the latter it lives up to the Modernist ideal of making the medium one with the message by deliberately, and indeed very self-consciously, working to close the 'gap between word and thing'. Think, for instance, of the way in which the proper nouns 'Jordan' and 'Mnetha' appeal to an innate taste for musicality, or of the cumulative effective of the sibilants in 'The false lips cursed me like an adder / Who bears his sting to wound the air', lines that certainly allow us to experience something of that sensation in the words themselves. Such lines are in fact typical of the 'process' poems, which were founded on Thomas's commitment to a belief that poetry should work from, rather than towards, words.

In such cases, it often seems that words don't appear to indicate things referentially so much as become those things in themselves.[39] And, although it is, as Walford Davies warns, perhaps too easy, at times, to emphasize this aspect of the poetry, there can be no doubt that a phrase like 'brambles wringing in the brains' (l. 24) can be palpably felt by the reader. The poem's impacted stanzas, which are, incidentally, rhymed on twenty-three words ending in 'er', overflow with images of various ghostly spectres, a 'fathering worm' and a betrayed, mortal Christ, who figures as a symbol of death. It thus provides ample illustration of what Desmond Hawkins meant when, less than two years later, in February 1935, he described Thomas as 'the *grateful heir* to Eliot's magical sense of the macabre and Auden's textual firmness'.[40] Hawkins thus showed a unique understanding of what he called Thomas's 'unborrowed language' as a kind of fusion of Modernist content and New Country, or 'Audenesque', form – a hybrid, as it were, of realist and experimental modes.

The consolidation of the hybrid 'process' style that can be seen in poems such as 'Before I knocked' marks an important point of departure in Thomas's development. For it is here, through the acquisition of a boldly authentic and strikingly original voice, that he truly achieves poetic synthesis, and finally breaks free from the Imaginary dyad that, as already shown, had tended to dominate the structures of the juvenilia. In Lacanian terms, the interruption of, or, to put it slightly differently, the movement away from, this prototypical dual relation marks the point of the inauguration of the speaking (or, in this case writing) subject and his Symbolic inscription. For Lacan, the Symbolic is the realm of radical alterity, which he also refers to as the Other:

> The unconscious is the discourse of the other, and thus wholly belongs to the symbolic order. The symbolic is also the realm of the Law which regulates desire in the Oedipus complex. It is the realm of *culture*, as opposed to the imaginary of nature. [And] whereas the imaginary is characterised by dual relations, the symbolic is characterised by triadic structures, because the inter-subjective relationship is always 'mediated' by a third term, the big Other.[41]

Clearly, then, in Lacan's account, the Oedipus complex is the paradigmatic triangular, or triadic, structure which contrasts with *all* dual relations. And its key function is thus that of the father, the third term whose intervention transforms the dual relation, or dyad, between the (m)other and child into a triadic, or ternary, structure. The Oedipus complex is then nothing less than the passage from the Imaginary order to the Symbolic order. It is, he says, 'the conquest of the symbolic relation as such'.[42] For Lacan this stage of subjective development occurs between the child's third and fifth years, the point at which he is first struck by a sense of Oedipal anxiety. Curiously, however, for the pre-natal speaker of 'Before I knocked' it seems that it is, in fact, within the womb itself that the subject's initial experience of Oedipal anxiety occurs. The second and third stanzas of the poem articulate the painful and traumatic consequences, for the child, of this first recognition of phallic authority, which, as Chris Wigginton suggests, is figured here in the most literal of terms of the 'father's penis'.[43]

> I who was deaf to spring and summer,
> Who knew not sun nor moon by name,
> Felt thud beneath my flesh's armour
> As yet was in a molten form,
> The leaden stars, the rainy hammer
> Swung by my father from his dome.

Here, then, we see the expression of the traumatic and agonizing fear of castration which, according to Lacan, will be enacted by the father, the Fore-figure of the Law, as punishment for the incestuous desire for the mother. Yet, unlike the pre-natal subject of Thomas's poem, whose Symbolic inscription is very clearly precipitated by a rival identification with the punitive 'Father of the Law', it seems that as poet he himself was propelled from the Imaginary into the Symbolic of literary tradition not through castration fear but, rather, through pleasure and excess – the pleasure, or jouissance, and excess both of influence and of language. For, as Thomas himself admitted, the initial infatuation with the material bases of language that prompted his decision to become 'a writer of words' never left him and, throughout his career, he continued to be both captured and captivated by their spell.[44] For Kristeva, in her further development of Lacanian thought, this would suggest that Thomas's own poetic transition to the Symbolic condition is presided over by the *Imaginary* Father, the affective pater, as Steve Vine calls him, the pre-historic 'mother-father conglomerate' who facilitates the movement from the self-falsifying ideal ego to the self-enabling ego ideal.[45] This structural position, the combined he/she/it that Kristeva has termed the archaic Imaginary Father, is what provides the support necessary for the child to move into the Symbolic. Importantly, says Kelly Oliver, '[t]his is a move from the mother's body to the mother's desire through the mother's love'.[46] She explains the process of identification with the 'maternal father' that enables the child's entrance into the rule-bound system of signs like this:

> Through the immediate transference onto the imaginary father, the child undergoes a transference to the site of maternal desire, which Kristeva claims is the desire for the phallus. It is an identification with the father who the child

imagines took part in the primal scene. But it is an identification with this imaginary father only insofar as he represents the phallus that satisfies the mother's desire. The child, then, is identifying with the father entering the mother; it is identifying with a reunion with the mother, with her *jouissance*, her satisfaction. Through its identification with the imaginary father, the child, in its imaginary, can re-place itself back inside its mother, in the mother's womb. The imaginary identification with the mother's body provides the support needed to lose the real identification with the mother's body and move to an identification with her desire, which is a move into the symbolic.[47]

In some sense, the identification with Kristeva's loving third allows for a *re*union with the mother in an altogether different guise and thereby facilitates both the separation from the maternal body and a 'playful [and jubilant, even,] entrance into the symbolic', which is precisely what we see in Thomas's hybridized poetic of excess.[48] For his ego ideal is founded upon a very heavily constructed, but at the same time playful and *near* parodic, fusion of the contemporary and near contemporary. From this perspective it is possible to read Thomas as a kind of signifier that embodies the fault lines that were beginning to develop within British poetry between realist and experimental modes.

There is, then, no evidence in the writing of any kind of Freudian or Bloomian agonistic struggle, just a jubilant or festive excess, a jouissance of influence, perhaps, as it reveals itself in Thomas's extension of Modernist practice, which evolves in what might well be described as a playful and uncanny simulacrum of avant-garde style. Perhaps the most outrageously striking example of this can be seen in what John Goodby describes as 'the calculated provocation' of 'Now', written in 1935.[49] The first stanza reads as follows:

> Now
> Say nay,
> Man dry man,
> Dry lover mine
> The deadrock base and blow the flowered anchor,
> Should he, for centre sake, hop in the dust,
> Forsake, the fool, the hardiness of anger.[50]

This hints at Dada, *zaum* and nonsense poetry, and Thomas's friend Trevor Hughes understood it to be a burlesque in the style of the Gertrude Stein of the *Tender Buttons*. But Hughes was quite mistaken to assume that it was written 'with little serious intent'.[51] For, as Goodby has insisted, '"Now" is a pseudo-avant-garde poem which mimics experimental form and transrationalism'. The main verbs – 'say', 'mine' and 'forsake' – are heavily disguised, but once they are uncovered the speaker can be seen as, perhaps, some kind of Hamlet figure 'trying to argue himself into turning his suicidal anger outwards against the world'. What particularly interests me here, however, is not so much the 'theme' (in its loosest possible sense) but, rather, the way in which Thomas's parodic intent reveals itself. For, quite remarkably, it seems that the peculiarly shaped stanzas can, in fact, be resolved into perfectly traditional or conservative forms: the total syllabic-count of the first four lines (one, two, three and four) adds up to that of an iambic pentameter, while the next three complete a symmetrical, quatrain pattern (ten and eleven alternately), pararhyming 'anchor'/'anger'. 'Nothing', says Goodby, 'reveals more clearly the value of formal regularity to the development of Thomas's poetry than this witty manipulation of readerly expectations'. And whilst he might agree with Maud and Davies 'that its significance may indeed come from its form and insistence on form', Goodby is keen to assert that this insistence is not 'mechanical', nor does it arise from 'a refusal to provide normal syntax', as they claim. For, as he correctly suggests, '"Now" offers a lively simulacrum of avant-garde style which is at once a mockery [of it] and a tribute to it; it is a parody of an avant-garde poem, and an avant-garde poem *as* parody.'[52]

This remarkable poem is just one of a plethora of examples that highlight the sheer delight with which Thomas curiously and uncannily haunts and parasitically appropriates established modes of poetic discourse, inhabiting them in order to deconstruct them from within. Hence, he cannot, with any degree of confidence, be fixed to any single poetic style or doctrine, not to surrealism, or even, as Don McKay asserts, to such fashionable revolutionary ideologies of his day as Marxism or Lawrentian sexual philosophy, which he sometimes arrogated but only to turn them to his own artistic advantage. Instead, he inhabits a diverse range of systems, both traditional and revisionist, in a purely provisional manner; but 'he does not, like Rimbaud or Artaud, place himself nakedly outside all structures as their exemplary inquisitor'.[53] He is, thus, best described as a gleeful saboteur of inherited system. For, unlike the Bloomian *ephebe*, or novice poet who, when confronted by the achievements of an immensely powerful precursor, experiences only a Freudian sense of the nightmare predicament of his own belatedness, Thomas seems to delight in the jouissance of influence as a recognition of the enhanced aesthetic opportunities made available by the legacy of his many 'literary fathers'. In Thomas's hybrid poetic, then, the radical alterity that is definitive of Symbolic subjectivity becomes a pleasurable excess rather than a painful and agonizing gap. And, as such, it is through this identification with the affective father, a father who, unlike Lacan's sternly prohibitive third term, 'loves' like a mother, that Thomas can become the 'imaginary' son, the rightful, or, as Hawkins puts it, 'grateful' heir to both T. S. Eliot and W. H. Auden.

This chapter has suggested that both the multiple influences that combine within the space of Thomas's richly intertextual verse and the *sheer delight* with which he sabotages inherited systems allow us to liberate the concept of literary influence from the Oedipal straightjacket within which it has been so long influentially and damagingly confined by Harold Bloom. The enigma of Thomas's relationship with Auden and Eliot can be fruitfully read in the alternative terms of the Lacanian Oedipal complex and of Kristeva's notion of the 'imaginary father'. According to the latter the father, of the third stage of Freud's nuclear complex, is transformed from the depriving and identificatory rival that he is in the grim economy of the Freudian model into a loving third term, or, in Kristevan parlance, the 'maternal-father', the 'he', 'she' or 'it' who presides over and facilitates the subject's movement into the Symbolic order. It was this affective *pater* that provided the necessary support to liberate Thomas from the primary dyad – and the inevitable misrecognition of 'self as other' it entails – which had tended to dominate the pages of the juvenilia. He was enabled to move forward in the direction of the pleasurable excesses of his mature work. In *Black Sun*, Kristeva's absorbing meditation on depression and melancholia, the figure of the loving third term acquires a certain religious resonance, and working within a 'Christian imaginary' Kristeva offers her archaic maternal-father, whom she links to 'the cult of the unpresentable', as a secular substitute for a dead God. Oliver explains her intriguing proposition like this:

> Kristeva seems to suggest that God is the Word and as such still exists. However, God is also Love [*sic*] and as such is dead. And without Love the word is empty ... mourning the loss of God the Loving Father, [she] creates his secular substitute in the loving imaginary father, [that] she also calls [in *Tales of Love*] the 'cult of the unpresentable'.[54]

This 'unpresentable' which paradoxically makes representation possible is represented, strangely enough, by Kristeva's prehistoric and loving third term. And attention will be paid to this in part two, even as it focuses primarily on her theory of abjection.

Part Two

'[A]nd I am dumb to tell': Presenting and Representing the Unpresentable

---

The postmodern would be that in which the modern puts forward the unpresentable in presentation itself: that which denies itself the solace of good forms, the consensus of taste which would make it impossible to share collectively the nostalgia for the unattainable; that which searches for new presentations, not in order to enjoy them but in order to impart a stronger sense of the unpresentable ... the artist and the writer, then, are working in order to formulate the rules of what will have been done. Hence the fact that work and text have the characters of an event ...

Jean François Lyotard, 1992

events are incorporeal transformations which are expressed in language but attributed to bodies and states of affairs. In so far as language serves to express such incorporeal transformations, it does not simply represent the world but intervenes in it ...

Paul Patton, 2002

All the words are lovely, but they seem so chosen, not struck out. I can see the sensitive picking of words, but none of that strong inevitable pulling that makes a poem an event, a happening, an action perhaps, not a still-life or an experience put down, placed, regulated ...

Dylan Thomas to Vernon Watkins, 1938

Chapter 4

In 1938, Thomas sent to Vernon Watkins a critique of the latter's poem 'Call It All Names But Do Not Call It Rest' in which he noted that 'A motive has been rarefied, it should be made common. I don't ask you for vulgarity, though I miss it; I think I ask you for a little creative destruction destructive creation: "I build a flying tower, and I pull it down."'[1] The inclusion of a destructive element, or, to borrow a phrase from Don McKay, of the 'trickster's demolition work', within Watkins's mythopoesis, would, for Thomas, have the desired effect of rescuing the poem from timeless ubiquity and drawing it back into the field of temporality, thus making it 'a "vulgar" event and not merely a structure'.[2] As it stood, Watkins's writing seemed to him less like real poetry than a kind of nostalgia for the traditionally 'poetic'. In thus shrewdly criticizing his friend's work Thomas was, of course, revealing concerns he had himself come to entertain about the insufficient originality of his own early poetry, concerns that had been allayed only when he eventually succeeded in breaking through to a mode of writing that gloried in the riotous free-play of language (not least in the 'vulgar' form of the 'vulgate' that Watkins so fastidiously avoided) even while his poetry was haunted by the ultimately self-enclosed character of the system of signifiers that made such prodigally fertile free-play possible.

Indeed, whereas, in Bloomian terms, the very locus of the Romantic problematic itself resides in the fearfully uncontrollable excess of the signified, what we find in Thomas is something entirely different.[3] For what motivates, and indeed infuses, the exorbitant, materialist exploitation of language that governed his work, and which is evident from the very first of the early Notebook Poems right through to the final, and incomplete *In Country Heaven* sequence, is an uninhibited passion for, and an excess of, the signifier, which rather than being 'modernist' seems far more compatible with the practice of a contemporary avant-garde or postmodern poetics.[4] Of course, given the vast amounts of critical ink that have been spilt in retailing a more easily digestible version of Dylan Thomas the unified and integrated Modernist, to the general public, the possibility of a postmodern *re*-reading, might, one imagines, meet with some resistance. Yet, to re-read his stylistically radical writing in terms of a contemporary avant-garde aesthetic, or indeed to re-think Thomas as a proto-postmodernist even, should not necessarily preclude a larger view of Thomas as a belated and marginal but positive and critically engaged Modernist.[5] For, as the French theorist Jean François Lyotard reminds us, the postmodern is, in fact part of the modern. Moreover, it is, as he says, modernism in its nascent state, modernism's moment of invention.[6]

AN AESTHETIC OF THE SUBLIME

Departing from Baudrillard, Jameson and other postmodern commentators who have seen a decisive break between the Modernist and the postmodernist periods, Lyotard makes no temporal disjunction between the two, insisting instead that they inhere within one another – inhabit each other, as it were. It is not the case, then, of Modernism and postmodernism representing different, incompatible, historical or different aesthetic forms. Rather, as Simon Malpas succinctly puts it, 'the postmodern is a modification of the modern that further radicalises the latter's challenges to realist representation'.[7] Lyotard defines modernism in the following terms:

> [It is] the art that devotes its 'trivial technique', as Diderot called it, to presenting the existence of something unpresentable. Showing that there is something we can conceive of which we can neither see nor show – this is the stake of modern painting.[8]

The very notion of presenting the fact that there is something unpresentable, something that remains inexpressible, or something which, in normal terms, would seem to resist symbolization, is a key feature of Lyotard's thought, and forms the basis for his definitions of both modernism and postmodernism. Influenced by Kant's discussion of the sublime, which he takes as his ultimate, though perhaps 'somewhat uneasy',[9] authority for the existence of the unpresentable, Lyotard maintains that modern art (including literature) has the unique capacity to (re)present – to communicate – a sense that the unpresentable exists: 'that there are things that are impossible to present in available language games, voices that are silenced in culture, ideas that cannot be formulated in rational communication'.[10] Thus, the (post)modern aesthetic that begins to emerge from Lyotard's work, and which is examined most conveniently in the appendix to his seminal essay 'Answering the Question: What is Postmodernism?', can be thought of as 'an investigative aesthetic of the sublime'.[11]

Faithful to the paradoxical nature of the sublime sentiment, which involves a curious intermingling of pleasure and pain or, better still, as he puts it, 'pleasure derived from pain', Lyotard maintains that the existence of the unpresentable can be evoked in two quite different ways, one of which he calls the modern and the other the postmodern:

> The nuance which distinguishes these two modes may be infinitesimal; they often coexist in the same piece, are almost indistinguishable; and yet they testify to a difference [*un différend*] on which the fate of thought depends and will depend for a long time between regret and assay.[12]

Clearly Modernism and postmodernism both 'allude to something that does not let itself be made present'.[13] But – and this difference, or *différend*, is crucial to what Lyotard would see as being a properly contextualized understanding of the distinction he makes between the two forms – if the Modernist sublime is inextricably tied to feelings of loss or regret, then, by way of contrast, the postmodern sublime works explicitly through a sense of jubilation and excitement. Lamenting the fact that current modes of discourse no longer provide an accurate, or indeed adequate, representation of the world, Modernism typically embodies a nostalgic yearning to return to the relative stability of a previous state. Postmodernism, on the other hand, actively embraces the enhanced aesthetic possibilities made available by the failure of contemporary language games. Moreover, it seems that this apparent failure is greeted as a welcome prelude to innovation and artistic experimentation by the avant-garde: 'the old rules have failed', it announces, 'so, let us discover new ones'.[14]

THOMAS AND THE POETIC SUBLIME

The distinction that Lyotard makes between Modernist nostalgia and postmodern jubilation is significant not least for the fact that it presents a way of identifying postmodern writers and tendencies within what would normally be seen as the strictly 'modern' period (the Joyce of *Finnegans Wake*, or the Gertrude Stein of *Tender Buttons*, for instance). But, even more importantly, perhaps, especially in terms of a writer like Dylan Thomas who has remained persistently, and notoriously, difficult to contextualize, it allows us to recover the distinctions between forms of a more closed and elitist high Modernism (as practised by the men of 1914: Pound, Eliot, Hulme, et al.*)* and a more open, playful and experimental Modernism, of the kind that we might find, for instance, in Thomas's most radically stylistic work.[15] Now although it is not being suggested that Thomas's writing is paradigmatically postmodern, what is being argued here is that the modern and the postmodern are tendencies, or modes, which occur, and coexist within the textual space of his verse. Certainly within the context of Thomas's hybrid poetics, where the writing is, as was shown in the previous chapter, radically suspended between realist and experimental modes, the postmodern impulse in the work signifies a further radicalization of the implicit and explicit challenge posed to realist representation. There are of course many examples of this distinctive intermingling of backward- and forward-looking currents, or trends, in the writing. Indeed, Thomas's second volume, *Twenty-five Poems*, with its very self-conscious, and deliberate, selection and juxtaposition of the radical and the conservative (the particularly obscure 'Today this insect', *CPDT*, p. 38, and, conversely, the positively 'Audenesque' stanzas of 'The hand that signed the paper', *CPDT*, p. 51, for instance) might well be read as the culmination of this process, that interestingly and very deliberately calls into question its own modes of construction and representation. But, before turning to specific examples from the body of Thomas's work, it is important to consider that, to some extent at least, Thomas was both embodying and responding to something of a more general, periodic concern with issues of presentation. As Marjorie Perloff has been keen to note:

> The shift that takes place at the turn of the decade [1930s] is one from the modernist preoccupation with form – in the sense of imagistic or symbolist structure, dominated by a lyric 'I' – to the questioning of representation itself. Discourse now becomes increasingly referential, but reference does not go hand in hand with the expected mimesis. Rather, the boundaries between the 'real' and the 'fantastic' become oddly blurred. The taste for the 'natural', as in Pound's insistence that 'the natural object is always the adequate symbol', gives way to artifice and a marked taste for abstraction and conceptualisation. In the same vein, irony – so central to modernist poetics – gives way to the parodic, but even parody is not often sustained, with abrupt tonal shifts and reversals in mood becoming quite usual. Indeed, this 'time of tension' ... exhibits a mannerist style as distinct from its modernist antecedents as from the social realism to come.[16]

This can, with qualification, be applied to Thomas. Moreover, since Thomas's poetic practice in its production of a 'simulacrum modernism' challenges the distinction between mimesis or copy and the 'real', it contests its own modes of representation, and indeed the very idea of representation itself.[17] And, furthermore, like the postmodern itself which, according to Bennett and Royle, 'defines itself in terms of liminal phenomena',[18] Thomas's hybrid poetics defies both categorization and finally expression as it seeks new forms, or modes, through which to impart a stronger sense of the unpresentable.[19]

Text as event
But just how exactly does Thomas communicate a sense of the fact that there is an unpresentable that exists? For the characteristic displays of linguistic excess – the surplus of poetic device, patterning and wordplay – by which Thomas mimicked something of the fragmentation and spatial dislocation of high Modernism, could not, ostensibly at least, be further removed from the abstract minimalism of, say, for example, Barnett Newman, Lyotard's exemplary artist of the sublime. And, does the fact that there is, undeniably, a recognizable consistency of form within Thomas's imploded Modernism mean that the writing resolves itself purely into some kind of nostalgic lament, whereby the unpresentable would exist only, to borrow Lyotard's words, as the 'missing contents'.[20]

The difficulties these questions present can be explained partially, at least, in terms of the status of the poems as events, a point that appears to emerge from Chris Wigginton's broadly historicist reading of Thomas. Discussing the radical and subversive elements of his work in the context of a mainstream 1930s response to the historical crisis that had encouraged a reaction against experimentalism, Wigginton points to the fact that 'Thomas's poetry of the 1930s has the disruptive quality of an event that is not immediately translatable into meaning'.[21]

In a general sense the notion of eventhood is, it seems, crucial to a properly contextualized understanding of any definition of the postmodern. For, in so far as it presents a challenge to established genres of discourse, calling for all that has led up to it to be rethought, the event is, we might say, the founding moment of any postmodernism.[22] But, what particularly interests Lyotard in terms of his theorizing on avant-garde aesthetics is the fact that its status as an event, or happening, its inherent incalculability, as it were, effectively liberates the art work from both the demands of mimesis and from the canon of the beautiful. And this is certainly true of Thomas's early verse, where the jouissance or textual effect of the writing derives largely from the rich polysemous fluidity of the writing – linguistic as well as thematic – in other words from a use of language not immediately translatable into meaning. In the poetry of Thomas's first two collections especially – *18 Poems* and *Twenty-five Poems* – the writing is typified by a use of language that resists interpretation, where meanings appear to suggest themselves only retroactively or belatedly. Think for instance of the plural possibilities hinted at by 'the bagpipe breasted ladies', 'a petrol face', '[y]our corkscrew grave centred in nipple and navel', and not forgetting, of course, the notorious 'atlas-eater with a jaw for news'.[23] The list, and the possibilities, seem endless. In fact, meanings often seem to suggest themselves only when read in the context of Thomas's other poems. It is almost as if his collections exist, on one level at least, as networks of signification; a kind of virtual textual/poetic space. Think, for instance, of the 'Altarwise' sequence, which represented the high point of Thomas's Modernist obscurity, a kind of self-parodying gesture, we might say, of all that had gone before.[24] This is sonnet VI:

> Cartoon of slashes on the tide-traced crater,
> He in a book of water tallow-eyed
> By lava's light split through the oyster vowels
> And burned sea silence on a wick of words:[25]

Yet, despite the fact that epistemological and semantic certainties are obscured to the extent where meanings appear arbitrary and relative, it would be quite wrong to assume that Thomas's poetic universe is an entirely self-contained, autonomous space. More conventional critics, primarily those who learnt to read under the auspices of New Criticism, have tended to see Thomas's images as having no 'real world referent'.[26] But, this is not to say that the poetry is wholly self-referencing, that it exists as some kind of autotelic system, a space, as it were, that knows no outside. For Thomas's early verse reaches way beyond the enclosures of structuralist poetics, in its attempt to communicate a world that is hypnotic, intuitive and sensory in its perception.

THE PROCESS POETIC: REACHING FOR THE REAL

With the obvious exception of the 1933 poem 'The hand that signed the paper', it is fair to say that Thomas's verse can only very rarely be read in terms of its referential, or denotative, effect.[27] In fact, as Stewart Crehan has been keen to point out, Thomas's lyricism actually appears to create its own world, 'rather than describing the world we know'.²⁸ Hence, one of the key features of the writing is an apparent, and acute, disdain for a poetry of the 'everyday' world, of 'reality', based on conversational and discursive norms. Rather than attempting to communicate, to articulate, or to describe even, something of the fabric of contemporary existence, Thomas's early poems consistently evoke a mysterious elemental grandeur that is generated through the felt identification of natural and bodily processes. Here, inner and outer worlds collide, in a perpetual overlapping of body, mind and cosmos that blurs – erases even – the normative distinction between interior and exterior landscapes, between inside and outside. And, in addition, subject and object are frequently fused, as in, for example, 'Light breaks where no sun shines':

> Light breaks where no sun shines;
> Where no sea runs, the waters of the heart
> Push in their tides;
> And, broken ghosts with glow-worms in their heads,
> The things of light
> File through the flesh where no flesh decks the bones.²⁹

It is typical of the early verse that even the most cursory reading of the poem's first two stanzas seems to evoke some sense of an idiosyncratic blurring together of the interior worlds of dream and body with the outer cosmic processes of water cycle, tides and planetary, or galactic, movement. This is the world of the 'process' poem, a term already mentioned and first coined by Ralph Maud to refer to a paradigmatic nexus of poems in Thomas's first collection.³⁰ Developing this line of thought in the direction of a 'process poetic', or a 'process metaphysic', whereby process exists not simply as the philosophy behind the text, but acquires a certain thematic and structural significance,³¹ John Goodby has described this central concept in terms reminiscent of one of Thomas's favourite poets, Whitman:

> [E]verything in the universe exists in a state of total flux, of spatial interconnectedness and temporal simultaneity, from atoms to galaxies, selves to the solar system. In this universe all things contain their opposites; whatever is living bears its death within it, for to be born is to begin the process of dying; light is comprehended by its negation, darkness, and vice versa; what is high, seen from an altered viewpoint, is low. It is a profoundly relativistic and materialist vision of the universe as a seething, amoral continuum of forces, and the 'dialectical method' of breeding contrary images described in the letter to Treece is its logical outcome at the level of poetic composition.³²

For Maud, the quintessential process poem, and, incidentally, the one that provided him with the source for his label, is 'A process in the weather of the heart'.[33] First appearing in the *Sunday Referee*, 11 February 1934, it is, arguably, the simplest of this handful of texts, and is particularly significant in so far as it functions as a kind of ideological signpost, announcing the theme of universal interconnection, and registering the plural possibilities that this enigmatic merging of human and natural forces might entail. The only poem to actually mention the word process, it opens like this:

> A process in the weather of the heart
> Turns damp to dry; the golden shot
> Storms in the freezing tomb.
> A weather in the quarter of the veins
> Turns night to day; blood in their suns
> Lights up the living worm.
>
> A process in the eye forwarns [*sic*]
> The bones of blindness; and the womb
> Drives in a death as life leaks out.[34]

Clearly this is not the familiar world picture presented to us by culture as 'reality'. Indeed, the vision articulated here is of a mysterious, and somewhat oddly un-peopled landscape, inhabited only, it seems by a couple of ghosts (l. 18) and a solitary living worm, and is certainly not one that corresponds to any recognizable world view. Interestingly, however, Thomas's curiously undifferentiated universe, a universe that is characterized by some kind of pre-Oedipal, or (in Lacan's term) pre-Symbolic (and thus symbiotic), unity does seem to gesture towards the 'un-sayable', the unpresentable, or that strange region that lies beyond culture, that undifferentiated mass which Lacan has called the 'Real'.[35]

Since reality, for Lacan, equals 'fantasy', drawing one into the realms of the Imaginary and the Symbolic, both of which are specifically human domains, the Real is most certainly not the same as reality. Like Freud's reality principle which was an action internal to the mind, and not an event of the external world, so too the Lacanian Real is no Kantian postulation of noumena.[36] It is thus a psychical order. And yet, Lacan insists 'there are no gaps in the [R]eal'. There is, as he says, nothing missing in the Real, no division between subject and object in this wholly undifferentiated mass. It is the universe, prior to symbolization, the world before being carved up, as it were, by language. According to Bruce Fink the Real is, for example, the body of the pre-Oedipal infant, before it comes under the sway of the Symbolic order, before it is subjected to, and instructed in, the ways of the humanly constructed world. It is certainly worth quoting Fink at length here, for his particularly lucid and candid account of the Real highlights a number of points of correspondence, that seem to resonate curiously with Thomas's hitherto untheorized 'process' metaphysic, and thus to shed a new and illuminating light on it.

> In the course of socialization, the body is progressively written or overwritten with signifiers ... pleasure is localized in certain zones, while other zones are neutralized by the word and coaxed into compliance with social, behavioural norms. Taking Freud's notion of polymorphous perversity to the extreme, we can view the infant's body as one unbroken erogenous zone, there being no privileged zones, no areas in which pleasure is circumscribed at the outset. So too, Lacan's real is without zones, subdivisions, localized highs and lows, gaps or plenitudes: the real is a sort of unrent, undifferentiated fabric, woven in such a way as to be full everywhere, there being no space between the threads that are its stuff. It is a sort of smooth, seamless surface or space which applies as much to a child's body as to the whole universe.[37]

In fact, one might even go so far as to say that the Order of the Real describes those areas of life which cannot be known. And given that all our knowledge of the world is necessarily, and inevitably, mediated by language, then it follows that we can never, as speaking subjects, know anything directly. It is in this sense that Lacan can claim that the Real is the world before it is carved up by language. It is here that the extraordinary resemblances between Thomas's writing and Lacan's account of the topological category of the Real become most apparent: for he too tells of a time before the process universe is carved up by language, a time of brute materiality that is, apparently, prior to, and remote from, the patriarchal order of language, symbolic castration and the comprehension of words: 'All world was one, one windy nothing, / ... And earth and sky were as one airy hill, / ... The sun and moon shed one white light.'[38]

Given the complex nature of the Real, a complexity that is undoubtedly compounded by the Real's innate and definitive resistance to symbolization, it is worth pausing for a moment to consider Tony Myers's succinct illustration of an imagined encounter with the impossible Real. Myers quotes from the American author Chuck Palahniuk's 2001 novel *Choke*, suggesting that the following description of Mommy's understanding of the mountain involves something of the experience of the Real:

> For one flash, the Mommy had seen the mountain without thinking of logging and ski resorts and avalanches, managed wildlife, plate tectonic geology, microclimates, rain shadow, or *yin-yang* locations. She'd seen the mountain without the framework of language. Without the cage of associations. She'd

seen it without looking through the lens of everything she knew was true about mountains. What she'd seen in that flash wasn't even a 'mountain'. It wasn't a natural resource, it had no name.[39]

What is significant for Myers is the fact that the Mommy apparently has access to a mountain in its immediacy, which, apart from the fact that she identifies the mountain in its singularity and difference from everything around it, 'approximates well to an encounter with the Real'.[40] In his 1944 poem 'Ceremony after a fire raid', Thomas conveys this sense of an undifferentiated, un-rent fabric of existence by the *undecidability* of voice, rather than by image or statement alone.

> Myselves
> The grievers
> Grieve
> Among the street burned to tireless death
> A child of a few hours.[41]

Remarkably within the space of just one word the first person singular reflexive pronoun, *my*, mutates to the second part of the first person plural, *selves*, gesturing towards and indeed embodying a kind of universal communal self. This is a point to which J. Hillis Miller alludes in his seminal text *Poets of Reality*:

> From the very first moment of its existence, even in the womb, even when the 'seed [is] at-zero,' the self, for Dylan Thomas, includes all the cosmos, lives its life and is lived by its life. There is no need to achieve by expansive stratagems of sensation or imagination an identification with all things. That identification is given with existence itself and can never be withdrawn. There is no initial separation between subject and object. The self is not set apart from things or people which are other than itself. Thomas' early poetry, according to the poet himself, 'with all its many lives and deaths,' describes events which took place 'in the tumultuous world of [his] own being.'[42]

In a poignant echo of Rimbaud's '*Je est un Autre*' – 'I is another' – Thomas once declared himself to be 'lots of people'. Yet, even when his poems appear as dialogues they do not, as Hillis Miller has suggested, involve the confrontation of distinct separate identities. Rather, these early poems provide an arena for the staging of the opposing parts of a singular continuous existence. Thus, it is not a question, as for Rimbaud, of a singular-first person self which becomes 'another', which appears in plural incarnations and thereby enters into an alternate existence. For the self-styled 'Rimbaud of Cwmdonkin Drive' it is very clearly a case of the self being contained, inhering within one might say, in the most remote cosmic processes.⁴³ The self in Thomas then is not available to any kind of specular imaging. And, any sense of boundary between self and other that the first person 'I' would suggest is extremely provisional, transient and ephemeral. So much so that as Hillis Miller succinctly puts it 'what exists for Thomas as soon as anything exists at all is one continuous realm which is at once consciousness, body, cosmos, and the words that express all three at once'.⁴⁴

In a lengthy critique of a Pamela Hansford Johnson poem, Thomas revealed something of this methodology:

> Though you talk all through of the relationship of yourself to other things, there is no relationship at all in the poem between the things you example. If you are one with the swallow & one with the rose, then the rose is one with the swallow. Link together these things you talk of; show, in your words & images, how your flesh covers the tree & the tree's flesh covers you. I can see what you have done, of course – 'I am one with the opposites', you say. You are, I know, but you must prove it to me by linking yourself to the opposites and by linking the opposites together.⁴⁵

But, as Thomas seems to implicitly suggest here, even if we were to map the structure of the Real onto an undifferentiated 'All', this is still not the same as being able to name the Real. Interestingly, this idea finds specific thematic significance in Thomas's much anthologized 'The force that through the green fuse', the poem that first catapulted him to fame on the London literary scene in 1933:

> The force that through the green fuse drives the flower
> Drives my green age; that blasts the roots of trees
> Is my destroyer.
> And I am dumb to tell the crooked rose
> My youth is bent by the same wintry fever.⁴⁶

A fairly simple poem by Thomas's standards, 'The force' has lent itself to straightforward interpretations: nature and the poem's speaker are both susceptible to, and implicated in, the same creative/destructive forces of life and death, of growth and decay. It thus evokes a close identity between the events of nature and the physical organic life of the human body. Indeed, here Thomas goes as far as to claim that the energies by which he lives and those of the universe are actually identical. And this point is made with variations in each stanza. The first very clearly refers to trees and flowers, the second to mountains and rivers, the third to water, wind and sand and the fourth to the galaxy and stars – so that the perspective expands metonymically outwards, from microcosm to macrocosm, to embrace and to encompass, or to embody, the entire universe, thus making a statement about the unity of human and natural life.[47] The conflation of the human and the non-human works by simultaneously personalizing the body of the world and de-personalizing the human body – with the exception of the fourth verse, each stanza follows the same syntactic formula whereby 'the force that does A also does B'. And even in the case of the final stanza it would seem plausible that the first three lines are working to combine an inner and outer event, 'The lips of time leech to the fountain head; / Love drips and gathers, but the fallen blood / Shall calm her sores', although not obviously doing so. The poem is perhaps best described as a vital articulation of the merging of human and natural forces. However its tone, the repeated refrain 'And I am dumb to tell' does, as Walford Davies has noted, seem to suggest something more; something that exceeds a simple statement about the unity of human and natural life. It is as if the desire to communicate, 'to tell' as it were, is constantly thwarted, leaving the poet excluded, separated, marooned on the shores of language, cut off from those things with which he nevertheless identifies;[48] a doomed desiring creature, much like the Kantian subject of Terry Eagleton's *Ideology of the Aesthetic*, a decentred subject of the sublime, a speaking being who is characterized by incompleteness and left standing on the edge of the ungraspable real.

'BURIAL UNDER THE SPELLING WALL': THE PROCESS PROBLEMATIC

Although Davies is obviously quite correct in claiming that what these early poems celebrate is 'a world of undifferentiated consciousness', a realm not yet broken down, we might say, into separate 'physical and rational compartments', it would be wrong to assume that this is restricted to the handful of texts that have specifically, and conveniently, been referred to as the process poems.[49] Nor, indeed, is the idea of a primal archaic unity limited solely to his earlier work. For even in the later 'Fern Hill', a poem that has incidentally become part of the common currency of twentieth-century poetry, we get that same sense of uninterrupted existence; a universal totality that precedes the castrating effects of the propositional and rule-bound symbolic order:

> All the sun long it was running, it was lovely, the hay
> Fields high as the house, the tunes from the chimneys, it was air
>   And playing, lovely and water
>   And fire green as grass.[50]

Here we are presented with a kind of all-inclusive realm, composed from consciousness, body, world and the participation of words, a mysterious elemental continuum that Thomas calls simply 'it'. The significant word here is, of course, 'it', 'the anonymous subject', as Hillis Miller puts it, 'of all possible activities or things' and it is connected with, and to, all of these through a form of the verb 'to be':

> 'All the sun long it was running, it was lovely, ... it was air / And playing.' To put it another way, the word 'it' is the fact that something is, the unnamable, unthinkable fact of existence itself, a property which might be attributed equally to anything that is. *It is*. All things which are share a single property: they exist, they are.[51]

Here the blissfully nostalgic vision of childhood is clearly mapped on to that familiar pre-Oedipal landscape of symbiotic unity that provided the pre-natal theme and intra-uterine locus of the early poems. What particularly interests me here is the way in which 'the anonymous "it"', to use Hillis Miller's words, highlights the central difficulty of naming the un-nameable, of presenting, as it were, the unpresentable, ineffable fact of existence, and, consequently, the 'near impossibility' that interpolating the Real in a verbal medium necessarily entails. For, as Lacan reminds us, by definition the Real cannot be represented. Structurally speaking it is that which resists symbolization, an excess, a meaningless leftover, 'the vanishing point exterior to language', as Patricia Waugh puts it, 'which the subject seeks to recover through repetition, which only succeeds in marking it off as unattainable'.[52] It is the hard kernel around which symbolization fails, but equally, and this is crucial to a properly contextualized understanding of Lacan's account, it is the unattainable substance around which every signifying network is constituted.

Like any poet, or writer, the only way Thomas may (re)present the un-presentable is in, or through, the system of language. But, given the Real's innate and indeed definitive resistance to symbolization it is necessarily impossible to interpolate it in a verbal medium. And, for a poet like Thomas whose declared aim was, as we have already seen, to make a poem an event, or a happening, that would retain something of that primal energy and vitality which is normally lost to the restraining force of discursive language, this presented a serious and persistent stumbling block. This was, in fact, the *process problematic*.

Gareth Thomas has commented on what he refers to as 'the near obsession in [Thomas's] poetry – either in whole poems or individual lines and phrases – with the inadequacy of language, the lapsing into inarticulateness, the impossibility of "true" communication, and even the futility of making any attempt'.[53] We might think, for instance, of the following:

> My busy heart ...
> Sheds the syllabic blood and drains her words ('Especially when the October wind', *CPDT*, p. 18)
>
> I shall not murder
> The mankind of her going with a grave truth ('A refusal to mourn the death, by fire of a child in London', *CPDT*, p. 85)
>
> How shall my animal ...
> Endure burial under the spelling wall ('How shall my animal?', *CPDT*, p. 75)

And so on. More recently, Stewart Crehan has made a similar case, and has, for instance, read 'The force that through the green fuse' as the dramatization of the psychic conflict between the id, ego and the punitive super-ego, that reminds the speaker of his inability to speak, effectively rendering him dumb to tell.[54] Yet, from a post-structuralist perspective, where the emphasis is placed quite explicitly on the role of language, the speaker's words signify the inevitable failure of a figurative language to communicate the literal – or, in Lacanian parlance, of the Symbolic – to (re)present the Real. For Thomas, as a writer whose declared aim was, as we've already seen, to make a poem an event, or a happening that would retain something of the energy or vitality normally castrated, lost or erased by the sanitizing force of the Symbolic, this obviously posed major difficulties, which he articulated specifically in the magnificent 'How shall my animal?', his poetic summation of the paradox of writing as self-expression.[55] In a letter to Henry Treece, Thomas wrote:

> Very much of my poetry is, I know, an enquiry and a terror of fearful expectation, a discovery and a facing of fear. I hold a beast, an angel, and a madman in me, and my enquiry is as to their working, and my problem is their subjugation and victory, downthrow & upheaval, and my effort is their self-expression. The new poem I enclose, 'How Shall My Animal', is a detailed enquiry; and the poem too is the result of the enquiry, and is the furthest I can, at present, reach or hope for.[56]

From this, Ralph Maud infers that the poem functions as 'a "detailed enquiry" into how the angel-intellect wrestles with the beast of inchoate poetic stuff while the madman of words fixes the fight in imagery', and consequently that it is explicitly about 'the creative act when it occurs on the extraordinary level that Thomas demands of himself'. Yet, for Walford Davies, the poem acquires a far broader frame of reference, which extends beyond the personal and into a radical questioning of the fundamental limitations of language as a mode of artistic expression. Thomas, he insists, 'found obstacles not only in his own individual way with words but also in what words are in the first place capable of expressing'.[57] Thus, from a post-structuralist perspective, the opus, at the level of theme, would signify a dramatization of the conflict between the orders of the Real, the Imaginary and the Symbolic, re-enacted in Thomas's articulation of the self-contradictory nature of writing poetry. Thomas immediately plunges the reader into the poem with a rhetorical question, which laments the death of his inner experience, as the inevitable consequence of its verbalization and reduction to a structure of words:

> How shall my animal
> Whose wizard shape I trace in the cavernous skull,
> Vessel of abscesses and exultation's shell,
> Endure burial under the spelling wall,
> The invoked, shrouding veil at the cap of the face,
> Who should be furious,
> Drunk as a vineyard snail, flailed like an octopus,
> Roaring, crawling, quarrel
> With the outside weathers,
> The natural circle of the discovered skies
> Draw down to its weird eyes?[58]

Developing directly from the word 'animal', the images of bestial energy become metaphors for Thomas's poetic fervour, a physicality that belongs exclusively to the literal (or the 'brute physicality' of Lacan's Real), and which he fears will be tamed, or even wholly suppressed, by the countervailing, prevailing force of a figurative language. At the onset of poetic creation, it seems that Thomas was plagued by apprehension, for as a poet he recognized his task as translating his inner experience into language, yet he remained sensitive to the fact that the figurative can never truly recapture the literal, but can at best only gesture towards it, in what is necessarily a structure of words. Hence the 'spelling wall' (a pun on the wailing wall) and the 'shrouding veil at the cap of the face' (a reference, perhaps, to the hood that the executioner places over the condemned person's head) become metaphors for the poet's mouth that can only memorialize past experience and obscure what it seeks to express.[59] Whilst Thomas knew, implicitly, that to fix this internal animal in words signified an ultimate, but necessary, act of betrayal, the rebellious nature of the mortal beast when finally dragged into the outside is perhaps a curious reflection of his own creative violation of the normative rules of language. For the sake of the image, the animal is conceived as being feminine, and with Lacan's configuration of the Symbolic as the patriarchal order of language, and correspondingly the Imaginary as a dimension haunted by the maternal, it is hardly surprising that Thomas's fears for its survival should be figured in terms of how it will 'magnetise, / Towards the studded male.' The pun on 'studded/studied' of course suggests an implicit parallel between the sexual act and the act of writing, where creativity is born out of cruelty as the poetic spirit mates first with the stallion and then the land, in a simultaneous Zen-like process of creation and destruction. Playing on this image of the poem as a self-sufficient thing, in the third stanza Thomas sets up an opposition that contrasts what he wants from his writing with the mere appearance of 'having been created', which signifies the kind of work that lesser, more decorative and superficial poets are perhaps content to accept:

> Fishermen of mermen
> Creep and harp on the tide, sinking their charmed, bent pin
> With bridebait of gold bread, I with a living skein,
> Tongue and ear in the thread, angle the temple-bound
> Curl-locked and animal cavepools of spells and bone,
> Trace out a tentacle,
> Nailed with an open eye, in the bowl of wounds and weed
> To clasp my fury on ground
> And clap its great blood down;

Yet despite the fervour of poetic activity, as the author wrestles with the inner beast, the text twists, showing his efforts to be doomed, for the mortal animal is dragged from the depths of the unconscious only to suffer the brutality and finitude of death, at the moment of poetic creation, when paradoxically it becomes 'immortalized' in words:

> Never shall beast be born to atlas the few seas
> Or poise the day on a horn.

As the poem draws towards its conclusion, Maud notes how a profound and overwhelming sense of fatality pervades the final stanza where the dying beast is directly addressed as it is finally fixed in writing:

> Sigh long, clay cold, lie shorn,
> Cast high, stunned on gilled stone; sly scissors ground in frost
> Clack through the thicket of strength, love hewn in pillars drops
> With carved bird, saint, and sun, the wrackspiked maiden mouth
> Lops, as a bush plumed with flames, the rant of the fierce eye,
> Clips short the gesture of breath.
> Die in red feathers when the flying heaven's cut,
> And roll with the knocked earth:

> Lie dry, rest robbed, my beast.
> You have kicked from a dark den, leaped up the whinnying light,
> And dug your grave in my breast.[60]

Thomas clearly invests his energy not so much in a 'statement' of ideas but in a 'powerful enactment' of them through images, to the effect that each part of the poem is not only texturally dense, but is also moving, mutating and constantly changing,[61] as the animal imagery, which is sometimes disguised, runs in a series of metamorphoses producing a distinctly surrealist effect. Although Thomas's surrealism is not of the pure 'cut-up' type, and is subordinated to his own ends, the poem does have a valid, if not programmatic, surrealist element, that adds a certain force and power to the writing. As the energies of the poem, embodied in the way that the mutations occur, continually threaten to push the grammar and syntax apart, the dynamic of a surrealist import generates some impression of that very vitality and physical consciousness that Thomas so often insisted was castrated by the authoritarian repression of discursive language. Paradoxically, therefore, the poem is, says Davies, 'a victory' that triumphs 'over its own misgivings'.[62] For as the 'poetic beast' finally expires in the last line of the poem, it dies into a complete shape, that is the passion of its making over, gesturing towards the possibilities registered in the linguistic experimentation of André Breton and the French surrealists, the possibilities of discovering through poetry a reality beyond reality, composed, we might say, of the poet's inner and outer worlds.

Thomas very clearly does something more than simply pay homage to Modernism's acknowledgement of the withdrawal of the Real. For his writing not only gestures towards Lacan's 'impossible Real' in its vital articulation of those moments normally deemed to be beyond the realm of language – coition, gestation, birth, death – but, even more importantly, as was demonstrated by the magnificently mobile 'How shall my animal?', Thomas, like Joyce, actually allows the unpresentable to become perceptible in the writing itself;[63] in the paradoxical sufferings and passions of the signifier. But even if the playful materiality of the writing would seem to declare, to embody even, something of that characteristically postmodern euphoria, a sense of jubilation at the prospect of the enhanced aesthetic opportunities made available by the plural possibilities of the signifier, this is not to say that the writing does not encompass its own nostalgic moment. For, as we have already seen, Thomas's verse does tend to oscillate between backward- and forward-looking trends, unstably blending both. There is undoubtedly a nostalgic moment in Thomas's verse although this is almost always felt at the level of theme, rather than in a desire to recapture the simulated truth of realism; it is more a lament for the inefficacy of discursive language that renders true communication impossible. Moreover, any sense of lament is overshadowed and eclipsed by the radical play of signification that occurs at the level of language and linguistic structure. Indeed, with the exception of Joyce and possibly Wallace Stevens, there are few twentieth-century English-language writers who have celebrated the power of the signifier with 'such festive radicalism', to borrow Catherine Belsey's words, as Dylan Thomas.

Chapter 5

'NOW THAT MY SYMBOLS HAVE OUTELBOWED SPACE': CELEBRATING THE SIGNIFIER

For many of those theorists who have been particularly influential in terms of contemporary thinking – writers such as Roland Barthes, Mikhail Bakhtin, Julia Kristeva and, of course, Jean François Lyotard – the material anarchy of the avant-garde has, in fact, been seen as the defining attribute of modern poetic discourse, revealing itself most conspicuously in their radical subversions of the normative or expected linguistic order. Poetic language, says Kristeva, is an 'unsettling process – when not an outright destruction – of the identity of meaning and speaking subject'.[1] Now, given that slippery instability of meaning, the way in which words, images and, on occasion, even whole syntactical units are susceptible to radical fluctuations of meaning in Thomas's work, it seems that the early poetry, that of his first two collections, *18 Poems* and *Twenty-five Poems*, is, in a general sense, marked by what, from a post-structuralist perspective, might well be described as an insistent resistance to system. Yet, the points in the Thomas canon where this 'rogue element', for want of a better expression, asserts itself most forcefully are precisely those areas of the writing that, curiously, seem to have generated only scant critical attention.[2]

Perhaps one of the most interesting examples, from the early work, of a poem that has suffered from this kind of unwarranted critical neglect, is 'Today this insect' – a particularly difficult poem that might be seen as the culmination of Thomas's characteristic blend of sonorous amplitude and wilful opacity, which lures the reader, even as it apparently thwarts interpretation:

> Today, this insect, and the world I breathe,
> Now that my symbols have outelbowed space,
> Time at the city spectacles, and half
> The dear, daft time I take to nudge the sentence,
> In trust and tale have I divided sense,
> Slapped down the guillotine, the blood-red double
> Of head and tail made witness to this
> Murder of Eden and green genesis.
>
> The insect certain is the plague of fables. (*CPDT*, 38)

Composed in three, variously rhymed, eight-line stanzas, which are divided by two oracular pronouncements, this brief elegy is, even by Thomas's standards, particularly resistant to précis. It is possible, however, to make a few general observations: the poem is speaking, in some sense, about insects and poems, about the relationship between reality and imagination, fact and fiction, and seems to be making its own obscurity, or 'divided sense', its subject. Given the immediate context of 'sense' and 'symbols' one can reasonably assume that 'this insect', which has its root meaning in 'segmented' or 'divided' creature, serves as a metaphor for this particular poem, and refers both symbolically, and in a general sense, to Thomas's 'process' poetic, as that dialectic of conflicting and resolving images, to which he so often referred.[3] Although the imposition of any one interpretation would necessarily truncate its subversive potentialities, the poem does seem to hint at a number of possible scenarios. For instance, if it is read in the context of poems such as 'From love's first fever', we might interpret this as yet another staging of linguistic subjectivity, in which the following four lines would appear to communicate something of the violence of symbolic castration and a concomitant loss of linguistic plenitude:

> I divided sense,
> Slapped down the guillotine, the blood red-doubled
> Of head and tail made witness to this
> Murder of Eden and green genesis.

In such a reading, of course, the poem's central figure, the serpent – 'This story's monster has a serpent caul' – functions as a crude Freudian motif for the phallus as transcendental or master signifier, circumscribing the phonetic territory of this pre-Oedipal landscape, as he 'scrams round the blazing outline, / Measures his own length on the garden wall.' Yet, even though the overdetermination of meaning in this richly inter-textual writing demands an unusually high degree of readerly engagement, and encourages an entire range of diverse, but equally plausible, interpretations, none of these seems capable of exhausting the plural possibilities of the text, or granting the reader the certainty he naturally desires. Of course the exorbitant excess of verbal ambiguity, combined with an apparent lack of congruence between Thomas's symbols and the space that they have 'outelbowed', makes it extremely difficult to pin down any referents whatsoever in this poem. As such, developing any one reading to its logical conclusion becomes virtually impossible for, as Thomas reminds us, 'The insect certain is a plague of fables', which, put another way, seems to warn that if we crave certainty in his poetry, we might find it, to borrow a phrase from Don McKay, only 'in the glum fact of entropy'.[4] This said what is particularly worthy of note here, is the way in which Thomas's antagonistic division of meaning is so interestingly inscribed in the rich polysemy of this peculiarly gnomic sentence, where each important word yields at least two possible connotations. 'Insect' might be taken as either a literal insect or intricate image, either whole or divided. 'Certain' functions as a noun, an adjective or an adverb. 'Plague' could be translated as a multitude, a destroyer, an annoyer, or an irritant, whilst 'fables' seems to suggest both lies and fictions, in Wallace Stevens's sense, as created things. Consequently, the sense of the oracle, as Tindall remarks, depends entirely on the reader's own arrangement of these various possibilities: 'The insect, for example, is the Biblical plague of locusts; the poem destroys lies or consists of multiple fictions; reality is myth or fatal to it.'[5] The enigmatic pronouncement certainly appears to be speaking about insects, poems, fact and fiction, in both senses of the word. Thus, if the insect is, as Tindall tentatively suggests, 'Christ or a child' then other interpretations of creator, creature, reality and myth seem plausible, which given the poem's strategic positioning, in direct succession to 'Incarnate Devil', might suggest, on one level at least, an iconoclastic subversion of the inherited biblical myth by granting Satan the more active role in cosmogenesis. In one sense, with its ambiguous interweaving, and intertextual references to such literary notables as Macbeth, Don Quixote, Homer and, typically of the early poetry, to Shakespeare's *Hamlet*, the poem might well be taken as a response to the 1930s' academization of Modernism, that was spearheaded by Empson and Leavis. From this perspective, of course, the text reads as a highly self-conscious and remarkably self-reflexive dramatization of poetry as the scene of linguistic struggle, played out between the poem's opposing voices of tradition and the avant-garde. As Don McKay has argued, in the superb article to which I am indebted, 'What Shall We Do with a Drunken Poet?', these opposing voices inhabit time in very different ways:

The diachronic voice which opens the poem ... wrestles in the present with the task at hand for two and a half very obscure stanzas. The synchronic 'ageless' voice which appears in the last four lines of the poem between inverted commas is of course able to surround or transcend time, and hence deliver a message about permanent patterns without diachronic drudgery or *angst*.[6]

A juxtaposition of these voices reveals a number of useful insights:

> (a) Today, this insect, and the world I breathe,
> Now that my symbols have outelbowed space,
> Time at the city spectacles, and half
> The dear, daft time I take to nudge the sentence,
> In trust and tale have I divided sense,
> Slapped down the guillotine, the blood-red double
> Of head and tail made witness to this
> Murder of Eden and green genesis.

> (b) 'Adam I love, my madman's love is endless,
> No tell-tale lover has an end more certain,
> All legends' sweethearts on a tree of stories,
> My cross of fables behind the fabulous curtain.'

The first voice clearly embodies a kind of anarchic energy or anterior materiality, characterized most notably in the dissolute syntax, which is busily engaged in not signifying at the level of the sentence, and in the images of dividing and guillotining, that actually work to convey and participate in the fracturing of meaning that appears to be the subject of this enigmatic text. In his more conventional exegesis, William York Tindall speculates that 'presumably [Thomas] had just killed an insect as it crossed the table where he wrote', and having then consulted a dictionary, discovered an obsolete adjectival use of the word insect, and so found the material for his poem.[7] Yet, as McKay remarks, if something like this is 'the insect fable' behind the poem 'Thomas has chosen to hide it so thoroughly that the very act of obscuring seems to control our reading experience'. Unlike Donne's flea, or Bruce's spider, which can become instant myths or fables because their symbolic value is foregrounded, Thomas's insect is, by contrast, entirely emptied of its symbolic significance, so that he seems at once to be 'proposing and banishing its meaning'. We might, however, as McKay suggests, characterize this procedure in 'Peircean terms', as the conversion of a symbol into an icon: 'By interrupting the conventions of symbolisation [Thomas] has forced the insect to represent itself, as a linguistic sign, iconically.' In this sense, then, it has 'outelbowed space'.[8] This synchronic voice that delights in obscurity and flaunts its ability to destabilize traditional modes of discourse evidently constitutes some kind of disruptive impulse in the writing. The 'ageless', or synchronic voice, on the other hand, appears, ostensibly, at least, to establish some sense of permanence and coherence in the text. There is, for instance, the conflation of Adam's tree with the cross, that Thomas draws from a well-established tradition of metaphysical poetry and, perhaps most significantly, the unifying symbol of infinite love. Curiously, however, the univocality of this omnipresent love is, as the poem suggests, predicated on the energies of various literary madmen, who are catalogued in the previous four lines:

> Death: death of Hamlet and the nightmare madmen,
> An air-drawn windmill on a wooden horse,
> John's beast, Job's patience, and the fibs of vision,
> Greek in the Irish sea the ageless voice

What is particularly interesting here is the way in which the poem seems to finally resolve its contesting impulses into some kind of mutually dependent relationship. From a more general perspective, there is, of course, an inextricable linking of creative and destructive energies in Thomas's writing, which seems to resonate quite remarkably with Lyotard's basic thesis that the failure of contemporary language games or, to put it another way, the shattering of discourse, is what provides the catalyst for the creative and innovative impulse of (post)modern art and literature. As such, it might well be argued that the text stages an encounter between tradition and the avant-garde, which, paradoxically perhaps, seems to imply that tradition is served best by acts of rebellion rather than meek veneration.

'ABSTRACT[ING] THE LETTERS OF THE VOID': FETISHIZING THE SIGNIFIER

Syntactically tortuous, and laden with pun, circumlocutions and obscure allusions 'Today this insect' is a tireless testimony to the gaps, absences and 'hesitations' that haunt our speech. A profoundly experimental and decidedly gnomic piece of writing, the poem typifies an avant-garde aesthetic by repudiating the illusions of realism and 'breaking the rules' in order to tell an altogether different kind of 'truth' in poetry. Its emphasis is, as has already been shown, ultimately self-referential, defining and foregrounding the signifier itself – not the object represented – as the material substance, or subject even, of literature. Things, however, are rarely that simple or straightforward in Thomas, and paradoxically at the same time that the writing is communicating, through the play of signifiers, a sense of the fact of the Real, it is working through an excess of signification to defend the reading/writing subject against the threat of being engulfed by that self-same Real.

Chris Wigginton has made a particularly suggestive allusion to this point when he refers, in his recently published monograph, *Modernism from the Margins*, to Thomas's 'linguistic surplus' as the 'euphoric aspect' of the postmodern sublime, a kind of '*baroque superabundance [that] skates over the void of a "yawning wound"*'.⁹ Regrettably Wigginton chooses not to pursue this point. Nor does he name the void. Given its immediate context, however, it is safe to assume that he is making some gesture towards the void or wound of the Real, the inassimilable kernel, the gaping hole, one might say, at the very heart of the Symbolic order that renders signification possible. What is being proposed in the current discussion then is that Thomas fetishizes language and, in Žižekian terms, raises the signifier to 'the dignity of the-thing-itself', making of it the sublime object,¹⁰ the 'something' that 'happens', as it were, that protects the speaking subject – the Lacanian *parle-être* – from annihilation, from the threat of collapsing back into the chaos of nothingness that any direct encounter or confrontation with the Real would necessarily involve.¹¹ Thomas is however not unique in this. Rainer Emig has made a similar point with reference to Gerard Manley Hopkins and the problem of the sign, when he argues that '[p]aradoxically, the only defence left to the subject is to take part in this orgy of signification, to jump on the train hurrying towards complete annihilation and then to take – at least limited – control. How? By signification.' ¹² At this point it is worth pausing to reconsider the question posed at the start of the previous chapter about the possibility and legitimacy of re-reading Thomas in terms of a proto-postmodern aesthetic of the sublime, given that his poetic of excess appears, ostensibly at least, to be radically at odds with (and even, at times, perhaps, diametrically opposed to) the kind of abstract minimalism that we would typically associate with the modern sublime of someone like Barnett Newman. But, on closer inspection, Thomas's linguistic superabundance is perhaps not so different in its impetus from what has been widely referred to as Newman's plastic nudity. For, despite their apparent differences, what Newman and Thomas do share is that absolute refusal to submit, or to concede even, to any wider cultural demand that a solid anchorage be restored to the referent. And, moreover, Newman's abstract minimalism does, after all, represent only one aspect of what might well be described as Lyotard's Janus-faced postmodern sublime.[13] The other, its other 'euphoric' or jubilatory aspect, is, as has already been suggested, figured in Thomas's poetic of excess. This said, what is of particular interest here is the stress that both place on the idea of the creative act as an 'event'.

At first glance Newman's work appears deceptively simple: large asymmetrical blocks of colour are divided by a series of rectilinear lines that the artist famously referred to as 'zips'. These zips introduce a border, a dividing line that intervenes between order and chaos, for were we to imagine one of Newman's expansive canvases as being devoid of these linear distinctions the experience of 'a pure colour field' would, as Philip Shaw asserts, 'overwhelm the viewer to the point of paralysis'. Thus, in Burke's sense the experience would be 'terrible', adds Shaw, since it announces that 'language, otherness, or life itself will soon be over'.[14] From this we can infer that Newman's zips function in precisely the same way as Thomas's excess of signification, by plugging the void, as it were, so that the threat of annihilation for the subject is, momentarily at least, suspended. Writing of Newman's fixation with artistic creation, as a symbol of creation itself as in the story of Genesis, Lyotard refers to the painter's celebrated dictum '[t]he subject matter of creation is chaos':

> The titles of many of his paintings suggest that they should be interpreted in a paradoxical idea of beginning. Like a flash of lightning in the darkness or a line on an empty surface, the Word separates, divides, institutes a difference, makes tangible because of that difference, minimal though it may be, and therefore inaugurates a sensible world. This beginning is an antimony. It takes place in the world as its initial difference, as the beginning of its history. It does not belong to this world because it begets it, it falls from a prehistory, or from an a-history. The paradox is that of performance, or occurrence. Occurrence is the instant which 'happens', which 'comes' unexpectedly but which, once it is there, takes its place in the network of what has happened. Any instant can be the beginning, provided that it is grasped in terms of its quod rather than its quid. Without this flash there would be nothing, or there would be chaos. The flash like the instant is always there and never, and never there [sic]. The world never stops beginning.[15]

The resonance with Thomas here is quite remarkable. For, like Newman, he too sees the process of cosmogenesis as being rooted firmly in 'the word', as his 1934 poem 'In the beginning' very clearly demonstrates:

> In the beginning was the pale signature,
> Three-syllabled and starry as the smile;

> And after came the imprints on the water,
> Stamp of the minted face upon the moon;
> The blood that touched the crosstree and the grail
> Touched the first cloud and left a sign.
> ...
> In the beginning was the word, the word
> That from the solid bases of the light
> Abstracted all the letters of the void;
> And from the cloudy bases of the breath
> The word flowed up, translating to the heart
> First characters of birth and death. (*CPDT*, pp. 22–3)

The remarkable opening line is all about beginnings and origins. Thematically, like many of the poems in Thomas's first two collections, it establishes the poem's concern with identity formation before birth.[16] But it is, like the opening line of each and every stanza thereafter, also about itself as a beginning: it is a poem that returns us again and again to the beginning, as it unsettles and disrupts any simple or easy notion of opening. Moreover, and even more paradoxically, it returns us to a time before the beginning: to a time, or period, of utter and absolute chaos, a wholly undifferentiated realm, as it were, where even heaven and hell are indistinguishable, 'mixed as they spun' together. It is also a beginning that is, ambiguously, not truly a beginning or prelude, in so far as the text repeatedly refers us back to other texts, to other moments of artistic creation, not only in its biblical references to the book of Genesis and the Gospel of St John[17] but also, perhaps, as Maud tentatively suggests, to D. H. Lawrence's *Fantasia of the Unconscious*,[18] as texts which are themselves supremely concerned with cosmogenesis, and the process of creation.

The title, 'like all titles is poised uncertainly between inside and outside. It both names the poem as if from outside and forms part of the poem itself.'[19] Though this is, perhaps, exaggerated or foregrounded here. For it should be noted that the title, like almost all of Thomas's titles, is taken from the first line of the poem which, as Stewart Crehan has very acutely observed, would seem to suggest that Thomas embarked on many of his poems equipped, 'not with a preconceived theme or subject, an "idea for a poem", but with intrinsically poetic material: *with words and phrases*, sounds and sound patterns, images and image clusters that emanated from deep psychic sources, and which formed part of an evolving symbolic universe'.[20] And, beginning as it does with the 'word', the poem entails a certain performativity that, in itself, seems to inscribe the text with the status of an *event*, as artistic creation becomes inextricably linked to, and even conflated with, the symbol of all creation and the founding biblical story of genesis. For the text actually creates, performs or enacts the very process that it describes – the beginning, or origin, that is the word. But, this 'creation' is not just a single, isolated event that occurs at the moment of writing: it 'happens' with every new reading of Thomas's poem, where time after time the reader is returned to a beginning, a beginning that *is* the word. Here, then, the signifier appears in all its plural incarnations as 'word', 'cipher', 'pale signature', 'symbol' and so on, and is pitted against the anarchic chaos that precedes signification, the empty page which permits everything, because it contains nothing. An all-engulfing void, as it were, that lacks the order of the right, written, black word. For Thomas it seems that the written word, like Newman's rectilinear lines, allows for the introduction of borderlines, a distance which is both temporal and spatial, within the act of signification. This distance seems necessary to escape this potential anarchy, the overwhelming power of the void – a power that is its tendency to become wholly autonomous, its own reality which does not know an outside. What is being suggested here is that Thomas's fetishization of the signifier, like Newman's rectilinear zip, creates a threshold, or border, that separates something from nothing, or, as Philip Shaw incisively puts it, 'the pleasure of creation from the terror of privation'.[21] The boundary may be slight but it is enough, according to Lyotard, to make us experience, to feel, as it were, some sense of the sublime.

The notion of the event is crucial here, for, arguably, Thomas's poetry exists like Newman's art, to prevent the sublime from 'succumbing to the domesticating effects of time and sensibility'.[22] With both Newman and Thomas, the viewing/reading subject is confronted with an event, a 'happening', perhaps, that resists the imposition of rules and categories. All we can be sure of is that something happens but we are left unable to judge or to decide just what it is exactly that happens. As Shaw explains, for Lyotard the difference between 'something happens' and 'what happens' is crucial:

> On the one hand, when we declare 'what happens,' we supply the sublime event or object with a concept and thereby shut down its capacity for transformation. On the other hand, if we remain open to the 'something happens' then we maintain the specificity of the event and respond to the challenge of its radical indeterminacy.[23]

As events, or happenings, Thomas's poems consist then, we might say, 'in the perception of an instant in which something happens to which we are called to respond without knowing in advance ... [how] to respond'.[24] Confronted with the overwhelming orgy of signification that is Thomas's verse we are immediately struck by the need, the inclination, as it were, to react or to respond in some way. Yet, the wilful opacity of this densely textured writing, that thwarts even as it invites interpretation, offers no clue as to just how it is that we, as readers, might respond.

The wider implications of Lyotard's theorizing on the (postmodern) sublime are explored in his seminal text 'Answering the Question: What is Postmodernism' (1984).[25] In this classic account Lyotard departs from the kind of temporal and chronological definitions advanced by Jameson and Baudrillard, and argues for what is, essentially, a far more subtle and nuanced understanding of the postmodern, which he sees as an event in itself, rather than a movement or a passage of time. In other words, like Thomas's process poetic, and like Newman's abstract minimalism, the postmodern works not to confirm the familiar, or even to reveal the transcendental, but rather, as Shaw has argued, to 'precipitate in the emergence of the "now"':

> Whenever, that is, modernity stalls in nostalgic reverie for the lost contents of the sublime, offering the reader or viewer the promise of some ultimate 'reconciliation of the concept of the sensible', it is then that the postmodern arises to impart a stronger sense of the impossibility of this task.[26]

It would appear that, in contrast to a Modernist aesthetic which allows the unpresentable to be put forward 'only as the missing contents' (while its form 'continues to offer the reader or viewer matter for solace or pleasure'), both Thomas and Newman, like the postmodern, 'pu[t] forward the unpresentable in presentation itself'.[27]

In this chapter it has been argued that even though Thomas might not be considered to be paradigmatically 'postmodern' we can detect a certain postmodern impulse at work within the contours and textures of the writing. Suggesting that Modernism and the postmodern are either tendencies or modes that occur and coexist within the textual space of his verse, the current discussion has attempted to show how, within the context of Thomas's hybrid poetics, where the writing is, as was shown in part one of the book, radically suspended between realist and experimental modes, the postmodern impulse contained within the work signifies a further radicalization of the implicit and explicit challenge posed to realist representation. The next chapter will return, again, to the notion of this postmodern impulse, and will endeavour to further extrapolate the idea of Thomas as a proto-postmodernist by suggesting that the hyper-visibility of the body, and of bodily or corporeal jouissance, in his poetry is entirely at odds with what Maud Ellmann has seen as T. S. Eliot's frenetic attempt to exclude, or to abject, the body – and the female body in particular – in *The Waste Land*. This can be read as further evidence of Thomas's ongoing attempt to critique and destabilize the closures of modernity, by exploring the 'un-sayable', the 'invisible' and the 'incommunicable'.

Part Three

'Toenails and Tumours': Re-routing Abjection, from Pessimism to Parody

---

Tell him I write of worms and corruption, because I like worms and corruption. Tell him I believe in the fundamental wickedness and worthlessness of man, and in the rot in life. Tell him I am all for cancers. And tell him, too, that I loathe poetry. I'd prefer to be the keeper of a morgue any day. Tell him I live exclusively on toenails and tumours. I sleep in a coffin too, and a wormy shroud is my summer suit.

Dylan Thomas, 1934

Let a body venture at last out of its shelter, take a chance with meaning under a veil of words. WORD FLESH.

Julia Kristeva, 1976

This kind of ironic, self-reflecting parody of the dialogism inherent in language is often in the style of the traditional fool, who mocks others' use of words by using them himself.

Mikita Hoy, 1992

Chapter 6

Modern psychoanalytic theory is anything but monolithic; rather it consists of a multiplicity of divergent and competing theories which often contradict one another. There is, however, one point, at least, upon which some of the most significant and innovative post-Freudian thinkers in this field have appeared to concur: the importance of the body, and of bodily representation, in both the construction and constitution of subjectivity. In a lucid summary of contemporary psychoanalytic thought on the nature of the relationship between corporeality and subjectivity – a relationship which, remarkably, although apparently crucial, still remains to be fully theorized – Elizabeth Grosz makes this challenging observation:

> In place of the mind/body dichotomy, the fundamental connectedness of the mind to the body, the creation of a physical 'interior' for the body's object-like status, the mapping of the body's interior on its exterior and its exterior on its interior, all need to be theorized. Kristeva's conception of the body's role in physical development and in signification provides a major, if undeveloped, contribution to such an understanding. Only if the body's psychical interior is projected outwards, and its material externality is introjected as necessary conditions of subjectivity, can the dualism of our Cartesian heritage be challenged.[1]

'[T]he fundamental connectedness of the mind to the body', '[the] conception of the body's role in physical development and in signification', and the idea of 'the body's psychical interior [being] projected outwards, [whilst] its material externality is introjected', are all terms that could well be applied to Thomas's early writing which, with its panorama of corporeality and radical linguistic materiality, can be understood as offering a poetic interrogation of prevailing liberal, humanist, masculinist or naturalist conceptions of subjectivity.

Clearly, there are a number of urgent and illuminating parallels to be drawn here, for Thomas's early work, too, posits a similar concern to challenge the ways in which the body has traditionally been relegated to a subordinate position relative to the primacy of the mind. Yet, if Thomas's fascination with the physical, which also, importantly, includes the materiality of discourses, seems to concur with current theoretical trends, his privileging of the body, 'the strong stressing of the physical', as he put it, coupled with what might well be described as an excessive emphasis on the acoustic tissues of the word, placed him immediately at odds with both his contemporaries and his near contemporaries alike.

Taking this as a starting point for the current discussion, and drawing specifically on Julia Kristeva's theory of abjection, in this chapter it will be argued that Thomas's return to the body offers a re-inscription of what Eliotic high Modernism, with its aesthetic of abstraction, impersonality, intellectuality and emotional distance had attempted, although not entirely successfully, to repress.

'A STRONG STRESSING OF THE PHYSICAL': THE BODILY MATERIALITY OF FLESH AND LANGUAGE

Between November 1933 and December 1936 Thomas wrote at least seven letters that referred specifically to his use of anatomical imagery.[2] The first of these, dated early November 1933, and written to Pamela Hansford Johnson, is particularly significant and worth quoting at length. Composed in fifteen subsections, section five, entitled 'Defence of Poesie', registers an early statement of the poetic principles associated with the body and reads as follows:

> What you call ugly in my poetry is, in reality, nothing but the strong stressing of the physical. Nearly all my images, coming as they do, from my solid world of flesh and blood, are set out in terms of their progenitors. To contrast a superficial beauty with a superficial ugliness, I do not contrast a tree with a pylon, or a bird with a weasel, but rather the human limbs with the human tripes. Deeply, of course, all these contrasting things are equally beautiful and equally ugly. Only by association is the refuse of the body more to be abhorred than the body itself. Standards have been set for us. What is little realised is that it was only chance that dictated these standards. It is polite to be seen at one's dining table, and impolite to be seen in one's lavatory. It might well have been decided, when the tumour of civilisation was first fostered, that

celebrations should be held in the w.c., and that the mere mention of 'eating and drinking' would be the height of impropriety. It was decided by Adam and Eve, the first society lawmakers, that certain parts of the body should be hidden and certain be left uncovered. Again, it was chance that decided them to cover their genital organs, and not, say, their armpits or throats. While life is based upon such chance conventions and standards as these, it is little wonder that any poetry dealing impartially with the parts of the anatomy, (not quite impartially, perhaps, for the belly emphasises an abstruse point better than the Atlas-bone), and with the functions of the body, should be considered as something rather, hideous, unnecessary, and, to say the least, indelicate. But I fail to see how the emphasising of the body can, in any way, be regarded as hideous. The body, its appearance, death, and diseases, is a fact, sure as the fact of a tree. It has its roots in the same earth as the tree. The greatest description I know of our own 'earthiness' is to be found in John Donne's Devotions, where he describes man as earth of the earth, his body earth, his hair a wild shrub growing out of the land. All thoughts and actions emanate from the body. Therefore the description of any thought or action – however abstruse it may be – can be beaten home by bringing it onto a physical level. Every idea, intuitive or intellectual, can be imagined and translated in terms of the body, its flesh, skin, blood, sinews, veins, glands, organs, cells, or senses.

Through my small, bonebound island I have learnt all I know, experienced all, and sensed all. All I write is inseparable from the island. As much as possible, therefore, I employ the scenery of the island to describe the scenery of my thoughts, the earthquakes of the body to describe the earthquakes of the heart.[3]

Although Thomas's immediate concern here is, clearly, to defend his use of anatomical imagery against the charge of 'ugliness' that had been levelled at his poetry, from a more general perspective the significance of this important piece of correspondence lies quite explicitly in its revelation of the extent to which he was vitally compelled by an almost obsessive fascination for the body and bodily processes. As far as Thomas was concerned there is, in fact, no rationale behind the arbitrary cultural dictates and social conventions that determine which parts of the body are deemed to be presentable in sociocultural terms, and those which are not – why '[i]t is acceptable to be seen at one's dining table, and not in one's lavatory'. Moreover, there is nothing, in his view, that is intrinsically abhorrent even about bodily waste or 'refuse'. For, it is only 'by association', he insists, that we become engulfed by a painful sense of loathing or revulsion when confronted with the experience of what in Kristevan terms would be referred to as 'abject matter'.[4] Hence, as Harri Garrod Roberts has observed, what Hansford Johnson identifies as 'ugly' in his poetry is, we might say, 'merely the transgression of such bodily proprieties and conventions' via the strong stressing of the physical – an emphasis that is essential, says Roberts, 'if we are to experience the abstract mediations of language on the *immediate* and *material* level of the body'.[5]

Although, in one sense, it might be argued that Thomas's staging of an often grotesque corporeality signifies a Modernist rejection of the norms of beauty, it was in fact his return to the body – both thematically and linguistically – that would place him immediately at odds with his Modernist precursors. A comparison with Eliot is inevitable here. For even though there is much to link Thomas with Eliot – we might think for instance of the enthusiasm with which Thomas was to seize upon the older poet's claim that 'meaning' in a poem was something that satisfied the rational mind of the reader while the poem was performing its 'real' work on him/her at an unconscious somatic level[6] – the often grim, biological reductionism of Thomas's early work totally opposes him to Eliot's rejection, in *The Waste Land*, of the body, and of the female body in particular, as material, devouring and engulfing.

In contrast, then, to Thomas's reification of the body and its refuse, *The Waste Land* can be read as revealing Eliot's paradoxical fear of, and fascination for, the body – and, especially, as is suggested above, the female body, whose adornment and inner workings are the subject of so much of the poem. Maud Ellmann, in *The Poetics of Impersonality* (1987), has described *The Waste Land* as 'one of the most abject texts in English literature'.[7] But, before going on to discuss the implications of Ellmann's assertion, it might be worth pausing to consider just what it is that Kristeva means by her notion of the essentially and unequivocally excessive 'abject'.

For Kristeva abjection, the state of 'abjecting' or rejecting what is essentially other to oneself, and thereby creating borders of an always tenuous or fragile 'I', is one of the most fundamental processes of what she calls *le sujet en procès* – the subject in process or 'on trial'.[8] Although Kristeva does agree with Lacan that the mirror stage may indeed bring about some sense of unity or synthesis, she is concerned to take us beyond, or behind, the mirror stage, and suggests that even prior to the onset of this crucial stage of ego-formation the infant begins to separate itself from the mother, and the unificatory dyad, in order to develop borders between 'I' and other. These boundaries are formed and further developed by the process she calls abjection, that is to say, the process of jettisoning what seems, paradoxically perhaps, to be part of oneself. The abject is, explains

Noëlle McAfee, 'what one spits out, rejects, [and] almost violently excludes from oneself: sour milk, excrement, even a mother's engulfing embrace':

> What is abjected is radically excluded but never banished altogether. It hovers at the periphery of one's own existence, constantly challenging one's own tenuous borders of selfhood. What makes something abject and not simply repressed is that it does not entirely disappear from consciousness. It remains as both an unconscious and a conscious threat to one's own boundaries of a clean and proper self. The abject is what does not respect boundaries. It beseeches and pulverises the subject.[9]

Kristeva provides a catalogue of graphic examples in an attempt to communicate some sense of the violence by which the subject jettisons phenomena that simultaneously threaten and create the always tenuous and fragile borders of the self. She speaks not only of bodily waste (most notably vomit and excrement) but also of curdling milk, the cadaver or corpse and even the 'abject mother' (her most pointed example of abjection), and of how it is that one retches at their very presence. This, then, is how she famously describes food loathing as perhaps the most archaic form of abjection:

> When the eye sees or the lips touch that skin on the surface of the milk – harmless, thin as cigarette paper, pitiful as a nail pairing – I experience a gagging sensation and, still farther down, spasms in the stomach, the belly; and all the organs shrivel up the body, provoke tears and bile, increase heartbeat, cause forehead and hands to perspire. Along with sight clouding dizziness, nausea makes me balk at that milk cream, separates me from the mother and father who proffer it. 'I' want none of that element, sign of their desire; 'I' do not want to listen, 'I' do not assimilate it, 'I' expel it. But since the food is not an 'other' for me, who am only in their desire, I expel myself, I spit myself out, I abject myself within the same motion through which 'I' claim to establish myself.[10]

What has to be acknowledged and repeatedly stressed, however, is that the object is neither the milk, the dung, the vomit, the corpse, the (m)other, nor indeed, as Julian Wolfreys asserts, any particular object as such: 'the subject rids itself of something other than itself and yet part of itself, thereby seeking in the process of "ab-jecting" to re-establish the boundaries of the self'.[11] So to reiterate then, abjection or, as Kristeva would have it, the active process of *ab-jecting*[12] names the work of a psychic traversal 'resulting in a corporeal, physiological and psychological response' which, 'due to the extremity and violence of subjective experience, breaks up the subject's sense of identity in the very process by which I [the subject] try to maintain myself, my identity, my life'.[13] As such, it would seem that the subjective self is, perhaps, continually returned to the drama of abjection, for, in attempting to maintain the essentially unstable borders of its own fragile identity, the subject finds him/herself forced to jettison, time and time again, that which is, as Norma Clare Moruzzi insists, ambiguously, most necessarily inescapable and, at the same time, rejected: 'the bodily reminders of physical dependency [on the maternal] and necessity'.[14]

This reflects interestingly on Ellmann's assertion that *The Waste Land* is, arguably, the most abject text in English literature. For in describing Eliot's poem as a text of abjection what is actually being said, both implicitly and explicitly, is that *The Waste Land* is a radically unstable work which delights in expelling waste, but which is, at the same time, haunted by a pervasive sense of its own failed exclusions: for abjection is, according to Georges Bataille, 'the inability to assume with sufficient strength the imperative act of excluding abject things', an act which, he insists, 'establishes the foundations of collective existence'.[15] Waste, then, is what a culture *must* cast away, what it must exclude or reject in order to establish its own limits, in much the same way as the subject, in Kristeva's psychoanalytic sophistication of Bataille, 'defines the limits of his/her body through the violent expulsion of its own excess'.[16]

In Ellmann's authoritative reading, *The Waste Land* is assumed to be about what it declares – waste. A kind of 'centrifugal dissemination of debris', Eliot's poem 'teems' with all sorts of *disjecta*. From the written detritus, the 'waste paper', of a literary past to the wreckage and desolation of Europe's ruined cities, 'London/Unreal' (l. 376),[17] to the 'empty bottles, sandwich papers, / Silk handkerchiefs, cardboard boxes, and cigarette ends' (ll. 175–7) that paste the banks of the Thames, the text is littered, it seems, with broken images.[18] But what particularly interests Ellmann, and what appears to fascinate her even more than the heap of broken images that the poem shores up, is the very act of 'casting out', the thrusting aside or 'laying waste' that the text performs. This 'abjection' is, ultimately, a rejection of the body and of femininity. Yet the abject, as has already been shown, is, according to Kristeva, never entirely safely discarded, and continues to exist both as a precondition of subjectivity, as that against which the subject must define itself, and as an ever present threat to the stability and integrity of this subjectivity. As Elizabeth Grosz puts it, '[this waste] can never be definitively and permanently externalised. It *is* the subject; it *cannot* be completely expelled.'[19] Endorsing this point, in a reading of Kristeva that is clearly very strongly influenced by Grosz's essay, Harri Roberts adds:

The abject can thus never be safely confined to the category of *object*, but continues to transgress the boundaries separating subject from object, self from other. Moreover, the very act of expelling the abject itself testifies to the frailty of the defining subject/object opposition. The expulsion of abject otherness is therefore what establishes the illusion of an autonomous unified self and what reveals the fragility, porosity and fundamental instability of that self ...[20]

Roberts's fundamental assertion is that 'the subject both abjects and is made abject in the same ambivalent motion', and goes some way at least to explaining the strange dual fascination with, and repulsion by, female flesh that Ellmann identifies when she notes that 'the poem is enthralled by the femininity that it reviles'.[21] For, in spite of the text's rigorously repeated attempts to purge itself of the odorous 'stench of female flesh', Eliot's fiercely misogynistic poem never ceases to be threatened by the encroachments of the material feminine – the aborted foetuses, broken fingernails, carious teeth, slime, effluvia, and so on.

Of course, the point that needs to be emphasized here is the crucial ambiguity that Kristeva's canonical formulation entails: that is her slippage between the operation *to abject* and the condition *to be abject*. Once again, to abject is to expel, to reject, to separate; to be abject, on the other hand, is to be 'repulsive, stuck, subject enough only to feel this subjecthood at risk'.[22] For Kristeva the operation to abject is 'fundamental to the maintenance of subject and society alike, while the condition to be abject is corrosive of both formations'.[23] Thus, in abjecting the distanced and displaced body, the text of *The Waste Land* is itself made abject, haunted, as it were, by the spectre of a nameless and 'shoreless' flesh, a kind of absent presence, in the Macherayan sense perhaps, that threatens to dissolve the bodily integrity and masculinist self-mastery of the work.

The contrast with the body-centredness of Thomas's early work is remarkable. For if Eliot had indeed attempted to abject or exclude the body in order, as Wigginton suggests, to 'stage the mind of Europe', then it might equally be said that Thomas actually foregrounds abjection or, to be more accurate, abject matter in order to reclaim the body as a site of subversive potentialities.[24] And, if we relate Eliot's definitive text to almost any of the poems in Thomas's first collection the dissimilarity is striking. For, it would appear that within the pages of his *18 Poems* the body is propelled back from the margins, to a position that Thomas regarded as its rightful place at centre stage. Think, for instance, of an early poem such as 'When once the twilight locks'. Published initially in *New Verse* in June 1934, this is one of Thomas's most striking 'womb and tomb' poems:

> When once the twilight locks no longer
> Locked in the long worm of my finger
> Nor dammed the sea that sped about my fist.
> The mouth of time sucked, like a sponge,
> The milky acid on each hinge
> And swallowed dry the waters of the breast.[25]

This is merely the beginning, of course. The entire poem proceeds in this same remarkable fashion, valorizing all the physical processes that Modernists like Eliot (although not Joyce, once more a rare exception) so fastidiously relegated to the margins and footnotes of their writing. The hyper visibility of human anatomy, figured here most prominently in the maternal feminine, very clearly reverses Eliot's repeated attempts to displace and efface the threat of what he perceived to be a sexually encoded female physicality in *The Waste Land*. Thomas's theme here is that of creation, which is positively linked to the maternal. As is the case with so many of his early works, the body-centredness of the writing radiates from its intra-uterine locus poetic. Galactic, a portmanteau word, that conflates lactation and cosmos, gives a positive charge to the process of weaning as an antecedent to poetic development and creative energies in this poem, where the creature could be Christ, child, poem or all three. Interestingly, there is a related point to be made here about language. For, if we take the creature to be the poem or poetic development, Thomas seems to be suggesting that the feminine or semiotic mode of discourse, that by its very definition subordinates connotative determinacy to the aural and oral pleasures of the word, is both a natural and necessary precursor to poetic development. Ultimately, this might even be read in terms of a challenge on Thomas's part, a revolt against the incipient misogyny of an élitist male modernism.

Throughout the course of her work Kristeva has returned again and again to her key theme of abjection. Interestingly, in *Powers of Horror* (1982) she forges a link between literature and abjection, calling literature 'abjection's privileged signifier':

> By suggesting that literature is [abjection's] privileged signifier, I wish to point out that, far from being a minor, marginal activity in our culture, as general consensus seems to have it, this kind of literature, or even literature as such, represents the ultimate coding of our crises, of our most intimate and most serious apocalypses. Hence its nocturnal power.[26]

Her general argument in *Powers of Horror* does seem to suggest that literature, in displaying the symptoms of abjection, offers the reading/writing subject some way of working through his own neuroses. And, whilst it would be quite wrong to suggest that Thomas's playful poetic of excess is in any sense cathartic, or that it might offer (either Thomas himself or the reader) some means of working through what she lyrically calls 'the maladies of the soul', her next point does appear to reflect interestingly on Thomas's staging of a grotesque corporeality. For, she adds that literature 'may also involve not an ultimate resistance to but an unveiling of the abject: an elaboration, a discharge, and a hollowing out of abjection through the Crisis of the Word'.[27] This certainly seems relevant to an understanding of the body-centredness of Thomas's early work for the writing does seem to gesture towards this kind of unveiling of the abject or, perhaps, to be more accurate, of abject visceral matter. Consider, for instance, the grim biological reductionism of a poem like 'Before I knocked', which is typical of Thomas's womb and tomb poems in so far as it traces the development of the not-yet-subject self from the moment of conception within the intra-uterine space of the maternal body. This is the poem's opening stanza:

> Before I knocked and flesh let enter,
> With liquid hands tapped on the womb,
> I who was shapeless as the water
> That shaped the Jordan near my home
> Was brother to Mnetha's daughter
> And sister to the fathering worm.[28]

Here the pre-natal speaker is shapeless and genderless, defined by neither physical distinction nor physiological attributes,[29] a he/she or it that is at once both 'brother to Mnetha's daughter / And sister to the fathering worm.' This is a being without borders who is entirely merged with the maternal other. For this is, we might say, a poetic summation of primary narcissism in its most literal guise, an unveiling as Kristeva would have it of the impossible body of the 'abject' mother. A similar example of Thomas's 'unveiling of abjection' can be seen in the poem that is placed immediately before this one in *18 Poems*, 'A process in the weather of the heart':

> A process in the weather of the heart
> Turns damp to dry; the golden shot
> Storms in the freezing tomb.
> A weather in the quarter of the veins
> Turns night to day; blood in their suns
> Lights up the living worm.
>
> A process in the eye forwarns [sic]
> The bones of blindness; and the womb
> Drives in a death as life leaks out.[30]

Here the womb is explicitly seen as driving in a death, which we might interpret as gesturing towards the inevitable and necessary dissolution of the narcissistic union as 'each mothered child / [s]its in their double shade', both seduced or longing for, and yet, at the same time, utterly repelled by, the memory of the abject mother's terrifying and all engulfing embrace.

It is here then that we see how Thomas differs so profoundly from the Eliot of *The Waste Land*. For, in its body-centredness, Thomas's writing might be said to stage the abject – not simply in its vital articulation of the 'abject mother', but also in its more general foregrounding of a vivid corporeality that includes the bodily waste of 'cancers', 'abscess', faecal matter ('the maggot in the stool'), 'bags of blood' and the various corpses and cadavers, which symbolize, for Kristeva, the most grotesque instance of death infecting life – but it is certainly not, like Eliot's poem, an abject text, or, a writing of abjection. For Thomas harnesses the body, celebrating and reclaiming it as a site of subversive potentiality, projecting the threat of an all too solid and 'fleshy' corporeality into what for male Modernists and mid-century critics alike was a horrible and menacingly close proximity.[31] Again, as was shown in chapters four and five in reference to Thomas's notion of the poem as 'event', there is something of a postmodern impulse at work here. And, this can be discerned in the 'ghastly, gothic anti-blazon', as John Goodby puts it,[32] of skin, eyes, teeth, ribs, bone, hair, blood, brain, nerves, womb, cock, nails, breasts, heart, 'manseed', sweat and other bodily fluids,[33] a vivid and visceral panorama of corporeality that immediately opposed him to the agendas of an élitist and profoundly masculinist Modernism with its narratives of absence, exclusion and concealment.[34]

Given that a sense of the bodily is crucially inscribed within the materiality of discourses, a kind of encoding, as it were, of the physical, a related comparison might be drawn here between Thomas's privileging of the semiotic in his anomalous use of language and what Chris Wigginton has observed as Eliot's 'rejection of the sonority, musicality and artistry in his critical work',[35] although, since it might be argued that Eliot was always quite ambiguous in this regard, Wigginton's point does seem to apply more satisfactorily to Eliot's pioneering essay 'Milton 1' (1936). As Maud Ellmann asserts, it is this severance of sound from sense that Eliot refers to as the 'dissociation of sensibility', and consequently regards as bearing the brunt of responsibility for the linguistic fall of man:

> Milton is his prime culprit, because his poetry obeys the witchery of music rather than the laws of sense, forsaking meaning for mellifluence. The pleasure, Eliot complains, arises from the 'noises': from a language that

refuses to efface itself, delighting in the 'mazes' of its own sonority. ... [For Eliot] Milton's poetry neglects the *meaning* of the language for its *art*. Eliot's arguments imply that all these 'heresies' begin with the fetishism of the signifier – of the written or acoustic tissues of the word – where literary pleasure overwhelms the stern demands of sense, replacing sound for meaning, form for content, rite for faith.[36]

Paradoxically, however, as Ellmann acutely observes, whilst Eliot accuses Milton of dividing sound from sense and bequeathing a fallen language to posterity, his own techniques of theft and bricolage entail the same displacements which haunt the text from within. His work *unconsciously* exemplifies

> the mutual contaminations of the past and present, of the dead letter and the living voice. Eliot's quotations demonstrate how written signs are necessarily displaceable, orphaned from their origins and meanings. Moreover, *The Waste Land* shows a Miltonic and perverse delight in the semiotic side of language, in the asemantic echolalias of words. Beneath the meaningful connections of the text a parodic underlanguage opens forth, based on the contagion between sounds.[37]

As such, Ellmann concludes that *The Waste Land* is a text of abjection in which both the body and the bodily materiality of language is repressed, demonized and finally expelled as waste. Thomas, of course, would certainly have endorsed the view of *The Waste Land* as a *truly* abject poem; in fact, as John Goodby avers:

> Rather than the heightened social reportage the Audenesque poets found in it, for Dylan Thomas Eliot's poem was an abject text requiring a restoration of the grisly poetry of the body – as mucous, skin, teeth, hormones, glands, blood, gristle, semen, milk, 'the maiden's slime' – to the body of the poetry.[38]

It is in *18 Poems*, the collection in which the rebellious materiality of flesh and language can be most palpably felt, that this 'restoration', as Goodby calls it, is performed most rigorously and most creatively. A poetic assertion, we might say, of Thomas's old adage that 'whatever is hidden should be made naked',[39] since the volume's subtext both promises and warns that 'Eliot's displaced, subaltern body cannot be so easily displaced'.[40]

Chapter 7

In the previous chapter it was shown that although Thomas's fascination with the physical seems to concur with current theoretical trends, his privileging of the body – the vivid and often grotesque panorama of corporeality that distinguishes his early work – placed him immediately at odds with both his contemporaries and his near contemporaries alike. Extending this line of thought to include linguistic materiality, in this chapter it will be argued that Thomas's return to the body and to bodily signification, whereby language coalesces with the orchestration of the drives, can be read as a parodic 'outing', a kind of carnivalesque re-inscription, perhaps, of what an élitist and profoundly male high modernism, as practised by Eliot and the men of 1914, had attempted to repress.

FROM SYMPTOM TO SINTHOME: RECLAIMING THE PHYSICAL

One way of thinking about the relationship between the two texts is to consider this first volume by Thomas as a kind of psychoanalysis of *The Waste Land*, in so far as Thomas moves (Eliot's) repressed symptom back into (poetic) discourse. Although it would be wrong to claim that *The Waste Land* is in itself a symptom, since as a discursive structure this would clearly be impossible, what is being suggested here is that Eliot's ravaged, fractured and thoroughly atomized text does, in fact, assume something of the status of the symptom, as does his repression of the body and bodily materiality in order to 'stage the mind of Europe'. It might be worth pausing here, briefly, to consider Lacan's topological elaboration of the Freudian symptom, for his conception of the symptom, or *sinthome*[1] as he later called this equivalent in the realm of the psyche for the physical symptom, seems particularly relevant to a more subtly nuanced understanding of Thomas's reclamation of all kinds of bodily experience. Significantly, it was, of course, Joyce, the Modernist with whom Thomas's own linguistic experimentation and virtuosic use of English has so often been compared, who was hailed by Lacan as the writer of the symptom par excellence. In fact, it was his forceful engagement with Joyce that allowed the later Lacan to move beyond the tri-partite schema, of the Imaginary, Symbolic and Real, and to develop his concept of the *sinthome*. Moreover – and this is particularly relevant to the way in which Thomas seizes upon the body as a site of subversive potentialities – for Lacan, the symptom is crucially, and inescapably, linked both to the body and to discourse, and to written discursive structures in particular. In fact, as early as 1957, and in radical opposition to the prevailing view of the symptom as being some kind of ciphered message, Lacan was provocatively claiming that the symptom was 'inscribed in a writing process'. As he went on to state in 1963, the symptom does not call out for interpretation: 'in itself, it is not a call to the Other but a pure *jouissance* addressed to no one':

> This move from conceiving of the symptom as a message which can be deciphered by reference to the unconscious 'structured like a language', to seeing it as the trace of the particular modality of the subject's *jouissance*, culminates in the introduction of the term *sinthome*. The *sinthome* thus designates a signifying formulation beyond analysis, a kernel of enjoyment immune to the efficacy of the symbolic.[2]

Rather than calling for some kind of analytic dissolution, the *sinthome* is, as Luke Thurston has observed, 'what "allows one to live" by providing a unique organisation of *jouissance*'.[3] And this is very clearly why, for Lacan, the task of analysis is, ultimately, to identify with the *sinthtome*. As Jean-Michel Rabaté has pointed out:

> Lacan develops his conception of the symptom by explaining that the symptom is what any patient will start by disclosing, often asking to be rid of it. But for his part, he will never promise that they can be ridden of the symptom. By that time Lacan had identified the symptom with 'the most proper element of the human dimension' and defined the psychoanalytic cure as the exploitation of puns and linguistic equivocation – without missing the sense of 'fun' (Lacan used the English word) provided by the unconscious – in order to reconnect the symptom with the symbolic order. In this sense psychoanalysts were invited to become Joyceans if they wanted to understand the right type of cure![4]

Now what Rabaté is actually claiming here is that in his later formulations, where Lacan was to establish the crucial difference between symptom and *sinthome*, the *sinthome* becomes something of an appeal, an exhortation as it were, to 'Enjoy your *symptom*!' Seen in this light, then, Thomas is, we might say, the *sinthome* to Eliot's *symptom*. For the early writing with its panoramic corporeality and linguistic exuberance seems to delight in the very thing that *The Waste Land* denies, extolling just what it is that Eliot finally expels – the rebellious materiality and fluid threat of flesh and language. An obvious example of Thomas's foregrounding of corporeality, and one that fully illustrates his Eliotic penchant for linguistic subversion would be 'I see the boys of summer'.[5] The poem, which is composed in three sections and which adopts a regular a, a, b, c, c, b rhyme scheme, takes the form of a debate between the opposing voices of youth and experience.[6] It begins typically with masturbation: Thomas's profligate youths 'lay the golden tidings [of their semen] barren', wasting the seed that might have been set in 'store' for the pro-creative 'harvest'. But, at the same time as there is an obvious sense of 'moral censure of their "folly"', as Katie Gramich has pointed out, there is also an implicit 'celebration' of their self-obsessed fecundity.[7] Interestingly, this is figured in the kind of universal elemental terms – tides and floods – generally reserved for the essentialist identification of the female with the flesh. In the poem's second stanza linguistic and onanistic subversions coalesce in the 'jacks of frost' ('jacking-off'). This same punning energy can be felt in the 'dams', a word that Thomas favoured for its multiple associations. Here, it clearly refers to the 'brawned womb' of the female and its 'weathers', and also might suggest the damming up of amniotic fluid in the uterus. Equally, however, and without negating any other possible associations, the auditory imagination might easily interpret the phrase as implying a curse.

What is of particular interest in terms of the present discussion, however, is the remarkable correspondence between Lacan's definition of the 'psychoanalytic cure' (see above) and those qualities of linguistic equivocation and stylistic excess that have been shown above and which Thomas had identified as the most distinctive features of his work, more than thirty years earlier, in what is known as the 'Poetic manifesto' (1951):

> I am a painstaking, conscientious, involved and devious craftsman in words ... I use everything and anything to make my poems work and move them in the directions I want them to: old tricks, new tricks, puns, portmanteau-words, paradox, allusion, paronomasia, paragram, catachresis, slang, assonantal rhymes, vowel rhymes, sprung rhythm. Every device there is in language is there to be used if you will.[8]

Significantly, and again in perfect accordance with Lacan's insistence on the importance of retaining the sense of 'fun' in order to reconnect the symptom to the Symbolic order, Thomas adds that '[p]oets have got to enjoy themselves sometimes, and the twistings and convolutions of words, the inventions and contrivances are all part of the joy that is part of the painful, voluntary work'.[9]

Joyce aside, there are, in fact, few twentieth-century writers who have, consistently, displayed such uninhibited pleasure in 'forcing and dislocating language' into their own meaning.[10] And, although in one sense it might be argued that Thomas's linguistic opportunism constitutes some kind of positive engagement with Modernism's own excesses of linguistic and metrical de-familiarization, Thomas certainly exceeds the twentieth-century norm. It would seem then that the jouissance or textual effect of the writing, which in a Barthesian vocabulary would undoubtedly be described as *scriptable* (writerly) rather than *lisible* (readerly), arises from the distinctive rhetorical innovations that 'jar' with the reader's 'everyday' understanding of words, bringing his/her relationship with language to a crisis. Consider, for instance, Thomas's 'key-less smiles', or the equally peculiar 'safe unrest', where the attributive use of the adjective, 'safe', modifies the noun, 'unrest', in an entirely unexpected and wonderfully weird way. This, along with a plethora of other oxymoronic expressions, serves to confirm and indeed accentuate the pervasive sense of connotative indeterminacy that underpins his unique mode of poetic signification and, importantly, helps maintain the poetry's resistance to précis. But, there is a point here that needs to be made in relation to the materiality of language. Broadly speaking, linguistic materiality is associated with what we might call the musicality of language; with sonority and rhythm, with the 'stuff of speech', in which language coalesces with the body. In Thomas's poetic of excess there is a crucial link, however, between the exorbitant play of device, which, in itself, tends to promote the palpability of the signifier, and the materiality of the writing; a dynamic fusion, we might say, that radically derails the logic of signification. Evidence of this kind of linguistic opportunism is copiously there in both the play of device and in the physical material basis of language which Kristeva called the semiotic mode of signification as a syntax that undercuts order. One striking example of this would be Thomas's 1934 'birthday' poem, the incantatory 'Especially when the October wind', which is, we might say, the apotheosis of his textualization of the world, as instanced by the following passage:

> Shut, too, in a tower of words, I mark
> On the horizon walking like the trees

> The wordy shapes of women, and the rows
> Of the star-gestured children in the park.
> Some let me make you of the vowelled beeches,
> Some of the oaken voices, from the roots
> Of many a thorny shire tell you notes,
> Some let me make you of the water's speeches.[11]

Although there is an obvious 'real-world referent' here, language and substance become curiously and, indeed, inextricably intertwined – as in, ('[t]he wordy shapes of women', 'the vowelled beeches', 'oaken voices', 'the water's speeches', 'the hours word', 'the meadow's signs', the busy heart that 'talks' and 'sheds the syllabic blood and drains her words'). The result is, as Harri Garrod Roberts says, 'the real world of things takes on the qualities of language', its ability, as it were, to construct meaning via the medium of the linguistic sign:

> In [this] process, the emptiness of language as simple referent is itself 'filled' by its association (and even identification) with the reality of physical objects. The distinction between signifier and signified is thus problematized in this poem: while words become real, physical objects themselves signify in a way that, in Walford Davies' words, 'is not divorcable [sic] from their simple presence' – what is termed [in the poem's second stanza] a 'neural meaning'. 'Especially when the October wind' therefore serves to fulfil Thomas' claim that '[w]hen I experience anything, I experience it as a thing and a word at the same time, both equally amazing'.[12]

As Roberts explicitly asserts, for Thomas words possess an affective material significance: 'they do not (or cannot) simply "stand in" for the objects they symbolise, but must become (or, rather, aspire to become) those objects in their own right': objects able, as he says, 'to speak the real by *being* [or, by being implicated within] the real'.[13]

This early, and now famous, poem by Thomas with its insistent rhythms, engaging half rhymes and thudding monosyllables, can be read, then, as a statement, a poetic summation, as it were, of Thomas's desire to re-invigorate language (with the affective drive) and thereby to 'redeem language', as Walford Davies puts it, to restore a nostalgic intimacy to the thing itself.[14] As such, then, it can be seen as gesturing towards what was part of a much broader attempt, on Thomas's part, to liberate words from their usual taxonomic (and semantic) restraints that not only derails the very logic of signification but actually jars with the reader's 'everyday understanding of words' in such a way as to bring his entire relation with language to a point of crisis. This combination of affective materiality and exorbitant play of device constitutes a dynamic fusion that is very consciously, and very cleverly, calculated to promote the palpability of the signifier. And it is, in fact, this distinctive 'way with words' – what the early Thomas suggestively described as the 'colour of saying' – that derives largely from affective material exploitation of language, and that Lacan deemed necessary for the transformation of the repressed symptom into the jouissance-packed *sinthome*, which constitutes his source of appeal as a poet. Certainly, the feature of the writing that is most likely to immediately strike the reader is this kind of festive radicalism and linguistic superabundance. Of course, at the level of verbal richness, the later poems are perhaps more colourful, and certainly more verbally 'musical', whereas the earlier poems, on the other hand, seem to lure the reader with the non-signifying delights and suasions which are derived, mainly, from an exorbitant play of device and the unmistakeable exploitation of language that has become Thomas's signature.[15]

Thomas's linguistic exploitation is copiously there in both the startling use of pun, which might be said to be the master trope for both him and Lacan alike, and the ingenious incorporation of slang phrases, from which the verbal wit of the poetry very often derives. Consider, for instance, his statement that the '[r]otating halves are horning as they drill / The arterial angel', or the memorable lines, from 'I in my intricate image', '[s]uffer, my topsie-turvies, that a double angel / Sprout from the stony lockers like a tree on Aran.'[16] In fact, many of Thomas's poems are actually constructed out of these kinds of slang expressions and puns. And this is true, to some extent at least, even in the later poems where the material bases of language are not, perhaps, foregrounded in quite the same way. Think, for instance, of the 1951 poem 'Lament' in which an extended use of pun and slang expression provide the source for Thomas's lively, working-class humour – the 'old ram rod', the 'wick- / Dipping moon', the 'black sheep with a crumpled horn', 'the jawing of the bells'.[17] A similar, but much earlier, example would be 'When like a running grave' which provides ample illustration of the architectonic purpose that lies behind the punning energies of the poems. Demanding an inordinately high level of readerly engagement, the first sentence extends over five stanzas, beginning as follows:

> When, like a running grave, time tracks you down,
> Your calm and cuddled is a scythe of hairs,
> Love in her gear is slowly through the house,
> Up naked stairs, a turtle in a hearse,
> Hauled to the dome,

> Comes, like a scissors stalking, tailor age,
> Deliver me who, timid in my tribe,
> Of love am barer than Cadaver's trap
> Robbed of the foxy tongue, his footed tape
> Of the bone inch,
>
> Deliver me, my masters, head and heart,
> Heart of Cadaver's candle waxes thin,
> When blood, spade-handed, and the logic time
> Drive children up like bruises to the thumb,
> From maid and head,[18]

Here 'love in her gear' gestures towards both apparel and equipment; 'dusters in my glove' meaning brass knuckles; 'Cadaver's trap' meaning the corpse's mouth; 'boxy shift' (stanza eight) meaning underpants or boxer-shorts (newly invented in 1925) as well as coffin. More alert than most to the accidental flash points created between words, Thomas recognized that pun allowed him to move his poems in more than one direction, so that with a wonderful economy he was able to capture, simultaneously, a multiplicity of often radically divergent possibilities, or to generate new clusters of meaning. For, what both these poems highlight is the way in which pun capitalizes the link between signifiers, so that meaning is forced to abandon the normal or safe route from signifier to signified, and comes to reside, as it were, in the 'play' of signifiers itself. And this was, of course, crucial for Thomas since, as was shown in 'Especially when the October wind', it is precisely the fossilization of the socially sanctioned bond between signifier and signified that he was keen to disrupt.[19] There is clearly a social dimension to this. For the emphasis on the acoustic tissues of the word that pun necessarily entails both involves and promotes an anterior or trans-linguistic materiality – a kind of inchoate energy, we might say, which re-surfaces as the memory of a, never truly forgotten, pre-moral delight in the aural and oral pleasures of the word that pre-dates the subject and his/her Symbolic inscription.

This goes some way at least to explaining just why it was that linguistic equivocation, and pun in particular, should have offered Lacan the means of reconnecting with the *sinthome* by allowing the analytic subject to tap into the jouissance of his hitherto repressed symptom. For in speaking of the punning energies of Thomas's poems, what we are really dealing with is a level of material signs that resists précis and paraphrase and establishes the kind of affective libidinal or material connection that, according to Slavoj Žižek's understanding of the *sinthome*, 'establishes connections not grounded in narrative symbolic structures' for they just relate, or connect in a kind of pre-symbolic cross-resonance. These trans-linguistic signs, then, are not signifiers, says Žižek, 'but elements of what, a decade or two ago, one would have called ... *écriture*'.[20] Now even though the libidinal investment and affective materiality of the poetry certainly establishes Thomas as a confident exponent of the kind of semiotic signifying practices that have come to define *écriture feminine*, in many ways his densely impacted writing places him immediately at odds with a writing practice that has, primarily, been concerned to communicate, and to embody within its own amorphous structures, a sense of the fluidity of the bodily pulsional flows. For, in contrast to the signifying practices of *écriture*, in Thomas's early poetry the 'undoing' of connotative determinacy is achieved not by suppressing syntax, but through the use of a radically wrenched and contorted syntax such as, for instance, in 'When like a running grave' (see above) where the main verb is delayed and stretched over thirty-four apposite clauses.[21] This heightens the 'tangibility' of the writing, by suspending meaning and forcing the reader to actively (re)connect with the trans-linguistic materiality of the signifier and, as such, with the hitherto repressed jouissance of the *sinthome*. For the *sinthome* is perhaps best described as a somewhat curious coagulation of signification and libidinal investment which, even though it is constitutive of the subject, has, in itself, no determinate meaning: 'it just gives body, in its repetitive pattern, to some elementary matrix of *jouissance*, of excessive enjoyment. [For] although *sinthomes* do not *have* sense, they do *radiate jouis*-sense, enjoy-meant'.[22]

But, even if the *sinthome* does have some kind of a definitive resistance to meaning and, as it were, means nothing, this 'nothing', according to Žižek, '[is] not an *empty* nothing, but the *fullness of libidinal investment*, a tic that [gives] body to a cipher of enjoyment'.[23] And, from a Lacanian perspective it is, as he says, clearly quite easy to associate this with a materialized jouissance, a 'jouissance turned into flesh'.[24] Evidencing his claim with a reference to the work of Hitchcock that appears to reflect quite remarkably upon Thomas's own signifying practice, Žižek suggests:

> Hitchcock's sinthoms [*sic*] are thus not mere formal patterns; they already condense a certain libidinal investment. As such, they determined his creative process: Hitchcock did not proceed from the plot to its translation in audio-visual terms. He rather started with a set of (usually visual) motifs that haunted his imagination, that imposed themselves as his sinthoms [*sic*]; he then constructed a narrative that served as the pretext for their use. The sinthoms [*sic*] provide the specific flair, the substantial density of the cinematic texture

of Hitchcock's films; without them we would have a lifeless formal narrative.[25]

There is a very clear parallel gesture here that links the jouissance, or textual effect, of Thomas's linguistic materiality to what Žižek calls the cinematic texture of Hitchcock's films. For, in Thomas's view words, themselves, as physical objects, were, like Hitchcock's own *sinthomes*, not simply formal symbolic patternings, since, at the level of the signifier they did of course condense a certain libidinal investment and, as such, determined a poetic practice that was calculated to work from words rather than towards words. Indeed, as has already been suggested in chapter 3, it often seems that Thomas embarked on many of his poems equipped, not, as Stewart Crehan says, with any kind of preconceived theme or subject, an 'idea for a poem', as it were, but with 'intrinsically poetic material': 'with words and phrases, sounds and sound patterns, images and image clusters that emanated from deep psychic sources, and which formed part of an evolving universe'.[26] It was as if the affective materiality of words, the very physicality of their object-like status that, to borrow a phrase from Žižek, 'haunted his imagination', 'imposed' itself as his *sinthome* which does seem to go some way at least to explaining the materialized jouissance of Thomas's linguistic equivocation.

The body-centredness of Thomas's poetic of excess, like that in Joyce's *Finnegans Wake*, entails a special relation to language; a destructive refashioning of it as *sinthome*, that might be thought of as the invasion of the Symbolic order by Thomas's own private jouissance. But this is not to say that the poetry does not have its own moment of unease or anxiety – although this, of course, is almost always offset by the playful materiality of the signifier. This contrast between exuberance and an unease that very often manifests itself as a kind of gloomy introspection in the early poetry does hint at something of the paradoxical nature of jouissance itself, as a pleasure that is, perhaps, beyond pleasure, a pleasure that is always and already tinged with pain. In fact, referring to 'Before I knocked and flesh let enter', a poem that presents a somewhat negative view of identity formation, Chris Wigginton points to what he describes as a kind of 'petit bourgeois bravado', a desire, as it were, 'to exorcise uneasiness by dramatizing it'. And, discussing 'My hero bears his nerves', a poem that charts the narcissistic onanistic sexual experience of a speaker who is both Christ as Logos, the Word and the poet-as-hero, Wigginton even goes so far as to suggest that the 'anxiety *is*', in fact, 'the poetry'.[27] Here, masturbation and the act of writing are conflated and figure both as 'an unnerving presence' and as a 'disquieting plenitude'. The poem ends as follows:

> My hero bares my side and sees his heart
> Tread, like a naked Venus,
> The beach of flesh, and wind her bloodred plait;
> Stripping my loin of promise,
> He promises a secret heat.
>
> He holds the wire from this box of nerves
> Praising the mortal error
> Of birth and death, the two sad knaves of thieves,
> And the hunger's emperor;
> He pulls the chain, the cistern moves.[28]

Although the tone of gloomy adolescent self-absorption cannot be denied, this is quite clearly offset by the punning energies of the text itself. The paper, for instance, that is both toilet paper and writing paper, is 'lovelorn' because, says Wigginton, 'it bears the evidence of an absent presence', the 'unruly scrawl' (of either semen or ink) which foregrounds, for the narrator, 'the deferral of real voice or love', as opposed to the more immediate bodily pleasures of his own auto-eroticism.[29] The bodily waste (semen and also, possibly, faeces), that the images of 'paper' and flushing suggest, makes this poem a striking example of the way in which Thomas tends to foreground the abject in the early poetry. And, as such it seems quite plausible that Thomas might well have been defending the supposed indelicacy of the 'lavatory image' of the final line when he wrote to Pamela Hansford Johnson on 5 November 1933, after having sent her this poem less than a month earlier (on 15 October 1933): '[i]t is polite to be seen at one's dining table, and impolite to be seen at one's lavatory. It might well have been decided, when the tumour of civilisation was first fostered, that celebrations should be held in the w.c.'[30] Interestingly, however, as Maud observes:

> [T]hough the word 'cistern' lays itself open to a sewage disposal interpretation, it is [in fact] the same word as the anatomical word 'cisterna': any sac in the body holding fluids ... [whilst] 'to pull one's wire' is in Eric Partridge's *A Dictionary of Slang and Unconventional English* as '(of the male) to masturbate; low; late C. 19–20.'[31]

Given that Thomas had already used the phrase 'cistern sex' in a similar context in the February 1933 notebook,[32] Maud argues that it is perhaps inevitable that we should be drawn to the view that the '"love hunger" being uttered in this poem, a forlorn response to the emptiness of life', involves the opening up to self-pleasure as the only release possible, which seems to suggest that it is not the poet's ego or his hand, even, but the penis which emerges as the true hero of this brave and magnificently indelicate poem.

In a sense then it might be said that 'My hero bares his nerves' is just one example of the way in which Thomas was to expose the darkness of Eliotic high modernism by dragging its distanced and demonized body into the clear naked light of ribald comedy. For, as John Goodby has suggested, what Thomas actually did, in *18 Poems*, was to seize upon Eliot's assertion that to write truly modern poetry '[O]ne must look into the cerebral cortex, the nervous system, the digestive tracts', which he then 'pushed ... to his [own] truly shocking un-Eliotic conclusion'.[33] For Thomas not only followed Eliot's advice but took it to a parodic point of self-contradiction, thereby establishing his own kind of body-centred originality, in a move that might well be said to re-route abjection from pessimism to parody.

'MY JACK OF CHRIST': THOMAS'S OBSCENE OBJECT

It has already been argued that Thomas's reclamation of the body as a site of subversive potentiality seemed to project the threat of an all too solid and 'fleshy' corporeality into what, for male Modernists and mid-century critics alike, was a horrible and menacingly close proximity. His vivid and visceral panorama of corporeality immediately opposed him to the agendas of an élitist and profoundly masculinist Modernism and, as was suggested in chapter 6, it seems to hint at something of a postmodern impulse at work in the writing. In order to strengthen this contention, at this point in the discussion it is worth pausing to consider the concept of 'the obscene object of postmodernity' articulated in Slavoj Žižek's *Looking Awry: An Introduction to Jacques Lacan through Popular Culture* (1991). Žižek's basic contention is that all modern art is organized around a central absence, whereas the postmodern, by way of contrast, is a matter of overwhelming presence; his text thus provides a useful starting point from which it becomes possible to begin to locate the literary-historical and cultural parameters of the critical idiom that led to Thomas being condemned for his 'glandular compulsion', 'false materiality' and his deployment of a profoundly 'feminine' mode of language that, it was claimed, prevented objectivity.[34]

As one of the many contemporary thinkers who have claimed that we are currently living in what has been popularly and, indeed loosely, described as the 'postmodern era', Žižek has been particularly anxious to provide a clear and precise definition of the term postmodern, in the face of its somewhat sloppy chronological usage. For Žižek, as for Lyotard, the term is not, in fact, reducible to any simple diachrony – a point that he is particularly concerned to emphasize in 'The Obscene Object of Postmodernity', a chapter from his prestigious survey of popular culture *Looking Awry*. An impressive intervention into philosophy, politics and aesthetics, the chapter, which draws on a diverse range of material – from film, drama, fiction and opera – is framed by an argument that focuses on the 'line of demarcation', or distinction he wishes to make between Modernism and postmodernism. According to Žižek, it is, in fact, Lacan who marks the postmodernist break 'by focusing upon that which lies outside the signifier and which is detectable only retrospectively, after language has failed in its reference'.[35] Hence, one of the ways in which an understanding of the postmodern might be characterized is as an over-proximity to the Real. In postmodern art Žižek identifies various manifestations of this, such as the technique of 'filling in the gaps', of 'telling it all', as it were. What Žižek means by this can be seen in his comparative analysis of Antonioni's *Blow Up*, which he describes as 'perhaps the last great modernist film', and a 'postmodernist' scene in Hitchcock's *Lifeboat*.[36] Elizabeth Wright very neatly summarizes the two scenes as follows:

> The theme of *Blow Up* is the disappearance of a body photographed by chance, the film's action centring upon the search for what is to fill this absence. A final sequence shows the photographer watching a 'tennis match' in which the non-existent 'ball' rolls to his feet; whereupon he 'throws' it back, joining in a game which 'works without an object'. In this fantasy, 'nothing' is taken to be 'something' – a fantasy concealing a gap.
>
> In the postmodernist scene, however, the reverse happens: there is 'something' where there was 'nothing'. In Hitchcock's film, a German U-boat sailor, while being picked up in a lifeboat, reveals himself as a cause of horror by showing in his face his response to the response of the British sailors.[37]

In Žižek's account, whereas Modernism works to conceal, or to repress, what he terms as the 'obscene object', in the postmodern, it is, in fact, the object of fear itself that is made fully explicit, becoming the focus for the camera, the object of the gaze as it were. Postmodernism consists, then, 'not in demonstrating that the game works without an object, that the play is set in motion by a central absence, but rather in displaying the object directly, allowing it to make visible its own indifferent and arbitrary character'.[38] Furthermore, as Žižek is particularly keen to point out, the same object can, in fact, 'function successively as a disgusting reject *and* as a sublime and charismatic apparition': the difference, is, he insists, 'strictly structural, [and] does not pertain to the "effective properties" of the object, *but only to its place in the symbolic order*'.[39]

Žižek's articulation of the obscene object as *Das Ding*, or, to put it slightly differently, the Lacanian 'thing', the incestuous maternal object, brought into a horrible and menacing proximity, is particularly relevant to a discussion of Thomas's staging of the corporeal. Indeed, if we recall the letter to Hansford Johnson, quoted at the start of the previous chapter, where Thomas very forcefully states that 'all these contrasting things are equally beautiful and equally ugly' and, that '[o]nly by association is the refuse of the body more to be abhorred than the body itself', and then compare this with Žižek's text, an obvious and remarkably similar strand of thought seems to emerge. For Thomas, too, is quite insistent that the perceived ugliness of the visceral in his poetry does not in any way pertain to the effective properties of the body as object, but rather to its positioning within the contemporary socio-symbolic network. But, what is perhaps even more significant is the fact that if we take Thomas's early verse that is characterized by an overwhelming presence of the flesh, and of bodily horror, and place it alongside *The Waste Land*, where the body is reduced to a 'disgusting reject', then almost immediately it becomes possible to discern a difference in structure that is very similar to the one that Žižek has identified as part of his ongoing attempt to distinguish the *post*modern from the modern.

As previously noted, critics were often virulent in their condemnation of these egregious aspects of Thomas's work, and it is perhaps revealing that such moralising attacks tended to persist even up until the early 1990s. For, as Harri Garrod Roberts observes, it would seem that the Leavisite legacy 'continues to inflect critical approaches to Thomas, even when an intention to break with this legacy is explicitly expressed'.[40] Thus, in his influential publication *English Poetry since 1940* (1993), Neil Corcoran, who begins his discussion of Thomas with the laudable assertion that the vivid corporeality in his early work is long 'overdue for a contemporary Bakhtinian reassessment', proceeds to what Roberts quite rightly describes as 'a more emotive appeal to personal pathology'.[41] Coming perilously close to the kind of crude psycho-biography that had underpinned David Holbrook's notorious three-volume attack on Thomas more than twenty years earlier, Corcoran concludes by dismissing the affective materiality of the early work as nothing more than an unhealthy adolescent obsession: 'a glandular compulsiveness' and 'mesmerised and self-obsessed narcissism'.[42]

Perhaps the most shocking and crudely spectacular manifestation of what Žižek might call Thomas's 'obscene object' is the blasphemous identification of Christ with the most literal symbol of phallic authority, the male member, the penis. In more conventional studies Thomas's 'Jack of Christ' has been read as a reference to his own father, D. J. or Jack Thomas, the Swansea school master. However, as previously noted, a darker and more iconoclastic interpretation suggests itself in the expression 'jacking-off' which denotes a sexualized self-pleasuring. Thus, within the textual space of the early poetry, the Holy Trinity is hijacked, shattered and supplanted by a grotesquely re-imagined Oedipal triangle, as God the Son, the symbol and embodiment of the Father's love, is shorn of any spiritual reference or *dignitas* and continues to exist purely, though purely is perhaps not quite right here, as 'an overwhelming presence of flesh'.[43] Thus in the final stanza of 'if I were tickled by the rub of love', the poet-Christ narrator is crucified on the phallic symbol of the cross which thereby becomes emblematic of the Oedipal fate of man:

> And what's the rub? Death's feather on the nerve?
> Your mouth, my love, the thistle in the kiss?
> My Jack of Christ born thorny on the tree?
> The words of death are dryer than his stiff,
> My wordy wounds are printed with your hair.
> I would be tickled by the rub that is:
> Man be my metaphor.[44]

These lines offer a shocking and crudely indelicate pun on 'stiff' as both the dead body of the mortal Christ and his (and the speaker's) erection: 'there is no faith', says John Goodby, 'that Christ offers salvation, and his stiffness takes us closer to death ("Death's feather" is "on the nerve" of the tumescent "penis")'.[45] Similarly, but even more blasphemously, 'My hero bears his nerves' charts the narcissistic, onanistic sexual experience of the adolescent Christ-narrator, who is figured as 'hunger's emperor', the de-tumescent penis that hangs between the testicles, of the 'the two sad knaves of thieves'.[46] Here Thomas's bodily and blasphemously re-imagined Christ becomes a spectacularly indecorous projection of the adolescent male ego onto the surrounding world. But whilst this perversely parodic and grotesquely imagined re-staging of the anthropomorphism of the New Testament Christ threatens the most sacred symbol of an organized and mainstream Christian faith, then the 'lovelorn paper' that bears the evidence of an absent presence – 'the unruly scrawl of ink/semen telling the narrator of the deferral of his real voice or love as opposed to his auto affectation'– might also be seen as an outright rejection of any kind of negative theology.[47]

In what Bennett and Royle describe as his 'influential' and 'characteristically religious' essay, 'The Function of Criticism at the Present Time' (1864),[48] Matthew Arnold described literature as 'the promised land' that contains 'the best that is known and thought in the world'.[49] And it is very much within this same Christian-spiritualistic critical tradition that F. R. Leavis propounded a theory of literature as the embodiment of 'our spiritual tradition ... the "picked experience of ages"'.[50] But if such conceptions have, as Bennett and Royle suggest, tended 'to epitomize the sorts of spurious claims traditionally made of ... "the authoritative, even redemptive qualities of literature"', then as Georges Bataille makes clear in his groundbreaking study, *Literature and Evil* (1953), an intermingling of creation, imagination and evil, or profanity, is characteristic of literary works.[51] 'Literature is not innocent', writes Bataille: 'Literature, like the infringement of moral laws, is dangerous'.[52] And this is certainly true of Thomas's early poetry. For the 'over-proximity' of both flesh and language, that is pushed to its parodic limit in the profanely blasphemous figure of Thomas's 'Jack of Christ', goes beyond any simple rejection of Thomas's own Welsh nonconformist roots, and towards what might be seen as a full frontal attack on the theological basis of Western culture as a whole.

Conclusion

According to Slavoj Žižek the entire field of theory is constructed around the exclusion of Lacan. Indeed, as Tony Myers suggests, one might even be tempted to say that Lacan is 'the *sinthome* of academic theory – he is the surplus that binds the otherwise disparate groupings of theorists together':

> Deconstructionists do not like him, the followers of Foucault do not like him, the feminists do not like him – nobody likes him, and despite their many internal differences, all these other theoretical groupings agree on one point. The life of a self-proclaimed Lacanian, such as Žižek, can therefore be a difficult one.[1]

Something similar might, in fact, be said of Thomas. For he too continues to exist as a surplus, a *sinthome*, a somewhat curious and uncanny excess jouissance perhaps, that, to put it bluntly, just doesn't seem to fit. And whilst there can be no doubt of his reputation as a major twentieth-century literary figure, Thomas remains, nonetheless, a particularly difficult poet to contextualize. Indeed, once we progress beyond an initial acquaintance with the writing, we are forced to confront what Goodby and Wigginton have identified as 'the problem of the yawning gap' that exists between his critical and popular reputations.[2] Added to this is the complex nature of Thomas's relationship with both Modernism and the more discursive 'Audenesque' poets who emerged as the vanguard of a politically left poetic norm during the 1930s, as well as his tactical disavowal but actual engagement with surrealism, that exasperates even the most cogent and sustained attempts to situate Thomas within the broader pantheon of English literature. Moreover, whilst each of these contexts has its own specific relevance for Thomas, in the early poetry, where the conventions of generic boundaries are flaunted to such an inordinate degree as to become an advertised feature of the writing, we can be certain that none will ever fully define or circumscribe his work. Considerations of Thomas's Welshness, of course, reveal the same kind of contradictions and ambiguities that we find when placing him in any other conventional contexts. Is he, for instance, Welsh in any significant way, or simply an English poet who was born and lived much of his life in Wales, and, as a monoglot English speaker, does the powerful and well-defined body of Welsh-language literature bear meaningfully in any way on his work? It is perhaps worth pausing here to consider how discussions of Thomas's Welsh contexts have been further complicated by the coexistence of two separate and distinct national literatures, both of which, it could be argued, were at their prime when Thomas's meteoric career was set to reach its height. For the more conservative tendencies amongst Welsh nationalists Thomas was castigated as the inauthentic un-Welsh product of English linguistic colonization,[3] whilst for those engaged in the attempt to define a tradition of Anglo-Welsh literature Thomas presents a specific set of problems. On the one hand as a lyric poet of international stature with poems such as 'The force that through the green fuse' and 'Do not go gentle into that good night' having become anthology staples, Thomas is of course far too important to be ignored. Yet, many scholars of the tradition have felt, like Gwyn Jones, that it is ironic that such an ambivalently Welsh writer as Thomas should be recognized as its most famous exemplar.[4] Thomas was certainly aware of his liminal status but as has already been suggested, it seems that he was apparently quite happy to exist in this semi-transitional space, and would on occasion even ridicule what he clearly recognized as his own dichotomous positioning:

> Regarded in England as Welsh and as a waterer of England's milk and living in Wales as an Englishman, I am too unnational to be here at all. I should be living in a small private leper-house in Hereford or Shropshire, one foot in Wales and my vowels in England, wearing red flannel drawers, a tall witches' hat and a coracle tiepin, and speaking English so Englishly that I sound like a literate Airedale, who has learned his 'a's and 'e's by correspondence course, piped and shagged and tweeded, but also with a harp, the look of all Sussex in my poached eye, and a whippet under my waistcoat. And here are Scotch writers at home, and greeted by writers of England and France, and a border case like myself ...[5]

As a border case Thomas was never, it seems, completely or entirely absorbed into either the English or the Anglo-Welsh canon, and is perhaps best described as a disruptive or destabilizing force, for paradoxically he exists as both the repressed symptom and as the surplus that neither tradition can ever hope to fully contain. Or rather, bearing in mind the foregoing discussion, he might perhaps be characterized as the *sinthome* of the Anglo-Welsh condition. In much the same way that the subject fends off enjoyment by delegating it to either a limb or pattern of behaviour, Anglo-Welsh writing, in adopting a selective view of Thomas's work that tends to focus on the middle and later periods, has failed to connect with its own repressed jouissance which it fends off by delegating Thomas to its margins. If Welsh writing in English is to have any kind of meaningful connection with Thomas then it is necessary that a more liberal approach be adopted that would give serious consideration to the linguistic materiality of the early work.

This study has, then, sought to argue that it is high time for critical attention to switch from the issue of Dylan Thomas's 'personality' – a subject that has all too often been discussed in heavily moralistic and ham-fistedly psychoanalytical terms – to the challenge of properly understanding Thomas's *poetic* personality. Models of psycho-poetic development particularly suited to this purpose may, it has been further suggested, be found in the work not of Freud (a tired favourite of the analysts of 'personality') but rather of such radical 'revisionists' as Lacan and Kristeva. While some of the key terms and categories of their thinking – such as the Real, the Imaginary and the Symbolic – may on first encounter appear unpromisingly rebarbative, on closer acquaintance and following fuller understanding they are, or so the argument here has run, capable of offering us valuable insights into the distinctive character of Thomas's poetic development. In particular, they can make available to us a way of understanding 'literary influence' that helps bring into focus the exact nature of Thomas's poetic maturation between the extant Notebook Poems and his first published collection, *18 Poems*.

These models of psycho-poetic development enable us to see how Thomas's relationship to important poetic precursors was not that of a struggle to the death with powerful 'father' figures, on the rather crude Freudian model so influentially popularized by Harold Bloom, but rather of exuberant, often playful, even affectionately parodic, appropriation and redirection of their creative energies to his own distinctive ends as a poet. To recognize this poetic of jouissance, it has been here suggested, is furthermore to understand how cunningly ambiguous in character was the 'belated' Thomas's indebtedness to the great masters of high Modernism, as indeed was his relationship to many of the most celebrated and weighty of his own immediate contemporaries. When viewed through this lens, his poetry appears to be stimulatingly hybrid in character, and furthermore to anticipate, in this as in other of its characteristic features, some of the defining characteristics of what nowadays tends to be classified as a 'postmodernist' poetics. Indeed, several of Lyotard's seminal comments on postmodernism seem perfectly to fit key aspects of Thomas's poetic practice. One such comment relates to postmodernism's response to the 'unpresentable' that resists every attempt to translate it into humanly intelligible terms. According to Lyotard's suggestive formulation, the Modernist response to 'the unpresentable' was always composed in the anxious key of wistful nostalgia, whereas that of postmodernism tends to be composed in the key of festive celebration. Whereas the former was far from being unsounded by Thomas, it is the latter, or so the preceding study has suggested, that is more often to be heard in the 'festive radicalism' of much of his writing, and it is this that at times makes it seem positively postmodernist *avant la lettre*.

It is also this 'festive radicalism' that is manifest in the 'orgy of signification', the 'rogue' feature of Thomas's writing that so many critics trained in the 'mainstream' ways of Modernist culture have found so difficult to understand and accept. His poetry insists always on the primacy of the materials – the words and images – out of which it is fashioned and (much more radically and controversially) in which its 'meaning' and 'significance' so stubbornly inhere. And in the process of foregrounding the promiscuous fecundity of the sign, these poems also register in their very being the infinite irreducible unknowableness of ultimate definitive meaning, thus generating an experience of the sublime that is uncannily postmodern in character.

As disconcerting as Thomas's seemingly 'undisciplined' devotion to language is, for connoisseurs of Modernism, his indiscriminate gratuitous wallowing in the body and all its processes. Often adduced as evidence of an 'infantilism', or a fixation on adolescent experience, the 'gross' physicality of his writing can, or so this study has proposed, be better understood as a 'body-centredness' calculated to reclaim what Thomas regarded as the 'maternal' source of all creativity, of limitless potentiality, from the 'abject' status to which it had been reduced by Eliot and others. And it is Kristeva's work on the abject, it is suggested, that provides us with the best guide to this crucial aspect of Thomas's work.

CONCLUSION

But when all is said and done, this whole study has in essence been founded on one simple fundamental fact about Dylan Thomas that, although self-evident (in more than one sense of that familiar expression), has tended perversely to be overlooked by so many of his biographers and critics. First and foremost, Dylan Thomas was an inordinate lover of words – not of women, or of drink, or of celebrity. In one, important, sense, both exhilarating and tragic, he was a man made of words, much in the way in which Wallace Stevens's celebrated Snow Man (itself an alter ego of sorts for Stevens the poet) was a MAN made 'purely' of Snow. And just as that Snow Man had a 'mind of winter', so, too, did Thomas have a 'mind of language', which it has been the consistent purpose of this study to explore. Many times did he rejoice in this – as we, too, have every reason a century after his birth and more than half a century after his passing to rejoice with him. But occasionally, too – and again in a manner strikingly similar to that of the poets of postmodernism – he also mourned it. Because what, in the end, was the status of words? What 'trust' exactly should he place in them? How much of his existential weight could they take? Or, to rephrase such concerns in his own, hauntingly tragic terms, 'Where have the old words got me?' It is surely this that constitutes the pathos that is the other side of Thomas's exhilarated and exhilarating life in language that this study has at least attempted to 'biographize'.

Notes

Introduction

1. Many of Thomas's poems have, in fact, become anthology staples. See, for example, 'The force that through the green fuse' (*CPDT*, p. 13), 'Do not go gentle into that good night' (*CPDT*, p. 148), 'Fern Hill' (*CPDT*, pp. 134–5), 'And Death shall have no dominion' (*CPDT*, p. 56), 'Poem in October' (*CPDT*, p. 86). Certain lines such as 'after the first death there is no other' and 'the force that through the green fuse drives the flower' are now part of the common currency of twentieth-century English-language poetry. *Under Milk Wood*, Thomas's enormously popular radio 'play for voices', has been adapted for several media – stage, film, cartoon. It has won international acclaim, and is still regularly performed and broadcast.
2. John Goodby and Chris Wigginton (eds), *Dylan Thomas: New Casebook* (Basingstoke: Palgrave, 2001), p. 1; Eynel Wardi, *Once Below a Time: Dylan Thomas, Julia Kristeva, and Other Speaking Subjects* (New York: State University of New York Press, 2000).
3. Walford Davies (ed.), *Dylan Thomas: New Critical Essays* (London: Dent, 1972), p. vii.
4. David Holbrook, *Llaregub Revisited: Dylan Thomas and the State of Modern Poetry* (London: Bowe and Bowes, 1962), p. 128. For further evidence of Holbrook's sustained attack on Thomas see also idem, *Dylan Thomas and Poetic Dissociation* (Carbondale: Southern Illinois University Press, 1964); and idem, *Dylan Thomas: The Code of Night* (London: Athlone Press, 1972).
5. For examples of the kind of sexual, and pseudo-sexual, imagery in Thomas's poetry that helped motivate Holbrook's attack, see, for example, stanzas 3 and 4 of 'Light breaks where no sun shines' (*CPDT*, p. 24). This poem was first published in *The Listener* on 14 March 1934. Thomas mentioned at the time in a letter to Glyn Jones that the poem was 'a very obscure one' (*CLDT*, p. 99). Some readers, however, thought it was quite clear: 'You'll be interested to know that the B.B.C. have banned my poetry. After my poem in the Listener ("Light Breaks Where No Sun Shines") the editor received a host of letters, all complaining of the

disgusting obscenity of two of the verses. One of the bits they made a fuss about was: "Nor fenced, nor staked, the *gushers* of the sky / *Spout* to the rod divining in the smile / The *oil* of tears." The little smut-hounds thought I was writing a copulatory anthem. In reality, of course, it was a metaphysical image of rain & grief. I shall never darken Sir John Reith's doors again, for all my denials of obscenity were disregarded' (*CLDT*, p. 108). It is worth noting however that Thomas was not, in fact really banned, and *The Listener* published 'Especially when the October wind' later that same year. Moreover, the publication of 'Light breaks' led to letters of interest from T. S. Eliot, Stephen Spender and Geoffrey Grigson, and thus launched Thomas onto the London literary scene.

[6] Goodby and Wigginton (eds), *Dylan Thomas: New Casebook*, p. 3.

[7] For a fine explanation of the classical model of applied psychoanalysis, according to which literature is seen as analogous to fantasy and treated as a symptom of a particular state of mind, see Elizabeth Wright, 'Modern Psychoanalytic Criticism', in Ann Jefferson and David Robey (eds), *Modern Literary Theory: A Comparative Introduction* (London: B. T. Batsford Ltd, 1995), pp. 145–65 (pp. 145–50).

[8] See Wardi, *Once Below a Time*, p. 27. Wardi soundly asserts that the methodological implication of her analysis of Thomas is founded on that formulated by Shoshana Felman: 'who pointing to the equal status of literature and psychoanalysis as both "bodies of knowledge" and "bodies of language," advocates a dialogical rather than an applicative psychoanalytic interpretation'.

[9] Wardi, *Once Below a Time*, p. 74. The letter to which she refers is an incomplete draft and was addressed to Princess Caetini (a patroness and publisher of Thomas) shortly before his death. See *CLDT*, pp. 115–16.

[10] Catherine Belsey, *Critical Practice* (London: Methuen, 1980), p. 12. '[I]n Leavis' criticism in general there is a recurring slide from text to author which manifests itself in a characteristic way of formulating his observations ... the text has disappeared entirely, leaving the assumption, not unfamiliar from commonsense accounts of the nature of communication, that discourse is intelligible primarily as a revelation of the qualities of the mind of its individual author or speaker'.

[11] Stewart Crehan, 'The Lips of Time', in John Goodby and Chris Wiggington (eds), *Dylan Thomas: New Casebook* (Basingstoke: Palgrave, 2001), pp. 46–64 (pp. 47–8).

[12] Holbrook, *Llareggub Revisited*, pp. 120, 140; emphasis added.

[13] For the purposes of the present study mention of the early poetry can loosely be taken as referring to that which Thomas published in his first two volumes, *18 Poems* (London: Parton Press, 1934) and *Twenty-five Poems* (London: Dent, 1936) respectively. Some attention will be paid to his third collection, *The Map of Love* (London: Dent, 1939), though this is limited to a discussion of those poems that precede a noticeable change in Thomas's style at around 1938; attention is also given to the body of poetry in Thomas's four extant notebooks, which is collected in *The Notebook Poems 1930–1934*, ed. Ralph Maud (London: Dent, 1989). To date the Notebook Poems have received only scant critical attention.

[14] Cited in Rainer Emig, *Modernism in Poetry: Motivations, Structures and Limits* (London: Longman, 1995), p. 133.

15. Freud's central concepts of narcissism and the Oedipus complex are perhaps the most prominent examples of the way in which psychoanalysis has both appropriated the subject-matter of literature and absorbed literary terms into its own vocabulary.
16. See Sigmund Freud, *The Penguin Freud Library*, vols 1–15, trans. J. Strachey (London: Penguin, 1990–3), vol. 4, p. 363. 'The action of the play consists in nothing other than the process of revealing, with cunning delays and ever-mounting excitement – a process that can be likened to the work of a psycho-analysis – that Oedipus himself is the murderer of Laius ... the son of the murdered man and of Jocasta.'
17. Steve Vine, *Literature in Psychoanalysis: A Reader* (Basingstoke: Palgrave, 2005), pp. 1–2.
18. Cited in Lionel Trilling, 'Freud and Literature' (1941), in David Lodge (ed.), *20th Century Literary Criticism* (London: Longman, 1972), pp. 275–90 (p. 276).
19. Emig, *Modernism in Poetry: Motivations, Structures and Limits*, p. 134.
20. Sue Vice (ed.), *Psychoanalytic Criticism: A Reader* (Cambridge: Polity, 1996), p. 1.
21. For a succinct overview and explanation of traditional applied psychoanalysis see Wright, 'Modern Psychoanalytic Criticism', pp. 145–8. In this model, explains Wright, either the author or the literary character is treated as if living in a fantasy, with a complex of his own: 'Freud's analysis of E. T. A. Hoffmann's *The Sandman*, in his essay "The Uncanny" ... is a case in point ... Although Freud briefly elaborates Hoffmann's biography in a footnote, he is concerned to analyse the uncanny effect of the story via the central characters infantile complex.' This, she says, all relates back to author's psyche and 'the assumption that the purpose of the work of art is the same as that which psychoanalysis had taken to be the purpose of the dream: the secret gratification of an infantile and forbidden wish, lodged in the unconscious' (p. 146).
22. J. W. Krutch, *Edgar Allan Poe: A Study in Genius* (New York: Knopf, 1926), pp. 234–5.
23. In his revision of Freudianism, Lacan used Poe's famous tale of a double theft to demonstrate the theory of repetition compulsion, claiming that *The Purloined Letter* offers an allegory of the psychoanalytic situation. Arguably, however, since his innovative interpretation was to have such profound implications for the reading process in general, it has become possible to describe Lacan's analysis of *The Purloined Letter* as presenting no less than an allegory of the reading process itself.
24. Jacques Lacan, *Écrits: A Selection*, trans. Alan Sheridan (London: Tavistock, 1977), p. 65.
25. *CPDT*, p. 23.
26. John Goodby and Chris Wigginton, '"Shut, too, in a tower of words": Dylan Thomas' Modernism', in Alex Davies and Lee M. Jenkins (eds), *Locations of Literary Modernism* (Cambridge: Cambridge University Press, 2000), p. 106.
27. Dylan Thomas, *Dylan Thomas: Early Prose Writings*, ed. Walford Davies (London: Dent, 1971), p. 158.
28. Crehan, 'The Lips of Time', p. 46.

[29] See, for example, Holbrook, *Dylan Thomas: The Code of Night*, p. 169, where Holbrook cites such lines as, 'in the groin's endless coil a man is tangled' ('I make this in a warring absence', *CPDT*, p. 68), and, '[o]ne womb, one mind, spewed out the matter' ('From love's first fever to her plague', *CPDT*, p. 22).

[30] Yet, Holbrook persistently strives for a *literal* meaning that ignores the complexity of Thomas's challenge at the level of language. Rather than *his reading Thomas*, the textual effect seems to be that of Holbrook *himself being read*, and caught out, so to speak, in a fiction of interpretive mastery.

[31] Crehan, 'The Lips of Time', p. 47.

[32] Slavoj Žižek, *How to Read Lacan* (London: Granta Books, 2006), chapter 6.

[33] See Thomas's 'Poetic Manifesto', in Dylan Thomas, *Dylan Thomas: Early Prose Writings*, ed. Walford Davies (London: Dent, 1971), pp. 154–60 (pp. 154–5).

Chapter 1

[1] Cited in R. B. Kershner, *Dylan Thomas: The Poet and His Critics* (Chicago: American Library Association, 1976), p. 76.

[2] John Ackerman, *A Dylan Thomas Companion: Life, Poetry and Prose* (London: Macmillan, 1994), p. 75.

[3] Kershner, *Dylan Thomas: The Poet and His Critics*, p. 76.

[4] Kershner, *Dylan Thomas: The Poet and His Critics*, p. 79.

[5] John Goodby, '"Eggs laid by tigers": the politics of a style' (unpublished manuscript, 2007), 1.

[6] Desmond Hawkins, 'Poetry', *Time and Tide*, XVI, 6 (9 February 1935), 204, 206.

[7] Sandra M. Gilbert and Susan Gubar, *The Madwoman in the Attic*, reprinted in *The Norton Anthology of Theory and Criticism* (New York: Norton, 2001), pp. 2023–35 (p. 2024).

[8] Mikkel Borch-Jacobsen, 'The Oedipus Problem in Freud and Lacan', *Critical Enquiry*, 20, 2 (winter 1994), 267–82 (280).

[9] Borch-Jacobsen, 'The Oedipus Problem in Freud and Lacan', 268.

[10] William York Tindall, *A Reader's Guide to Dylan Thomas* (Syracuse: Syracuse University Press, 1962), p. 57.

[11] See, for instance, the explications proffered by Maud and Tindall, in Ralph Maud, *Where Have the Old Words Got Me?* (Cardiff: University of Wales Press, 2003), pp. 101–3, and the earlier Tindall, *A Reader's Guide to Dylan Thomas*, pp. 57–9.

[12] *CPDT*, p. 21.

[13] *CPDT*, p. 21.

[14] Terry Eagleton, *Literary Theory: An Introduction* (1983–96; London: Blackwell, 2002), p. 145.

[15] This crucial difference is partly why I wish to refrain from over-inflating the thematic correspondence between Thomas and Lacan, a point to which I shall return during the course of this chapter.

[16] *CPDT*, p. 21.

[17] Harri Garrod Roberts, *Embodying Identity: Representations of the Body in Welsh Literature* (Cardiff: University of Wales Press, 2009), p. 105.

[18] See, for instance, 'Before I knocked' (*CPDT*, pp. 11–12), which catalogues a far more negative view of identity formation:

> As yet ungotten, I did suffer;
> The rack of dreams my lily bones
> Did twist into a living cipher

[19] See, for instance, Thomas's letter to Pamela Hansford Johnson, dated 9 May 1934: '[m]y lines, *all* my lines, are of the tenth intensity. They are not the words that express what I want them to express; they are the only words that I can find that come near to expressing a half. And that's not good. I'm a freak user of words, not a poet.' *CLDT*, p. 130.

[20] *CPDT*, p. 22.

[21] Eagleton, *Literary Theory*, p. 145.

[22] Given the relative simplicity of the poem as a whole, the final stanza is fairly difficult to unpack, William York Tindall, however, offers a useful gloss (*A Reader's Guide to Dylan Thomas*, pp. 58–9): 'Oneness has produced this manyness. From learning that the sky is distinct from the earth, above from below, he has learned "double" talk. But the "two framed globe" becomes a "score" of worlds. The "million minds" of the past have suckled the "bud" that "forks" his compound eye. Here, bud, sometimes phallic, may be tongue or mouth about to flower. "Forks," sometimes piercing or fixing, also means dividing here. His eye sees double as his forked tongue tries double talk. But "score" and "forks" together, bringing tuning forks to mind, could imply the music of poetry.'

[23] The original version ended quite differently with an additional eleven lines (*Notebook Poems*, p. 205):

> Now that drugged youth is waking from its stupor,
> The nervous hand rehearsing on the thigh
> Acts with a woman, one sum remains in cipher:
> Five senses and the frozen brain
> Are one with the wind, and itching in the sun.
> Stone is my mate? Who shall brass be?
> What seed to me?
> The soldered world debates.

[24] The father is not a simple concept but a complex one for Lacan, who repeatedly stresses the importance of distinguishing between the Symbolic father, the Imaginary father and the Real father. Not a real being but a position or function within the symbolic order the purpose of the Symbolic father (also referred to variously as both the Name-Of-The-Father and the paternal function) is to impose the law and to mediate desire in the Oedipus complex. As an imago, the imaginary father is a composite of all those illusory constructs that the subject builds up in a fantasy around the figure of the father. He can be constructed as the 'ideal father' or as the agent of privation, and in both these guises he is figured as omnipotent. Again, like the Symbolic father, the Imaginary construction often bears little relationship to the father as he is in reality. For a more detailed explanation see Dylan Evans, *An Introductory Dictionary of Lacanian Psychoanalysis* (London: Routledge, 2005), pp. 61–3, 119, 137.

NOTES

25 For a fine account of Julia Kristeva's heretical notion of this 'imaginary father', see Elizabeth Grosz, 'Julia Kristeva', in Elizabeth Wright (ed.), *Feminism and Psychoanalysis: A Critical Dictionary* (Oxford: Blackwell, 1992), p. 199.

Chapter 2

1 Critical attention has rested, largely, on Ralph Maud's scholarly, though limiting, forty-four page editorial preface and introduction to Dent's 1968 edition *Poet in the Making: The Notebooks of Dylan Thomas*. It is perhaps revealing that, even here, the emphasis is placed firmly on the status of the poems 'as first drafts'. See *Poet in the Making: The Notebooks of Dylan Thomas*, ed. Ralph Maud (London: Dent, 1968), p. 9. The implication here is that the notebooks were simply quarried, as it were, to supply the material for Thomas's first three volumes.
2 *18 Poems* (London: Parton Press, 1934), *Twenty-five Poems* (London: Dent, 1936) and *The Map of Love* (London: Dent, 1939), respectively.
3 A fifth notebook was rediscovered and acquired at auction in December 2014 by Swansea University. In addition to the four notebooks in the collection of the State University of New York at Buffalo, the fifth notebook forms part of the Swansea University collection held in the Richard Burton Archives.
4 Dylan Thomas, *Dylan Thomas: Early Prose Writings*, ed. Walford Davies (London: Dent, 1971), pp. 154–5.
5 See *CLDT*, pp. 163, 191.
6 Harold Bloom, *The Anxiety of Influence: A Theory of Poetry* (New York and Oxford: Oxford University Press, 1997), p. 30.
7 See Jacob Blevins, 'Influence, Anxiety, and the Symbolic', *Intertexts*, 9, 2 (fall 2005), 123–38 (123).
8 Malcolm Bowie, *Lacan* (London: Fontana, 1991), p. 33.
9 Bowie, *Lacan*, p. 33; emphasis added.
10 *CPDT*, p. 109.
11 Dylan Evans, *An Introductory Dictionary of Lacanian Psychoanalysis* (London: Routledge, 2005), pp. 144–5; emphasis added.
12 Jacques Lacan, 'Some reflections on the ego', *International Journal of Psycho-Analysis*, 34 (1953), 61–73 (15). Yet, as Lacan is keen to note, this jubilatory moment can be accompanied by some form of 'depressive reaction' when the child is forced to compare its own precarious and 'inadequate' sense of mastery with the obvious omnipotence it perceives in the (m)other. See Evans, *An Introductory Dictionary of Lacanian Psychoanalysis*, p. 146.
13 Bowie, *Lacan*, p. 22.
14 Of course, it should be remembered that Bloom's poetics of conflict essentially seeks to theorize the literary genealogy of Romanticism and, as such, cannot account for Modernism's ideas of the fragmentation, disruption and the 'divided' self.
15 In 1956 Lacan referred specifically to the 'conflictual nature' of the ego. See Evans, *A Dictionary of Lacanian Psychoanalysis*, p. 115.
16 Maud Ellmann, *The Poetics of Impersonality: T. S. Eliot and Ezra Pound* (Cambridge, Mass.: Harvard University Press, 1987), pp. 95–6.

17 Lacan, 'Some reflections on the ego', 15.
18 *Dylan Thomas: Early Prose Writings*, p. 156.
19 See Sue Vice (ed.), *Psychoanalytic Criticism: A Reader* (Cambridge: Polity, 1996), pp. 99–100. 'Lacan begins with the infant in an amorphous state, with no boundaries to its experience of sense or of need, as a jumble he punningly calls "l'hommlette" – *home-lette*, "little man"; *omelette*, "shapeless mass" of egg.'
20 Cited in *Poet in the Making: The Notebooks of Dylan Thomas*, ed. Ralph Maud (London: Dent, 1968), p. 12. Maud quotes Thomas in his introduction to the volume but gives no reference for this citation.
21 Maud (ed.), *Poet in the Making*, p. 12.
22 See *The Notebooks of Dylan Thomas*, pp. 47–8. Whilst this is clearly a serious poem reminiscent of the Celtic Twilight, at the same time in April 1930 Thomas produced and published a precocious and deftly turned parody of Yeats entitled 'In Borrowed Plumes' in *Swansea Grammar School Magazine*, XXVII (April 1930), 25–6:

> There was a pearl-pale moon that slid
> Down oceans of ambrosial sky,
> Under the drooping of the day's dusk-lid
> Where darkness and her wine-waves lie ...

Further parodies include 'The Children's Hour, or Why the B. B. C. Broke Down', *Swansea Grammar School Magazine* (December 1930) and 'The Sincerest Form of Flattery', *Swansea Grammar School Magazine* (July 1931).
23 *Poet in the Making*, p. 58.
24 The essay entitled 'Modern Poetry' first appeared in the *Swansea Grammar School Magazine* in December 1929. It has subsequently been reprinted in *Dylan Thomas: Early Prose Writings*, pp. 83–6. See *Dylan Thomas: Early Prose Writings*, pp. 84–5.
25 See *Poet in the Making*, pp. 13–14.
26 This selection is listed as an example by Maud in *Poet in the Making*.
27 Richard Aldington, *Exile and Other Poems* (London: George Allen & Unwin, 1923), pp. 29–30; Sachervell Sitwell, *The Hundred and One Harlequins* (London: Duckworth, 1929), p. 27; Thomas's 1930 Notebook Poems, 14, 24 and 30. See *Poet in the Making*, pp. 66–8, 77–8 and 85–6.
28 See, for instance, 'Light breaks where no sun shines' (*CPDT*, pp. 23–4). First published in *The Listener* on 14 March 1934, this audacious poem led to letters of enquiry from such notables as T. S. Eliot, Stephen Spender and Geoffrey Grigson.
29 Sean Homer, *Jacques Lacan* (London: Routledge, 2005), p. 25.
30 Homer, *Jacques Lacan*, p. 25; emphasis added. As Homer points out, Lacan is placing himself here in direct opposition to the dominant strain of ego psychology, according to which the ego is not only given priority over the unconscious processes, but is also seen as being synonymous with the self. For in Lacan's account the ego is, to put it simply, an 'imaginary function'; it is the 'effect of images'.
31 See Kelly Oliver, *Reading Kristeva: Unraveling the Double-bind* (Bloomington and Indianapolis: Indiana University Press, 1993), p. 37.

[32] Jacques Lacan, *The Seminar of Jacques Lacan, Freud's Papers on Technique, 1953–54*, trans. John Forrester (Cambridge: Cambridge University Press, 1988), p. 147.
[33] Lacan, *The Seminar of Jacques Lacan*, p. 170.
[34] *Reading Kristeva: Unraveling the Double-bind*, p. 37.
[35] *CPDT*, pp. 42–3.
[36] *CPDT*, p. 42.
[37] For Lacan, the constitution of the ego by (an imaginary) identification with something which is external to (and even against, or in conflict with) the subject is what 'structures the subject as a rival with himself'. See Jacques Lacan, *Écrits: A Selection*, trans. Alan Sheridan (London: Tavistock, 1977), p. 22.
[38] It is important not to confuse Lacan's ideal ego (*moi idéal*) with the ego-ideal (*idéal du moi*): The ego-ideal is a symbolic introjection, whereas the ideal ego is the source of an imaginary projection. For further clarification see Evans, *An Introductory Dictionary of Lacanian Psychoanalysis*, p. 52.
[39] *Poet in the Making*, p. 97.
[40] See *CPDT*, pp. 75–7.
[41] For a more detailed explanation see Ralph Maud's introductory preface to *Poet in the Making*, pp. 13, 15.
[42] Thomas regarded 'word' and 'image' as being inseparable. A poetic summation of this assertion can be seen in 'Especially when the October wind' (*CPDT*, pp. 18–19), which is the apotheosis of his 'textualization' of the world.
[43] *CLDT*, pp. 181–2.
[44] *CLDT*, p. 282.
[45] Evans, *An Introductory Dictionary of Lacanian Psychoanalysis*, p. 52.

Chapter 3

[1] *Poet in the Making: The Notebooks of Dylan Thomas*, ed. Ralph Maud (London: Dent, 1968), p. 103.
[2] John Goodby '"Eggs laid by tigers": the politics of a style' (unpublished manuscript, 2007), 11. As Goodby adds, it is this 'northern Gothic-expressionism that makes Thomas difficult to assimilate to "Anglo-American notions of modernism"'.
[3] *Poet in the Making*, pp. 144–5. There is, as I have already argued, evidence to suggest that these new sources of imagery began to appear in the writing more than six months earlier. A further, though arguably less impressive, example of the way in which Thomas's interest in 'darker' subjects began to manifest itself can be seen in poem XXVI, 28 July 1931:

> And whose affections aren't corrupt? –
> Listen and lie;
> The head's vacuity can breed no truth
> Out of its sensible tedium,
> ...
> For I shall turn the strongest stomach up
> With filth I gather ...

4. See Caradoc Evans, *My People*, ed. John Harris (Bridgend: Seren, 1997). For further explanation of the Gothic and grotesque elements of Thomas's work, and a detailed account of what he describes as Thomas's '*surregionalism*', see Chris Wigginton, '"Birth and copulation and death": Gothic Modernism and Surrealism in the Poetry of Dylan Thomas ', in *Dylan Thomas: New Casebook*, ed. John Goodby and Chris Wigginton (London: Palgrave, 2001), pp. 85–105.
5. Tony Conran, *Frontiers in Anglo-Welsh Poetry* (Cardiff: University of Wales Press, 1997), p. 113. It should be noted, however, that Conran's use of the Welsh word *buchedd*, which denotes a sense of rural cultural and community values, is itself grotesque in its distortion of its meaning.
6. Jacob Blevins, 'Influence, Anxiety, and the Symbolic', *Intertexts*, 9, 2 (fall 2005), 123–38 (123).
7. The problem here is that Blevins sees Bloom's 'strong poet' as existing only within the Symbolic, and fails to recognize the fact that no matter how well a subject is interpolated within Lacan's system of signs he/she can never entirely escape the Imaginary just as he/she can never truly rid him/herself of the pressures of the Real.
8. See, for instance, John Ackerman's penetrating study, *Welsh Dylan: Dylan Thomas's Life, Writing and his Wales* (Bridgend: Seren, 1979), James A. Davies, *A Reference Companion to Dylan Thomas* (Westport, CT: Greenwood Press, 1998), Walford Davies, *Dylan Thomas*, Writers of Wales (1990; Cardiff: University of Wales Press, 2014) and M. Wynn Thomas, *Corresponding Cultures* (Cardiff: University of Wales Press, 1999).
9. 'I am Going to Read Aloud', *The London Magazine*, 3, 9 (1952).
10. Ackerman, *Welsh Dylan*, p. 58.
11. *New Signatures* and *New Country*, anthologies edited by Michael Roberts, and the collections by poets represented in them – William Empson, William Plomer, Bernard Spencer, John Lehmann, Cecil Day Lewis, Stephen Spender – swiftly established a formally non-experimental, discursive and politically left poetic norm. Michael Roberts (ed.), *New Signatures: Poems by Several Hands* (London: Hogarth Press, 1932); Michael Roberts (ed.), *New Country: Prose and Poetry by the Authors of New Signatures* (London: Hogarth, 1933).
12. 'New Country' (much like the term 'pylon poets') quickly became established as a term that was used generically to describe the new generation of social realist poets.
13. *CPDT*, pp. 18–19.
14. Dylan Thomas, *The Notebook Poems 1930–1934*, ed. Ralph Maud (London: Dent, 1989), pp. 121–2. Hereafter all references to *The Notebook Poems* will be given in the abbreviated form *NP*.
15. Goodby, 'Eggs laid by tigers', 12.
16. *NP*, pp. 146–7.
17. See also 'Do not go gentle into that good night' (*CPDT*, p. 148); 'After the funeral' (*CPDT*, pp. 73–4); 'A Refusal to Mourn' (*CPDT*, pp. 85–6).
18. Maud, however, has claimed that it is not 'And death shall have no dominion', but the slightly later 'Find meat on bones', that provides the very first instance of the emergence of the process metaphysic.
19. Jacob Korg, *Dylan Thomas* (Washington: Hippocrene Books, 1965), pp. 29–32.

20 Goodby, 'Eggs laid by tigers', 14.
21 Goodby, 'Eggs laid by tigers', 14. The biblical source of the refrain is Romans 6:9: 'Death hath no more dominion', whilst the idea of rising again from the sea in the first and second stanzas is based on Revelation 20:13: 'the sea gave up the dead'.
22 Jacques Lacan, *Écrits: A Selection*, trans. Alan Sheridan (London: Tavistock, 1977), p. 22. This was the founding proposition of Lacan's 1948 paper 'Aggressivity in psychoanalysis'.
23 For full discussion see previous chapter.
24 Standard literary histories have tended to see the supersession of high Modernism by new, formally non-experimental and discursive styles as characterizing the British poetry scene in the 1930s, and have thus tended to exclude writers such as Louis MacNeice and Dylan Thomas who, along with the many women writers of the decade, have consequently continued to exist as marginal figures. This fact is attested to by recent critical work on the period. In their introduction to *Rewriting the Thirties: Modernism and After*, Steven Matthews and Keith Williams write: 'Our reason for putting this anthology together is that we thought it long overdue to challenge the persistent aftermath of the thirties as a homogeneous anti-modernist decade. Outdated cultural maps of the time sustain a damagingly restricted canon centred on a narrow genealogy of polarized relations between aesthetics and politics, or between difficulty and accessibility.' Steven Matthews and Keith Williams (eds), *Rewriting the Thirties: Modernism and After* (London: Longman, 1997), p. 1.
25 *Sunday Referee*, 3 September 1933. Ralph Maud dates 'That sanity be kept' to August 1933, and whilst it exists as a transcript, it is identical in style to a number of poems entered into the third notebook in spring and summer 1933.
26 *Sunday Referee*, 3 September 1933.
27 Goodby, 'Eggs laid by tigers', 4.
28 Lacan makes a distinction between the 'ideal ego' and the 'ego ideal'. He associates the former with the Imaginary order and the latter he associates with the Symbolic order. Lacan's ideal ego is the ideal of perfection that the ego strives to emulate: it first affects the subject when it sees itself reflected in a mirror during the mirror stage. Seeing that image of oneself creates a discord between the idealizing image in the mirror (bounded/complete/whole) and the chaotic reality of one's own bodily experience at this early juncture, thus setting up the founding logic of the Imaginary's fantasy construction. For a full discussion and explanation of the mirror stage see chapter 2.
29 See *CLDT*, p. 131.
30 *CLDT*, p. 339.
31 What is of significance here is the fact that within Thomas's 'process' universe language had to be made to match the universal flux. As he would inform Pamela Hansford Johnson, in a letter dated 25 December 1933, 'by the magic of words and images you must make it clear to the reader that the relationships are real. If you are one with the swallow & one with the rose, then the rose is one with the swallow ... show, in *your* words & images, how your flesh covers the tree & the

tree's flesh covers you.' Thomas does this by exploiting the inherent pre-existing metamorphic, or 'processual', attributes of language and discourse.

32 Goodby, 'Eggs laid by tigers', 16.
33 *Poet in the Making*, p. 225.
34 *NP*, p. 179.
35 The August 1933 notebook is generally referred to as the fourth notebook.
36 'I see the boys of summer' (p. 267); 'When once the twilight locks' (p. 255); 'A process in the weather of the heart' (p. 262); 'Before I knocked' (p. 231); 'The force that through the green fuse' (p. 249); 'My hero bares his nerves' (p. 266); 'Where once the waters of your face' (p. 266); 'If I were tickled by the rub of love' (p. 270); 'Our eunuch dreams' (p. 264); 'From love's first fever' (p. 259); 'In the beginning' (p. 240); 'Light breaks where no sun shines' (p. 257); 'I fellowed sleep' (p. 258). These page numbers refer to Ralph Maud's *Poet in the Making*, and not to *18 Poems*.
37 *CLDT*, p. 22.
38 '[T]here is more in the poem, "Before I knocked", more of what I consider to be of importance in my poetry. Please this isn't boasting. I'm incurably pessimistic and eternally dissatisfied.' See *CPDT*, pp. 39–40.
39 See *CLDT*, pp. 147–8: '[H]ave I ever told you of the theory of how all writers either work towards or away from words? ... [a]ny poet or novelist you like to think of – he either works *out* of words or *in the direction of them*. The realistic novelist – Bennett, for instance – sees things, hears things, imagines thing (& all things of the material world or materially cerebral world), & then goes towards words as the most suitable medium through which to express these experiences. A romanticist like Shelley, on the other hand, is his medium first & expresses out of his medium what he sees, hears, thinks & imagines.' He repeated numerous versions of this, mantra-like, to various correspondents: thus 'the structure of the poem should arise out of the words and the expression of them' (*CLDT*, p. 43); '[Poetry] should work from words, from the substance of words and the rhythm of substantial words set together, not towards them' (*CLDT*, p. 208).
40 Desmond Hawkins, 'Poetry', *Time and Tide*, XLV, 6 (9 February 1935), 204; emphasis added.
41 Dylan Evans, *An Introductory Dictionary of Lacanian Psychoanalysis* (London: Routledge, 2005), p. 202.
42 Evans, *An Introductory Dictionary of Lacanian Psychoanalysis*, p. 202.
43 See Chris Wigginton, *Modernism from the Margins: The 1930s Poetry of Louis MacNeice and Dylan Thomas* (Cardiff: University of Wales Press, 2007), pp. 36–7. Wigginton executes a particularly suggestive and illuminating reading of Oedipal anxiety in 'Before I knocked' though his analysis does come from a strictly Freudian – rather than a Lacanian – perspective.
44 See 'The Poetic Manifesto', in Dylan Thomas, *Dylan Thomas: Early Prose Writings*, ed. Walford Davies (London: Dent, 1971), pp. 154–60.
45 What has occurred here is that the individual's Imaginary identifications (or 'ideal egos') that exclusively characterized its infantile years have been supplemented by an identification of an entirely different order: what Lacan calls a Symbolic identification with an 'ego ideal'. This points to an identification with and *within*

something that cannot be seen, touched, devoured or mastered: namely, the words, norms and directives of its given cultural collective. Symbolic identification is always identification with a normatively circumscribed way of organizing the social-intersubjective space within which the subject can take on its most lasting identifications.

46 Kelly Oliver, 'Kristeva's Imaginary Father and the Crisis in Paternal function', *Diacritics*, 21, 2/3, *A Feminist Miscellany* (summer–autumn 1991), 43–63 (44).
47 Oliver, 'Kristeva's Imaginary Father and the Crisis in Paternal function', 53.
48 Oliver, 'Kristeva's Imaginary Father and the Crisis in Paternal function', 56.
49 Goodby, 'Eggs laid by tigers', 9.
50 *CPDT*, pp. 45–6.
51 Goodby, 'Eggs laid by tigers', 9.
52 Goodby, 'Eggs laid by tigers', 9–10.
53 Don McKay, 'Crafty Dylan and the Altarwise Sonnets: "I build a flying tower and I pull it down"', *University of Toronto Quarterly*, 55, 4 (summer 1986), 381.
54 Oliver, 'Kristeva's Imaginary Father and the Crisis in the Paternal Function', 55.

Chapter 4

1 Central to the dialectical insight that informed his poetics was Thomas's insistence that each image 'must be born and die in another'. Negation thus becomes an essential part of the creative or, to be more accurate, of his 'creative/destructive' process. The origin of poetry is the negation of poetry, 'destructive and constructive at the same time', and it is this negation to which poetry must testify at the same time that it testifies to the inexhaustible fecundity of its source. Poetry, like its origin, must be 'creative destruction, destructive creation'. *CLDT*, pp. 281, 27.
2 Don McKay, 'Crafty Dylan and the Altarwise sonnets: "I build a flying tower and I pull it down"', *University of Toronto Quarterly*, 55, 4 (summer 1986), 375–94 (382).
3 Arguably, the paradigmatic text here would be Coleridge's *Kubla Khan*, which as the poetic summation and apotheosis of imaginative excess gestures explicitly towards a Romantic sublime.
4 Ihab Hassan has interestingly remarked that the postmodern may be summarized by a list of words prefixed by 'de-' and 'di-': 'deconstruction, decentering, dissemination, dispersal, displacement, difference, discontinuity, demystification, delegitimation, disappearance'. See Ihab Hassan, 'Beyond Postmodernism? Theory, Sense, and Pragmatism', in Gerard Hoffmann (ed.), *Making Sense: The Role of the Reader in Contemporary American Fiction* (Munchen: Wilhelm Fink, 1989), p. 309.
5 This is the view advanced in part one, 'A jouissance of influence', where it was suggested that Thomas's radical style might be interpreted as a near parody of high Modernism.
6 Jean-François Lyotard, *The Postmodern Explained: Correspondence 1982–1985*, trans. Don Barry, Bernadette Maher, Julian Pefanis, Virginia Spate and Morgan Thomas (Minneapolis: University of Minnesota Press, 1992), p. 11.

7. Simon Malpas, *Jean-François Lyotard* (London: Routledge, 2006), p. 46.
8. Lyotard, *The Postmodern Explained*, pp. 10–11.
9. See Catherine Belsey, *Culture and the Real: Theorizing Cultural Criticism* (London: Routledge, 2005), pp. 126–8. Belsey's own unease, as she explicitly states, stems partly from the view that we need not return to eighteenth-century notions of the Kantian sublime in order to theorize the relationship 'between the signifier and that which exceeds it'. See Belsey, *Culture and the Real*, p. 127. Although Belsey does concede that Lyotard's Kant does in fact turn out to actually anticipate Lacan's distinction between the Symbolic and the Real, and as such she maintains that Kant bears a close resemblance to Lacan's rereading of Saussure.
10. Malpas, *Jean-François Lyotard*, p. 47.
11. Raman Seldon and Peter Widdowson, *A Reader's Guide to Contemporary Literary Theory* (Brighton: Harvester Press, 1985), p. 184.
12. Jean-François Lyotard, 'Answering the Question: What is Postmodernism?', in James Docherty (ed.), *Postmodernism: A Reader* (New York: Columbia University Press, 1993), pp. 38–46 (p. 44).
13. Lyotard, *The Postmodern Explained*, p. 13.
14. It is in this sense that conception, according to Simon Malpas, 'runs ahead of presentation, as the collapsing structure of the realism challenged by the work of art indicates the possibility of a new, different, "inhuman" way of experiencing and thinking about the world'. Malpas, *Jean-François Lyotard*, p. 48.
15. Consider, for instance, Thomas's 1935 poem 'Now' (*CPDT*, p. 45), and also the 'Altarwise' sonnet sequence (*CPDT*, pp. 45–63).
16. Marjorie Perloff, '"Barbed-Wire Entanglements": The "New American Poetry", 1930–1932', in eadem, *Poetry On & Off the Page: Essays for Emergent Occasions* (Evanston: Northwestern University Press, 1998), pp. 53–4.
17. Perloff is referring to a similarly imploded improvization of high Modernism when she speaks of a mannerist Modernism, although her references are specifically transatlantic.
18. Andrew Bennett and Nicholas Royle, *An Introduction to Literature, Theory and Criticism* (Harlow: Pearson Longman, 2004), p. 98.
19. The word 'form' is used here not in the strict poetic sense of the term to denote versification, but as a more general reference to forms or modes of writing.
20. Here Docherty cites Lyotard's seminal text, 'Answering the Question: What is Postmodernism?', on the difference between modern and postmodern aesthetics:

    Here, then, lies the difference: modern aesthetics is an aesthetic of the sublime, though a nostalgic one. It allows the unpresentable to be put forward only as the missing contents; but the form, because of its recognisable consistency, continues to offer the reader or viewer matter for solace and pleasure. Yet these sentiments do not constitute the real sublime sentiment, which is an intrinsic combination of pleasure and pain: The pleasure that reason should exceed all presentation, the pain that imagination or sensibility should not be equal to the concept. (Docherty (ed.), *Postmodernism: A Reader*, p. 46)

21. Chris Wigginton, *Modernism from the Margins: The 1930s Poetry of Louis MacNeice and Dylan Thomas* (Cardiff: University of Wales Press, 2007), p. 9.

NOTES 143

22 The idea of the event is crucial to many of the themes in Lyotard's thought. Bill Readings, one of the most incisive commentators on his work, has defined the event in the following terms:

> An event is an occurrence, as such ... That is to say, the event is the fact or case that something happens, after which nothing will ever be the same again. The event disrupts any pre-existing referential frame within which it might be represented or understood. The eventhood of the event is the radical singularity of happening, the 'it happens' as distinct from the sense of 'what is happening'.

For further explanation see Bill Readings, *Introducing Lyotard: Art and Politics* (London: Routledge, 1991), p. xxxi.

23 *CPDT*, pp. 61, 34, 58.
24 *CPDT*, pp. 58–63.
25 *CPDT*, p. 61.
26 Walford Davies, *Dylan Thomas* (Milton Keynes: Open University Press, 1986), p. 114. Listing a number of poems including 'Where once the waters of your face' (*CPDT*, p. 112), 'When like a running grave' (*CPDT*, p. 111), 'I fellowed sleep' (*CPDT*, p. 24), 'I, in my intricate image' (*CPDT*, p. 53) and 'Altarwise by owl-light' (*CPDT*, pp. 58–63) – his most extreme example, to illustrate his argument – Davies claims that Thomas writes out of a narrative that 'never had a real-world equivalent that could stand in as a referent in the first place'.
27 *CPDT*, p. 51. This is a revised version of a notebook poem of 17 August 1933 (*The Notebook Poems 1930–1934*, ed. Ralph Maud (London: Dent, 1989), p. 181). It was sent to Geoffrey Grigson, probably in late November 1934, and subsequently published in *New Verse* in December 1935. Significantly, the notebook version was dedicated to 'A.E.T.', Labour party activist and fellow Swansea poet Bert Trick whom Thomas once jocularly referred to as 'the communist grocer'. Given that he stimulated Thomas's own left-wing views it is appropriate that he should be the dedicatee of Thomas's one acknowledged political poem. Treece wrote that the poem was unique in this regard, and evoked the following response from Thomas in a letter of July 1938 (*CLDT*, p. 310): 'I was interested in what you said about my lack, except in that little finger-poem, of any social awareness. I suppose I am, broadly, (as opposed to regimented thinkers and poets in uniform) antisocial, but I am extremely sociable. But, surely it is evasive to say that my poetry has no social awareness – no evidence of contact with society – while quite a good number of my images come from the cinema & the gramophone and the newspaper, while I use contemporary slang, cliché, and pun. You meant, I know, that my poetry isn't concerned with politics (supposedly the science of achieving and "administrating" human happiness) but with poetry (which is unsentimental revelation, and to which happiness is no more important – or any other word than misery): – (I'll elaborate that, if you'd like me to. Not that it's obscure, but it may, in some way, be helpful to add to it) but the idea you gave me was that you actually consider me unaware of my surroundings, out-of-contact with the society from which I am necessarily outlaw. You are right when you suggest that I think a

squirrel stumbling at least of equal importance as Hitler's invasions, murder in Spain, the Garbo-Stokowski romance, royalty, Horlick's lynchlaw, pit disasters, Joe Louis, wicked capitalists, saintly communists, democracy, the Ashes, the Church of England, birthcontrol, Yeats' voice, the machines of the world I tick and revolve in, pub-baby-weather-government-football-youthandage-speed-lipstick, all small tyrannies, means tests, the fascist anger, the daily, momentary lightnings, eruptions, farts, dampsquids, barrelorgans, tin whistles, howitzers, tiny death-rattles, volcanic whimpers of the world I eat, drink, love, work, hate and delight in – but I am aware of these things as well.'

28 Stewart Crehan, 'The Lips of Time', in Alan Norman Bold (ed.), *Dylan Thomas: Craft or Sullen Art* (London: Vision, 1990), pp. 34–58 (p. 38).

29 *CPDT*, pp. 23–4.

30 See Ralph Maud, *Entrances to Dylan Thomas's Poetry* (Pittsburgh: Pittsburgh University Press, 1963), p. 45. Maud's is the classic account. He first introduces the idea of 'process' in his 1963 study *Entrances to Dylan Thomas's Poetry*, where he defines 'process poems' as those which explore, and articulate, the duality of the world, and the struggle between black and white: 'HERE IN ITS SIMPLEST TERMS is the duality of the world portrayed in *I see the boys of summer* and the larger part of *18 Poems*. It is convenient to treat this struggle between black and white "process poems".'

31 What is of particular significance in terms of Goodby's reading is the fact that language is made to match the theme of process. Thomas does this, says Goodby, by drawing on, and exploiting the inherent pre-existing metaphoric, or 'proces-sual' attributes of language and discourse. This is an important point and one to which I intend to return during the course of this chapter.

32 John Goodby, *No Work of Words: The Critical Fates of Dylan Thomas* (unpublished manuscript). For further reading, see John Goodby, *The Poetry of Dylan Thomas: Under the Spelling Wall* (Liverpool: Liverpool University Press, 2013).

33 *CPDT*, pp. 10–11.

34 *CPDT*, p. 10.

35 Lacan's use of the term 'Real' as a substantive dates back to 1936. However it was not until 1953 that he elevated it to the status of a fundamental psychoanalytic category; henceforth, as Dylan Evans has observed, the Real is one of the three orders under which all psychoanalytic phenomena can be classified, the other two being the Imaginary order and the Symbolic order (both defined in previous chapters): the Real is no longer simply opposed to the Imaginary, but is also located beyond the Symbolic '[in] these formulations of the period 1953–5, the real emerges as that which is outside language and inassimilable to symbolisation. It is "that which resists symbolisation absolutely"; or, again the real is the domain of "whatever subsists outside symbolisation".' This theme remains a constant throughout the rest of Lacan's work, and leads him to link the Real with the concept of impossibility. For further explanation, see Dylan Evans, *An Introductory Dictionary of Lacanian Psychoanalysis* (London: Routledge, 2005), pp. 159–60.

36 Significantly, however, as Malcolm Bowie has observed, all three of Lacan's orders, the Imaginary, the Real and the Symbolic, have the capacity to,

momentarily at least, 'slip their human moorings altogether, and become warring principles in a grandiose cosmological allegory'. See Malcolm Bowie, *Lacan* (London: Fontana, 1991), p. 91.

[37] Bruce Fink, *The Lacanian Subject: Between Language and Joiussance* (New Jersey: Princeton University Press, 1995), pp. 24–5.

[38] *CPDT*, p. 21.

[39] Chuck Palahniuk, *Choke* (London: Jonathon Cape, 2001), p. 149.

[40] Tony Myers, *Slavoj Žižek* (London: Routledge, 2003), p. 25.

[41] *CPDT*, p. 107.

[42] J. Hillis Miller, *Poets of Reality: Six Twentieth-century Poets* (Harvard: Harvard University Press, 1965), p. 190.

[43] Thomas was of course not unique in this, and in many ways there is a resemblance here with Walt Whitman's great 'Song of Myself'.

[44] Miller, *Poets of Reality: Six Twentieth-century Poets*, pp. 190–1.

[45] *CLDT*, p. 75.

[46] *CPDT*, p. 13.

[47] For a conventional but very thorough exegesis, see Davies, *Dylan Thomas*, pp. 28–31.

[48] On one level at least it might seem possible to interpret the apparent failure of communication in terms of poetic impotency: 'And I am dumb to tell the lover's tomb / How at my sheet goes the same crooked worm.' Read in this way the sheet is clearly a sheet of paper, whilst the worm would signify the poet's scrawl. However to reduce the text in this way, to impose any kind of single coherent meaning onto the poem, would necessarily truncate its subversive potentialities. Moreover 'process' itself hinges on undecidability and an openendedness that keeps meaning(s) in play, rather than resorting to any neo-Kantian postulation of ambiguity

[49] See Davies, *Dylan Thomas*, p. 117. The process of separation or, in Lacanian terms, the withdrawal of the Real, is quite clearly seen by Thomas as having been caused by the subject's entry into language. See, for instance, 'From love's first fever' (*CPDT*, pp. 21–2).

[50] *CPDT*, p. 134.

[51] Miller, *Poets of Reality*, p. 197.

[52] Patricia Waugh (ed.), *Literary Theory and Criticism* (Milton Keynes: Open University Press, 2006), pp. 284–5.

[53] Gareth Thomas, 'A Freak User of Words', in Alan Norman Bold (ed.), *Dylan Thomas Craft or Sullen Art* (London: Vision, 1990), pp. 65–87 (p. 84).

[54] Crehan's reading is significant in so far as it was the first to register the possibilities of reading the poetry in the light of critical theory. However, his theoretical framework is drawn largely from Freudian models of psychosexual development which he uses in tandem with Saussurian linguistics to mount what is essentially a Marxist critique of the social and ideological interpolation of the subject. Strangely he makes no explicit reference to post-structuralist psycholinguistic accounts of the genesis of the speaking subject.

[55] *CPDT*, p. 75.

[56] See Thomas's letter to Henry Treece, dated 16 May 1938, *CLDT*, p. 296.

57. Davies, *Dylan Thomas*, p. 18.
58. *CPDT*, p. 75.
59. See Davies, *Dylan Thomas*, p. 17.
60. *CPDT*, p. 76.
61. Davies, *Dylan Thomas*, p. 18.
62. Davies, *Dylan Thomas*, p. 19. This is a point that Thomas himself appeared to endorse. In the above quoted letter to Treece, Thomas went on to claim that '[t]he poem is, as all poems are, its own question and answer, its own contradiction, its own agreement ... The aim of the poem is the mark that the poem itself makes; it's the bullseye; the knife, the growth, and the patient. A poem moves only to its own end, which is the last line.' Letter to Henry Treece, 16 May 1938, *CLDT*, p. 297.
63. For Lacan Joyce was, of course, the writer most supremely able to embody something of the jouissance that is inextricably linked to the impossible Real within the textures of his writing.

Chapter 5

1. Julia Kristeva, 'From One Identity to Another', in *Desire in Language*, trans. Leon S. Roudiez (New York: Columbia University Press, 1980), pp. 124–5.
2. Only one critic, David Holbrook, has written at length on the rogue element in Thomas (see David Holbrook, 'The Code of Night', in Walford Davies (ed.), *Dylan Thomas: New Critical Essays* (London: Dent, 1972)). As Don Mckay points out, he shares the broad assumptions of New Criticism: 'works of art ought to be unified and integrated', and so he deplores the fact that Thomas's are to him manifestly not. Rather they are the work of a schizoid personality suffering from a Laingian ontological uncertainty, a disability registered in his aberrant behaviour. This version is '"Dylan Thomas, the case study", a horrible example of the symptoms deriving from the contemporary crisis of consciousness.' See Don McKay, 'What Shall We Do with a Drunken Poet: Dylan Thomas' Poetic Language', *Queen's Quarterly*, 93, 4 (winter 1986), 794–804.
3. See for instance Thomas's letter to Henry Treece, dated 23 March 1938 (*CLDT*, p. 281), where Thomas seems to say that the creation of poetry is the destruction of poetry. 'Each image holds within it the seed of its own destruction, and my dialectical method, as I understand it, is a constant building up and breaking down of the images that come out of the central seed, which is itself destructive and constructive at the same time.'
4. Don McKay, 'What Shall We Do with a Drunken Poet: Dylan Thomas' Poetic Language', *Queen's Quarterly*, 93, 4 (winter 1986), 794–804 (799).
5. William York Tindall, *A Reader's Guide to Dylan Thomas* (Syracuse: Syracuse University Press, 1962), p. 89.
6. McKay, 'What Shall We Do with a Drunken Poet: Dylan Thomas' Poetic Language', 794–804 (799).
7. Tindall, *A Reader's Guide to Dylan Thomas*, p. 89.
8. McKay, 'What Shall We Do with a Drunken Poet: Dylan Thomas' Poetic Language', 800.

9   See Chris Wigginton, *Modernism from the Margins: The 1930s Poetry of Louis MacNeice and Dylan Thomas* (Cardiff: University of Wales Press, 2007), pp. 122–3; emphasis added. Although it is my contention that the idea of the postmodern sublime is perhaps most relevant to the early poems, Wigginton extends this argument to include the later work, reading Thomas's development from the early work of *18 Poems* (London: Parton Press, 1934) and *Twenty-five Poems* (London: Dent, 1936) to the later volumes such as *Deaths and Entrances* (London: Dent, 1946) and the final and incomplete *In Country Heaven* sequence as chronicling a journey 'from a Modernist search for autonomy towards a postmodernist recognition of its impossibility'. Regrettably, however, as Wigginton himself does admit, he does not trace the full implications that such a postmodern reading would require.
10 See Slavoj Žižek, *The Sublime Object of Ideology* (London: Verso, 1989), p. 194. Žižek says that, according to Lacan, the sublime object is an 'ordinary, everyday object which, quite by chance, finds itself occupying the place of what he calls *das Ding*, the impossible-real object of desire. The sublime object is "an object elevated to the level of *das Ding*". It is the structural place – the fact that it occupies the sacred/forbidden place of *jouissance* – and not its intrinsic qualities that confers on it its sublimity.'
11 Inextricably linked to the idea of trauma and its catastrophic effects for the subject, there is for Lacan only ever a glimpse of the Real as a kind of *après coup*, an after blow, as Julian Wolfreys puts it, 'or effect of a catastrophic event leaving its mark on the subject' (*Critical Keywords in Literary and Cultural Theory* (London: Palgrave, Macmillan, 2004), p. 112). According to Lacan then: 'the function of the *tuché*, of the real as encounter – the encounter in so far as it may be missed, in so far as it is essentially the *missed encounter* – first presented itself in the history of psycho-analysis in a form that was in itself enough to arouse our attention, *that of the trauma*' (my own emphasis added). See Jacques Lacan, *The Four Fundamental Concepts of Psycho-Analysis*, ed. Jacques-Alain Miller, trans. Alan Sheridan (1973; London: Penguin, 1994), p. 55.
12 See Rainer Emig, *Modernism in Poetry: Motivations, Structures and Limits* (London: Longman, 1995), pp. 20–1.
13 Although it might be argued that Newman's 'zipping' is, in fact, an affirmation, even exaltation, rehearsing the creative moment of the sublime, as it were.
14 Philip Shaw, *The Sublime* (London: Routledge, 2006), pp. 120–3.
15 Jean François Lyotard, *The Inhuman: Reflections on Time*, trans. Geoffrey Bennington and Rachel Bowlby (Cambridge: Polity Press, 1984), pp. 81–2.
16 See also 'When once the twilight locks' (*CPDT*, pp. 9–10), 'I dreamed my genesis' (*CPDT*, pp. 25–6), 'A process in the weather of the heart' (*CPDT*, pp. 10–11), 'All, all and all' (*CPDT*, p. 29), 'My world is pyramid' (*CPDT*, p. 42) and 'Do you not father me' (*CPDT*, p. 42).
17 The opening line of stanza 4: 'In the beginning was the word' is a deliberate echo of the Gospel of St John 1:1, 'In the beginning was the Word, and the Word was with God, and God was the Word' – which is itself, of course, an echo of the first words of Genesis.
18 Ralph Maud, *Where Have the Old Words Got Me?* (Cardiff: University of Wales Press, 2003), pp. 154–6. In his foreword to the text Lawrence describes himself as

'trying to stammer out the first terms of a forgotten knowledge ... the real truth, the clue to the cosmos': 'in the beginning – there never was any beginning, but let it pass. We've got to make a start somehow. In the beginning of all things, time and space and cosmos and being, in the beginning of all these was a little living creature.'

19   Andrew Bennett and Nicholas Royle, *An Introduction to Literature, Theory and Criticism* (Harlow: Pearson Longman, 2004), p. 5.
20   Stewart Crehan, 'The Lips of Time', in John Goodby and Chris Wiggington (eds), *Dylan Thomas: New Casebook* (Basingstoke: Palgrave, 2001), pp. 46–64 (p. 47).
21   Shaw, *The Sublime*, p. 122.
22   Shaw, *The Sublime*, p. 122.
23   Shaw, *The Sublime*, pp. 122–3.
24   Simon Malpas, *Jean-François Lyotard* (London: Routledge, 2006), p. 101.
25   See James Docherty (ed.), *Postmodernism: A Reader* (New York: Columbia University Press, 1993), pp. 38–47.
26   Shaw, *The Sublime*, p. 23.
27   'Answering the Question: What is Postmodernism?', in *Postmodernism: A Reader*, pp. 38–46 (p. 46). Lyotard illustrates his argument by contrasting the melancholia of the German Expressionists with the quixotic inventiveness of Braque and Picasso; the reconciliatory aesthetics of Proust's *A La Recherche du Temps Perdu* with the disruptive novation of Joyce's *Ulysses*.

Chapter 6

1   Elizabeth Grosz, 'The Body of Signification', in John Fletcher and Andrew Benjamin (eds), *Abjection, Melancholia and Love: The Work of Julia Kristeva* (London: Routledge, 1990), p. 82.
2   See *CLDT*. In his general index to the letters, Paul Ferris devotes a section to Thomas's 'anatomical' imagery, pp. 38–9, 72, 77–9, 90, 98, 102–3, 117, 243.
3   *CLDT*, pp. 38–39.
4   See Julian Wolfreys, *Critical Keywords in Literary and Cultural Theory* (London: Palgrave, Macmillan, 2004), p. 3. Julian Wolfreys offers this particularly succinct explanation of Kristeva's theory of abjection:

> 'Abjection is used by [Kristeva] in an effort to destabilize the binary logic of much psychoanalytic thought, where the notions of (desiring) subject and object (of desire) often represent a co-dependent oppositional pairing. In order to understand [her] point it is necessary that we recognise "subject" and "object" not only as supposed locations or two halves of a logical model, but also as supposedly discrete and complete identities in and of themselves. Each figure in the pair is accorded its own self-sufficient meaning with definable boundaries. Such boundaries are the psychic limits by which the self separates itself from the *other* within the psychoanalytic framework of Kristeva's text ... another way of positing the subject/object dyad would be to comprehend it, as is already implied, in terms of "self/other". The abject, says Kristeva, is

"neither subject nor object"; instead it opposes the ego by "drawing me to the place where meaning collapses". While the subject/object structure makes logical meaning possible, the abject produces, or is otherwise comprehensible as, an uncanny effect of horror, threatening the logical certainty of either the subject/object or self/not-self binarism. Abjection is thus the process or psychic experience of a slippage across the boundaries of the self, and with that a partial erasure across the borders of the psyche which define the ego. The abject is, amongst other things [then], the fluid locus of forbidden desires and ideas whose radical exclusion is the basis of the subject's cultural determination; in comprehending the process of abjection thus, we ... see ... that which threatens the self is not simply necessarily locatable outside the self but rather emerges or erupts within subjectivity ... it is clear from this term [abjection] that there is, in one sense, an intimate relationship between the psychic construction of the human body and that which both revolts it and yet in some manner belongs to that body.' Emphasis added.

5   See Harri Garrod Roberts, *Embodying Identity: Representations of the Body in Welsh Literature* (Cardiff: University of Wales Press, 2009), pp. 102–3; emphasis added. I am indebted to Roberts for his provocative reading of Thomas's subversive poetics of the body, where he maintains that whilst the foregrounding of language's non-syntactical, intonational qualities in Thomas's first two collections (*18 Poems* (London: Parton Press, 1934) and *Twenty-five Poems* (London: Dent, 1936)) poses a threat to the social contract with its fossilization of the signifier/signified bond, this is accompanied by an overt emphasis on the body and bodily processes that in itself constitutes a form of resistance to the perceived tyranny of the social compact.

6   See, for example, *CLDT*, p. 97: '[A]ll good poetry is bound to be obscure. Remember Eliot: "The chief use of the 'meaning' of a poem, in the ordinary sense, may be to satisfy one habit of the reader, to keep his mind diverted and quiet, while the poem does its work upon him."' Similarly, one cannot deny the obvious appeal for Thomas of Eliot's account, in his seminal essay on Matthew Arnold, of the 'auditory imagination', a feeling for 'syllable, rhythm, penetrating far below the conscious levels of thought and feeling, invigorating every word; sinking back to the most primitive and forgotten, returning to the origin and bringing something back [fusing] the most ancient and most civilised mentality'. It should be noted however that Eliot was to recant his faith in the auditory imagination only three years later, in 1936 as he grew increasingly conservative.

7   Maud Ellmann, 'Eliot's Abjection', in John Fletcher and Andrew Benjamin (eds), *Abjection, Melancholia and Love: The Work of Julia Kristeva* (London: Routledge, 1990), p. 181.

8   The notion of *le sujet en procès* is one of Kristeva's key ideas, and was hinted at early on in her epochal text *Revolution in Poetic Language*, that was first presented as a doctoral thesis in 1973. Here, she suggests that the speaking being, Lacan's *parle être* is not a stable subject, but something else altogether: a subject in process/on trial. She suggests that a dialectical notion of a signifying practice would show how 'significance puts the subject in process / on trial'. See Julia

Kristeva, *Revolution in Poetic Language*, trans. Leon S. Roudiez (New York: Columbia University Press, 1984), p. 22.
9   Noëlle McAfee, *Julia Kristeva* (London: Routledge, 2004), p. 46.
10 See Julia Kristeva, *Powers of Horror: An Essay on Abjection*, trans. Leon S. Roudiez (New York: Columbia University Press, 1982), p. 3.
11 Wolfreys, *Critical Keywords in Literary and Cultural Theory*, p. 5.
12 Kristeva's hyphenated gerund underlines the fact that she is speaking not simply of a subject-object, self-other, relation but of a 'process or movement that defines the very structurality, as it were, of that structure'. For further clarification see Wolfreys, *Critical Keywords in Literary and Cultural Theory*, pp. 3–4.
13 Wolfreys, *Critical Keywords in Literary and Cultural Theory*, p. 6.
14 Norma Clare Moruzzi, 'National Abjects: Julia Kristeva on the Process of Political Self-Identification', in Kelly Oliver (ed.), *Ethics, Politics and Difference in Julia Kristeva's Writing* (New York: Routledge, 1993), pp. 135–49 (pp. 144–5).
15 Quoted in Kristeva, *Powers of Horror*, p. 56.
16 Ellmann, 'Eliot's Abjection', p. 181.
17 See T. S. Eliot, *The Waste Land*, in *Selected Poems* (London: Faber, 1961), p. 58.
18 See Ellmann, 'Eliot's Abjection', pp. 180–2. There is a point to be made here that relates to the linguistic registers of the text; for the same sense of fragmentation can be discerned in the poem's 'broken', radically fractured language.
19 Grosz, 'The Body of Signification', p. 91.
20 Roberts, *Embodying Identity*, p. 5.
21 John Goodby, *No Work of Words: The Critical Fates of Dylan Thomas* (unpublished manuscript). For further reading, see John Goodby, *The Poetry of Dylan Thomas: Under the Spelling Wall* (Liverpool: Liverpool University Press, 2013).
22 Hal Foster, *The Return of the Real* (Massachusetts and London: The MIT Press, 1996), p. 156.
23 Foster, *The Return of the Real*, p. 156.
24 See Chris Wigginton, *Modernism from the Margins: The 1930s Poetry of Louis MacNeice and Dylan Thomas* (Cardiff: University of Wales Press, 2007), p. 36.
25 *CPDT*, pp. 9–10. Reading the poem in its entirely gives some sense of the extent of Thomas's bodily inflected lexis: 'finger', 'fist, 'mouth', 'breast', 'hair', 'bone', 'rib', 'heart', 'eyes', 'cataract[s]', 'cancer', 'jaws', 'blood', 'limbs', 'cock', 'fluids', 'mother's milk'.
26 Kristeva, *Powers of Horror*, p. 208.
27 Kristeva, *Powers of Horror*, p. 208.
28 *CLDT*, p. 11.
29 See Roberts, *Embodying Identity*, pp. 107–8.
30 *CPDT*, p. 10.
31 It was the menacing proximity of flesh and affective materiality that mid-century critics found so provocative. This, for example, was Grigson in 1957:

> 'While Mr Eliot's poems live tightly above the waste, those of Mr Thomas live, sprawl loosely, below the waist. Mr Eliot is a reasoning creature. The self in Mr Thomas's poetry seems inhuman and glandular. Or rather like water and mud and fumes mixed in a volcanic mud-hole ... not to worry the metaphor

too far, one would prefer a man's poetry to break out of the common fury like a geyser, at least with the force and cleanness of form, at least with the meaning of a pillar: not with the meaningless hot sprawl of mud.' Cited in E. W. Tedlock (ed.), *Dylan Thomas: The Legend and the Poet* (London: Heinemann/Mercury Books, 1963),, p. 96.

[32] Goodby, *No Work of Words*.
[33] See, for example, *CLDT*, p. 78.
[34] I shall return to the idea of the postmodern during the course of this chapter when I shall fully elaborate the point that I've made here.
[35] Christopher Wigginton, 'Modernism from the Margins; A Study of the 1930s Poetry of Louis MacNeice and Dylan Thomas' (unpublished PhD thesis, Swansea University, 2003), 67.
[36] Ellmann, 'Eliot's Abjection', p. 187.
[37] Ellmann, 'Eliot's Abjection', p. 187.
[38] John Goodby, 'The Blitz sublime: Dylan Thomas, T. S. Eliot and the poetry of the 1940's' (unpublished paper, St Andrew's University, March 2010).
[39] See 'Answers to an Enquiry', in Dylan Thomas, *Dylan Thomas: Early Prose Writings*, ed. Walford Davies (London: Dent, 1971), p. 150. When asked, in 1934, if he had been influenced by Freud, Thomas replied '[y]es. Whatever is hidden should be made naked. To be stripped of darkness is to be clean, to strip of darkness is to make clean. Poetry, recording the stripping of the individual darkness, must inevitably, cast light upon what has been hidden for too long, and, by so doing, make clean the naked exposure. Freud cast light on a little of the darkness he had exposed. Benefiting by the sight of the light and the knowledge of the hidden nakedness, poetry must drag even further into the clean nakedness of light more even of the hidden causes than Freud could realise.'
[40] Goodby, 'The Blitz sublime'.

Chapter 7

[1] For a fine explanation of the radical difference between the symptom and Lacanian *sinthome* see Sarah Kay, *Žižek: A Critical Introduction* (Cambridge: Polity, 2003), pp. 80–2. Kay asserts that:

'A psychoanalytic symptom is not just like a medical one, a sign that betrays the existence of some underlying disturbance, though it is that too. It is also a way in which the subject denies and fends off enjoyment by delegating it to, for example, a limb or a repeated pattern of behaviour. In this way, unlike a fantasy, which seals over a split in the subject and conceals its relation to enjoyment, the symptom draws attention to the existence of this split and presents its enjoyment for the Other to see. In Lacan's later thinking, the symptom becomes the sinthome, the manifestation of the subject's enjoyment which he cannot give up but should embrace as "what is in him more than himself". At this point, its symbolic dimension declines, and the subject's imaginary relation with enjoyment correspondingly increases in importance.'

2   See Dylan Evans, *An Introductory Dictionary of Lacanian Psychoanalysis* (London: Routledge, 2005), p. 189.
3   Evans, *An Introductory Dictionary of Lacanian Psychoanalysis*, p. 189.
4   Evans, *An Introductory Dictionary of Lacanian Psychoanalysis*, p. 189.
5   See *CPDT*, pp. 7–8.
6   In chapter 5, comparing the poem with 'Today this insect', it was argued that these opposing voices might be those of tradition versus the avant-garde, thus making the text itself a scene of linguistic struggle.
7   Katie Gramich, '"Daughters of Darkness": Dylan Thomas and the Celebration of the Female', in John Goodby and Chris Wigginton (eds), *Dylan Thomas: New Casebook* (Basingstoke: Palgrave, 2001), pp. 65–84 (p. 69).
8   Dylan Thomas, *Dylan Thomas: Early Prose Writings*, ed. Walford Davies (London: Dent, 1971), p. 158. William Moynihan noted that to Thomas's own exuberant list, '[w]e must add dialectical words, clichés, words based on hidden metaphors, grammatical shifts and wrenched syntax'. For a full account see William T. Moynihan, *The Art of Dylan Thomas* (Ithaca, New York: Cornell University Press, 1968), p. 78.
9   Moynihan, *The Art of Dylan Thomas*, p. 78.
10 The exception here would be those avant-garde practitioners who responded to Eugene Jolas's 'revolution of the word'.
11 *CPDT*, pp. 18–19. This is the first in Thomas's series of 'birthday poems', and began as an early draft, 'Especially when the November wind' (see chapter 1), extant in a British Library typescript. It was revised for publication in *The Listener*, 24 October 1934, with the title 'Poem in October' before appearing in *18 Poems* (London: Parton Press, 1934) as 'Especially when the October wind'.
12 Harri Garrod Roberts, *Embodying Identity: Representations of the Body in Welsh Literature* (Cardiff: University of Wales Press, 2009), pp. 108–9.
13 Roberts, *Embodying Identity*, pp. 108–9. Whilst Roberts speaks of 'objects able to speak the real by *being* the real' (emphasis added) he does not define that real, and it does seem to me that he is referring, in a more general sense, to some kind of physical *reality* rather than to any specifically Lacanian notion of the order of the Real.
14 *Dylan Thomas: Early Prose Writings*, p. 117.
15 Compare, for example, the obvious verbal richness of a later poem like 'Fern Hill' (*CPDT*, pp. 34–5) with the densely impacted sonnet stanzas of the earlier 'Altarwise by owl-light' (*CPDT*, pp. 58–63), which can be read as representing the high point of Thomas's Modernist obscurity.
16 *CPDT*, pp. 27, 35.
17 *CPDT*, pp. 148–50. Thomas wittily described this as a 'crotchety poem' that was 'coarse and violent [and] not quite clean, but worked at, between the willies, very hard' (*CLDT*, p. 791). The first stanza gives some sense of the way in which pun and slang expression provides the source of Thomas's lively humour:

> When I was a windy boy and a bit
> And the black spit of the chapel fold,
> (Sighed the old ram rod, dying of women),
> I tiptoed shy in the gooseberry wood,

> The rude owl cried like a telltale tit,
> I skipped in a blush as the big girls rolled
> Ninepin down on the donkeys' common,
> And on seesaw sunday nights I wooed
> Whoever I could with my wicked eyes,
> The whole of the moon I could love and leave
> All the green leaved little weddings' wives
> In the coal black bush and let them grieve.

[18] *CPDT*, pp. 19–21.
[19] *CPDT*, pp. 18–19.
[20] Slavoj Žižek, *Enjoy Your Symptom!* (1992; London and New York: Routledge, 2001), p. 226.
[21] *CPDT*, pp. 19–21.
[22] Žižek, *Enjoy Your Symptom!*, p. 226; emphasis added.
[23] Žižek, *Enjoy Your Symptom!*, p. 27; emphasis added.
[24] Žižek, *Enjoy Your Symptom!*, p. 27.
[25] Žižek, *Enjoy Your Symptom!*, p. 227.
[26] Stewart Crehan, 'The Lips of Time', in John Goodby and Chris Wiggington (eds), *Dylan Thomas: New Casebook* (Basingstoke: Palgrave, 2001), p. 47.
[27] Chris Wigginton, *Modernism from the Margins: The 1930s Poetry of Louis MacNeice and Dylan Thomas* (Cardiff: University of Wales Press, 2007), p. 39.
[28] *CPDT*, pp. 13–14.
[29] See Wigginton, *Modernism from the Margins*, pp. 39–40.
[30] *CLDT*, p. 39.
[31] Ralph Maud, *Where Have the Old Words Got Me?* (Cardiff: University of Wales Press, 2003), p. 183. Maud notes that in one of Thomas's short stories, 'The Holy Six', we have a man who eschewed female flesh 'and the male nerve was pulled alone' (Dylan Thomas, *The Collected Stories*, ed. Walford Davies, introduced by Leslie Norris (London: Phoenix, 2000), p. 97).
[32] See *The Notebook Poems 1930–1934*, ed. Ralph Maud (London: Dent, 1989), p. 154. The third stanza of poem twenty-seven, which was fair-copied into the February notebook on 23 April 1933, reads as follows:

> A one-legged man ascending steps
> Looks down upon him with regrets
> That whips and stools and cistern sex
> Have yet to add to that that mother strips
> Upon her knee and shields from metal whisper
> Of wind along the cot,
> Sees cool get cold and childmind darker
> As time on time sea ribbon rounds
> Parched shires in dry lands.

[33] John Goodby, 'The Blitz sublime: Dylan Thomas, T. S. Eliot and the Poetry of the 1940's' (unpublished paper, St Andrew's University, March 2010). 'Again TSE opined in anti-humanist, anti-Romantic mode, that "Look[ing] into our hearts and writ[ing]" is all very well ... But one can sense the glee with which Dylan Thomas

seized on this not quite convincing attempt to shock and pushed it to his truly shocking un-Eliotic conclusion, his Welsh modernist gothic spectacularly upping the ante on Eliot's tame little "bats with baby faces" with "dead [who] undid their bushy jaws, and bags of blood let out their flies", an embryo "smel[ing] the maggot in my stool" and "words of death ... dryer than his stiff" for a Christ who may be dead, suffering an erection, or both.'

34 A key point in Žižek's *oeuvre* is 'The Obscene Object of Postmodernity', a text that has been cited and re-printed, in part, in a number of prestigious theoretical readers. It first appeared, however, as a chapter in Slavoj Žižek, *Looking Awry: An Introduction to Jacques Lacan through Popular Culture* (Cambridge, Mass. and London: MIT Press, 1991), pp. 141–53.

35 Elizabeth Wright and Edmond Wright (eds), *The Žižek Reader* (1999; London: Blackwell, 2007), p. 40.

36 Žižek gives a further example of the technique of 'filling in the gaps' in a comparative analysis of the book and film versions of *The Talented Mr. Ripley*. See Slavoj Žižek, *The Fright of Real Tears:Krzysztof Kieślowski Between Theory and Post-Theory* (London and Bloomington: British Film Institute and Indiana University Press, 2001), pp. 146–9. In the novel, says Žižek, Ripley's homosexuality is indirectly proposed. In the film version, however, he is presented as being explicitly 'gay'. Hence, in Minghella's film version, the repressed content of the novel, the 'absence' around which it centres, as it were, is covered over, or 'filled in'.

37 Wright and Wright (eds), *The Žižek Reader*, p. 38.

38 Slavoj Žižek, 'The Obscene Object of Postmodernity', in Wright and Wright (eds), *The Zizek Reader*, p. 41.

39 Žižek, 'The Obscene Object of Postmodernity', p. 41; emphasis added.

40 Roberts, *Embodying Identity*, pp. 97–8.

41 Neil Corcoran, *English Poetry Since 1940* (London: Longman, 1993), p. 43; Roberts, *Embodying Identity*, p. 98.

42 Corcoran, *English Poetry since 1940*, pp. 43, 45.

43 John Goodby, 'The Blitz sublime'.

44 *CPDT*, p. 16.

45 John Goodby, *No Work of Words: The Critical Fates of Dylan Thomas* (unpublished manuscript), p. 15. For further reading, see John Goodby, *The Poetry of Dylan Thomas: Under the Spelling Wall* (Liverpool: Liverpool University Press, 2013).

46 *CPDT*, p. 14.

47 See *Modernism from the Margins*, p. 40.

48 Andrew Bennett and Nicholas Royle, *An Introduction to Literature, Theory and Criticism* (Harlow: Pearson Longman, 2004), p. 193.

49 Matthew Arnold, 'The Function of Criticism at the Present Time', in idem, *Essays in Criticism* (New York: Everyman's Library, 1964), pp. 34, 33.

50 F. R. Leavis and Denys Thompson, *Culture and the Environment: The Training of Critical Awareness* (London: Chatto and Windus, 1964), p. 82.

51 See *An Introduction to Literature, Theory and Criticism*, op. cit.

52 Georges Bataille, *Literature and Evil*, trans. Alistair Hamilton (London: Marion Boyars, 1985), pp. x, 25.

Conclusion

[1] Tony Myers, *Slavoj Žižek* (London: Routledge, 2003), pp. 111–12.
[2] John Goodby and Chris Wigginton (eds), *Dylan Thomas: New Casebook* (Basingstoke: Palgrave, 2001), p. 1.
[3] These include, most notably, the early (but not the late) Saunders Lewis and, more recently, Bobi Jones.
[4] Gwyn Jones, *The First Forty Years* (Cardiff: University of Wales Press, 1957), p. 14. From a somewhat different perspective, however, the distinguished poet/critic Tony Conran implicitly suggests that such ambivalences actually spring from the cultural dislocation of the Anglo-Welsh writer, whose predicament, he insists, is epitomized in Thomas's own dichotomous positioning: '*the poet is caught between two fires. He is neither English nor Welsh;* neither a member of the anglicised middle-class, nor of the Welsh-speaking peasantry. Indeed, he may despise both ... What is there left for him to praise and mourn but his own self's legend, the glory of himself and the pathos of his bewilderment?' Tony Conran, 'The English Poet in Wales', *Anglo-Welsh Review*, 10, 26 (1960), 11–21 (14–15).
[5] E. W. Tedlock (ed.), *Dylan Thomas: The Legend and the Poet* (London: William Heinemann, 1960), p. 8.

Bibliography

Ackerman, John, *Welsh Dylan: Dylan Thomas's Life, Writing and his Wales* (Bridgend: Seren, 1979).
Ackerman, John, *A Dylan Thomas Companion: Life, Poetry and Prose* (London: Macmillan, 1994).
Aldington, Richard, *Exile and Other Poems* (London: George Allen & Unwin, 1923).
Althusser, Louis, 'Ideology and the state', in idem, *Essays on Ideology* (London: Verso, 1984).
Arnold, Matthew, 'The Function of Criticism at the Present Time', in idem, *Essays in Criticism* (New York: Everyman's Library, 1964).
Baruch, Elaine and Lucienne Serrano (eds), 'Interview with Julia Kristeva', in eadem, *Women Analyse Women* (New York: New York University Press, 1988).
Bataille, Georges, *Literature and Evil*, trans. Alistair Hamilton (London: Marion Boyars, 1985).
Belsey, Catherine, *Critical Practice* (London: Methuen, 1980).
Belsey, Catherine, *Culture and the Real: Theorizing Cultural Criticism* (London: Routledge, 2005).
Bennet, Andrew and Nicholas Royle, *An Introduction to Literature, Theory and Criticism* (Harlow: Pearson Longman, 2004).
Blevins, Jacob, 'Influence, Anxiety and the Symbolic', *Intertexts*, 9, 2 (fall 2005), 123–38.
Bloom, Harold, *The Anxiety of Influence: A Theory of Poetry* (New York and Oxford: Oxford University Press, 1997).
Borch-Jacobsen, Mikkel, 'The Oedipus Problem in Freud and Lacan', *Critical Enquiry*, 20, 2 (winter 1994), 267–82.
Bowie, Malcolm, *Lacan* (London: Fontana, 1991).
Conran, Tony, 'The English Poet in Wales', *Anglo-Welsh Review*, 10, 26 (1960), 11–21.

Conran, Tony, *Frontiers in Anglo-Welsh Poetry* (Cardiff: University of Wales Press, 1997).
Corcoran, Neil, *English Poetry since 1940* (London: Longman, 1993).
Corpet, Oliver and François Matheron (eds), *Psychoanalysis: Freud and Lacan*, trans. Jeffrey Mehmlan (New York: Columbia University Press, 1996).
Crehan, Stewart, 'The Lips of time', in Alan Norman Bold (ed.), *Dylan Thomas: Craft or Sullen Art* (London: Vision, 1990).
Crehan, Stewart, 'The Lips of Time', in John Goodby and Chris Wiggington (eds), *Dylan Thomas: New Casebook* (Basingstoke: Palgrave, 2001).
Davies, James A., *A Reference Companion to Dylan Thomas* (Westport, CT: Greenwood Press, 1998).
Davies, Walford (ed.), *Dylan Thomas: New Critical Essays* (London: Dent, 1972).
Davies, Walford, *Dylan Thomas* (Milton Keynes: Open University Press, 1986).
Davies, Walford, *Dylan Thomas*, Writers of Wales (1990; Cardiff: University of Wales Press, 2014).
Eagleton, Terry, *Literary Theory: An Introduction* (1983–96; London: Blackwell, 2002).
Eliot, T. S., *The Waste Land*, in idem, *Selected Poems* (London: Faber, 1961).
Ellmann, Maud, *The Poetics of Impersonality: T. S. Eliot and Ezra Pound* (Cambridge, Mass.: Harvard University Press, 1987).
Ellmann, Maud, 'Eliot's Abjection', in John Fletcher and Andrew Benjamin (eds), *Abjection Melancholia and Love: The Work of Julia Kristeva* (London: Routledge, 1990).
Emig, Rainer, *Modernism in Poetry: Motivations, Structures and Limits* (London: Longman, 1995).
Evans, Caradoc, *My People*, ed. John Harris (Bridgend: Seren, 1997).
Evans, Dylan, *An Introductory Dictionary of Lacanian Psychoanalysis* (London: Routledge, 2005).
Fink, Bruce, *The Lacanian Subject: Between Language and Joiussance* (New Jersey: Princeton University Press, 1995).
Foster, Hal, *The Return of the Real* (Massachusetts and London: The MIT Press, 1996).
Freud, Sigmund, *Sigmund Freud, Complete Works: Standard Edition*, vol. 17 (London: Hogarth, 1953).
Freud, Sigmund, *The Penguin Freud Library*, vols 1–15, trans. J. Strachey (London: Penguin, 1990–3).
Gilbert, Sandra M. and Susan Gubar, *The Madwoman in the Attic*, reprinted in *The Norton Anthology of Theory and Criticism* (New York: Norton, 2001).
Goodby, John, *'uncaged sea'* (Hove: Waterloo Press, 2008).
Goodby, John, *The Poetry of Dylan Thomas: Under the Spelling Wall* (Liverpool: Liverpool University Press, 2013).
Goodby, John and Chris Wigginton, '"Shut, too, in a tower of words": Dylan Thomas' Modernism', in Alex Davies and Lee M. Jenkins (eds), *Locations of Literary Modernism* (Cambridge: Cambridge University Press, 2000).

Goodby, John and Chris Wigginton (eds), *Dylan Thomas: New Casebook* (Basingstoke: Palgrave, 2001).
Grosz, Elizabeth, 'The Body of Signification', in John Fletcher and Andrew Benjamin (eds), *Abjection, Melancholia and Love: The Work of Julia Kristeva* (London: Routledge, 1990).
Grosz, Elizabeth, 'Julia Kristeva', in Elizabeth Wright (ed.), *Feminism and Psychoanalysis: A Critical Dictionary* (Oxford: Blackwell, 1992).
Gramich, Katie, '"Daughters of Darkness": Dylan Thomas and the Celebration of the Female', in John Goodby and Chris Wigginton (eds), *Dylan Thomas: New Casebook* (Basingstoke: Palgrave, 2001), pp. 65–84.
Hassan, Ihab, 'Beyond Postmodernism? Theory, Sense, and Pragmatism', in Gerard Hoffmann (ed.), *Making Sense: The Role of the Reader in Contemporary American Fiction* (Munchen: Wilhelm Fink, 1989).
Hawkins, Desmond, 'Poetry', *Time and Tide*, XVI, 6 (9 February 1935).
Holbrook, David, *Llaregub Revisited: Dylan Thomas and the State of Modern Poetry* (London: Bowe and Bowes, 1962).
Holbrook, David, *Dylan Thomas and Poetic Dissociation* (Carbondale: Southern Illinois University Press, 1964).
Holbrook, David, *Dylan Thomas: The Code of Night* (London: Athlone Press, 1972).
Homer, Sean, *Jacques Lacan* (London: Routledge, 2005).
Jefferson, Ann and David Robey (eds), *Modern Literary Theory: A Comparative Introduction* (London: B. T. Batsford Ltd, 1995).
Jones, Gwyn, *The First Forty Years* (Cardiff: University of Wales Press, 1957).
Kay, Sarah, *Žižek: A Critical Introduction* (Cambridge: Polity, 2003).
Kershner, R. B., *Dylan Thomas: The Poet and His Critics* (Chicago: American Library Association, 1976).
Korg, Jacob, *Dylan Thomas* (Washington: Hippocrene Books, 1965).
Kristeva, Julia, 'From One Identity to Another', in *Desire in Language*, trans. Leon S. Roudiez (New York: Columbia University Press, 1980).
Kristeva, Julia, *Powers of Horror: An Essay on Abjection*, trans. Leon S. Roudiez (New York: Columbia University Press, 1982).
Kristeva, Julia, *Revolution in Poetic Language*, trans. Leon S. Roudiez (New York: Columbia University Press, 1984).
——, *Tales of Love*, trans. Leon S. Roudiez (New York: Columbia University Press, 1987).
Krutch, J. W., *Edgar Allan Poe: A Study in Genius* (New York: Knopf, 1926).
Lacan, Jacques, 'Some reflections on the ego', *International Journal of Psycho-Analysis*, 34 (1953), 61–73.
Lacan, Jacques, *Écrits: A Selection*, trans. Alan Sheridan (London: Tavistock, 1977).
Lacan, Jacques, *The Seminar of Jacques Lacan, Freud's Papers on Technique, 1953–54*, trans. John Forrester (Cambridge: Cambridge University Press, 1988).

Lacan, Jacques, *The Four Fundamental Concepts of Psycho-Analysis*, ed. Jacques-Alain Miller, trans. Alan Sheridan (1973; London: Penguin, 1994).
Leavis, F. R. and Denys Thompson, *Culture and the Environment: The Training of Critical Awareness* (London: Chatto and Windus, 1964).
Lyotard, Jean-François, *The Inhuman: Reflections on Time*, trans. Geoffrey Bennington and Rachel Bowlby (Cambridge: Polity Press, 1984).
Lyotard, Jean-François, 'Answering the Question: What is Postmodernism?', in James Docherty (ed.), *Postmodernism: A Reader* (New York: Columbia University Press, 1993), pp. 38–46.
Lyotard, Jean-François, *The Postmodern Explained: Correspondence 1982–1985*, trans. Don Barry, Bernadette Maher, Julian Pefanis, Virginia Spate and Morgan Thomas (Minneapolis: University of Minnesota Press, 1992).
Malpas, Simon, *Jean-François Lyotard* (London: Routledge, 2006).
Matthews, Steven and Keith Williams (eds), *Rewriting the Thirties: Modernism and After* (London: Longman, 1997).
Maud, Ralph, *Entrances to Dylan Thomas's Poetry* (Pittsburgh: Pittsburgh University Press, 1963).
Maud, Ralph, *Where Have the Old Words Got Me?* (Cardiff: University of Wales Press, 2003).
McAfee, Noëlle, 'Abject Strangers: Toward an Ethics of Respect', in Kelly Oliver (ed.), *Ethics, Politics and Difference in Julia Kristeva's Writing* (New York: Routledge, 1993).
McAfee, Noëlle, *Julia Kristeva* (London: Routledge, 2004).
McKay, Don, 'Crafty Dylan and the Altarwise Sonnets: "I build a flying tower and I pull it down"', *University of Toronto Quarterly*, 55, 4 (summer 1986), 375–94.
McKay, Don, 'What Shall We Do with a Drunken Poet: Dylan Thomas' Poetic Language', *Queen's Quarterly*, 93, 4 (winter 1986), 794–804.
Miller, J. Hillis, *Poets of Reality: Six Twentieth-century Poets* (Harvard: Harvard University Press, 1965).
Moi, Toril, *The Kristeva Reader* (Oxford: Blackwell, 1986).
Moruzzi, Norma Clare, 'National Abjects: Julia Kristeva on the Process of Political Self-Identification', in Kelly Oliver (ed.), *Ethics, Politics and Difference in Julia Kristeva's Writing* (New York: Routledge, 1993).
Moynihan, William T., *The Art of Dylan Thomas* (Ithaca, New York: Cornell University Press, 1968).
Myers, Tony, *Slavoj Žižek* (London: Routledge, 2003).
Oliver, Kelly, 'Kristeva's Imaginary Father and the Crisis in the Paternal Function', *Diacritics*, 21, 2/3, *A Feminist Miscellany* (summer–autumn 1991), 43–63.
Oliver, Kelly, *Reading Kristeva: Unraveling the Double-bind* (Bloomington and Indianapolis: Indiana University Press, 1993).
Palahniuk, Chuck, *Choke* (London: Jonathon Cape, 2001).

Perloff, Marjorie, '"Barbed-Wire Entanglements": The "New American Poetry", 1930–1932', in eadem, *Poetry On & Off the Page: Essays for Emergent Occasions* (Evanston: Northwestern University Press, 1998).

Readings, Bill, *Introducing Lyotard: Art and Politics* (London: Routledge, 1991).

Roberts, Harri Garrod, *Embodying Identity: Representations of the Body in Welsh Literature* (Cardiff: University of Wales Press, 2009).

Roberts, Michael (ed.), *New Signatures: Poems by Several Hands* (London: Hogarth Press, 1932).

Roberts, Michael (ed.), *New Country: Prose and Poetry by the Authors of New Signatures* (London: Hogarth, 1933).

Roland, Childe, *Ham and Jam and a Pearl* (Swansea: Hafan Books, 2010).

Sarup, Madan, *Jacques Lacan* (Hertfordshire: Harvester Wheatsheaf, 1992).

Seldon, Raman and Peter Widdowson, *A Reader's Guide to Contemporary Literary Theory* (Brighton: Harvester Press, 1985).

Shaw, Philip, *The Sublime* (London: Routledge, 2006).

Sitwell, Sachervell, *The Hundred and One Harlequins* (London: Duckworth, 1929).

Swrdwal, Ieuan ap, 'Hym to the Virgin', in Halshs Archive, *http://halshs. archives-ouvertes.fr/docs/00/47/44/20/PDF/German_PDGalles_.pdf* (accessed 11 April 2014).

Tedlock, E. W. (ed.), *Dylan Thomas: The Legend and the Poet* (London: William Heinemann Books, 1960).

Thomas, Dylan, *18 Poems* (London: Parton Press, 1934).

Thomas, Dylan, *Twenty-five Poems* (London: Dent, 1936).

Thomas, Dylan, *The Map of Love* (London: Dent, 1939).

Thomas, Dylan, *New Poems* (Connecticut: New Directions, 1943).

Thomas, Dylan, *Deaths and Entrances* (London: Dent, 1946).

Thomas, Dylan, *Twenty-six Poems* (London: Dent, 1950).

Thomas, Dylan, *Collected Poems 1934–1952* (London: Dent, 1952).

Thomas, Dylan, 'I am Going to Read Aloud', *The London Magazine*, 3, 9 (1952).

Thomas, Dylan, *In Country Sleep* (New York: New Directions, 1952).

Thomas, Dylan, *Poet in the Making: The Notebooks of Dylan Thomas*, ed. Ralph Maud (London: Dent, 1968).

Thomas, Dylan, *Dylan Thomas: Early Prose Writings*, ed. Walford Davies (London: Dent, 1971).

Thomas, Dylan, *Selected Poems*, ed. Walford Davies (1974; London: Dent, 1993).

Thomas, Dylan, *The Poems*, ed. Daniel Jones (London: Dent, 1979).

Thomas, Dylan, *Collected Poems 1934–1953*, ed. Walford Davies and Ralph Maud (1989; London: Dent, 1998).

Thomas, Dylan, *The Notebook Poems 1930–1934*, ed. Ralph Maud (London: Dent, 1989).

Thomas, Dylan, *The Collected Stories*, ed. Walford Davies, introduced by Leslie Norris (London: Phoenix, 2000).
Thomas, Gareth, 'A Freak User of Words', in Alan Norman Bold (ed.), *Dylan Thomas Craft or Sullen Art* (London: Vision, 1990).
Thomas, M. Wynn, *Corresponding Cultures* (Cardiff: University of Wales Press, 1999).
Tindall, William York, *A Reader's Guide to Dylan Thomas* (Syracuse: Syracuse University Press, 1962).
Trilling, Lionel, 'Freud and Literature' (1941), in David Lodge (ed.), *20th Century Literary Criticism* (London: Longman, 1972).
Vice, Sue (ed.), *Psychoanalytic Criticism: A Reader* (Cambridge: Polity, 1996).
Vine, Steve, 'Mary Shelley's *Mathilda*', in Tony Pinkney, Keth Handley and Fred Botting (eds), *Romantic Masculinities: News From Nowhere 2* (Lancaster: Keele University Press, 1992).
Vine, Steve, *Literature in Psychoanalysis: A Reader* (Basingstoke: Palgrave, 2005).
Wardi, Eynel, *Once Below a Time: Dylan Thomas, Julia Kristeva, and Other Speaking Subjects* (New York: State University of New York Press, 2000).
Waugh, Patricia (ed.), *Literary Theory and Criticism* (Milton Keynes: Open University Press, 2006).
Wigginton, Chris, '"Birth and copulation and death": Gothic Modernism and Surrealism in the Poetry of Dylan Thomas', in *Dylan Thomas: New Casebook*, ed. John Goodby and Chris Wigginton (London: Palgrave, 2001).
Wigginton, Chris, 'Modernism from the Margins; a Study of the 1930s Poetry of Louis MacNeice and Dylan Thomas' (unpublished PhD thesis, Swansea University, 2003).
Wigginton, Chris, *Modernism from the Margins: The 1930s Poetry of Louis MacNeice and Dylan Thomas* (Cardiff: University of Wales Press, 2007).
Wolfreys, Julian, *Critical Keywords in Literary and Cultural Theory* (London: Palgrave, Macmillan, 2004).
Wolfreys, Julian (ed.), *Feminism and Psychoanalysis: A Critical Dictionary* (Oxford: Blackwell, 1992).
Wolfreys, Julian, 'Modern Psychoanalytic Criticism', in Ann Jefferson and David Robey (eds), *Modern Literary Theory: A Comparative Introduction* (London: B. T. Batsford Ltd, 1995).
Wolfreys, Julian and Edmond Wright (eds), *The Žižek Reader* (1999; London: Blackwell, 2007).
Žižek, Slavoj, *The Sublime Object of Ideology* (London: Verso, 1989).
Žižek, Slavoj, *Looking Awry: An Introduction to Jacques Lacan through Popular Culture* (Cambridge, Mass. and London: MIT Press, 1991).
Žižek, Slavoj, *Enjoy Your Symptom!* (1992; London and New York: Routledge, 2001).
Žižek, Slavoj, *How to Read Lacan* (London: Granta Books, 2006).

Žižek, Slavoj, 'The Obscene Object of Postmodernity', in Elizabeth Wright and Edmond Wright (eds), *The Žižek Reader* (1999; London: Blackwell, 2007).
Žižek, Slavoj, *The Fright of Real Tears:Krzysztof Kieślowski Between Theory and Post-Theory The Fright of Real Tears* (London and Bloomington: British Film Institute and Indiana University Press, 2001).

Unpublished works
The following unpublished works are cited with permission of the author:
Goodby, John, '"Shape of sound": language and style' (unpublished manuscript, 2006).
Goodby, John, '"Eggs laid by tigers": the politics of a style' (unpublished manuscript, 2007).
Goodby, John, 'The Blitz sublime: Dylan Thomas, T. S. Eliot and the poetry of the 1940's' (unpublished paper, St Andrew's University, March 2010).
Goodby, John, *No Work of Words: The Critical Fates of Dylan Thomas* (unpublished manuscript).

Index

'A process in the weather of the heart' (Thomas) 16, 17, 74, 107–8
'A refusal to mourn the death' (Thomas) 80
abjection 16–18, 95, 102–9, 119, 120, 128
Ackerman, John 21, 50–1
adolescence 12, 26
affect 45–6
Aivaz, David 53
Aldington, Richard 42–3, 45–6, 55
alienation 43–4, 54–5
'Altarwise' sequence (Thomas) 72
anatomic imagery *see* human body
'And death shall have no dominion' (Thomas) 13, 51, 52–5, 58
animal imagery 41, 46, 81–3
Antonioni, Michelangelo 121
Arnold, Matthew 124
Auden, W. H. 12, 14, 22–3, 24, 59, 60, 64
avant-garde 14, 39, 56–7, 62–3, 68, 71, 85, 87–9

Bakhtin, Mikhail 85, 122
Barthes, Roland 85, 113
Bataille, Georges 104, 124
Baudrillard, Jean 68, 94
'Before I knocked' (Thomas) 17, 55, 59–61, 107, 118

belatedness 11–12, 22, 23, 30, 35, 63, 68, 128
Belsey, Catherine 4–5, 84
Bennett, Andrew 71, 124
Birds, Beasts and Flowers (Lawrence) 41
birth 12, 16, 26, 83
Black Sun (Kristeva) 64
Blevins, Jacob 36, 49–50
Bloom, Harold
  the *ephebe* 32, 35–6, 63
  theory of influence 12, 23–4, 30, 35–6, 38, 49, 50, 64, 127
Blow Up (Antonioni) 121
body, the 11, 16–18, 57, 95, 99–109, 110–13, 118–24, 128
Borch-Jacobsen, Mikkel 24
Borges, Jorge Luis 21
Bowie, Malcolm 36–7
Breton, André 83

'Call It All Names, But Do Not Call It Rest' (Watkins) 14–15, 67
Cantos (Pound) 38
castration
  fear of 13, 32, 61
  symbolic 11, 26, 29, 75, 80
'Ceremony after a fire raid' (Thomas) 76
Choke (Palahniuk) 75–6

Christianity 52, 54, 64, 123–4
conception 12, 16, 26, 83
Conran, Tony 49
Corcoran, Neil 122
Crehan, Stewart 5, 9, 72–3, 80, 92, 118
cultural consciousness 49–51

Dada 14, 62
Dali, Salvador 53
Davies, James A. 50
Davies, Walford 3, 50, 60, 63, 78, 80–1, 83, 114
death 16, 52–4, 82–3
desire 44, 45–6, 61–2
difference 15, 27–8, 30
'Do not go gentle into that good night' (Thomas) 126
'Do you not father me?' (Thomas) 44–5
Donne, John 57, 88, 101
drives 11, 16, 45, 110

Eagleton, Terry 27, 78
'Ears in turrets hear' (Thomas) 57–8
écriture féminine 117
ego 27, 37–8, 40, 43–5, 54
ego ideal 13, 61–2
18 Poems (Thomas) 17, 21–2, 39, 43, 55–8, 72, 85, 105, 109, 120, 127
Eliot, T. S.
 and abjection 17–18, 95, 102, 104–6, 108–9, 122, 128
 and the body 16, 17–18, 95, 100, 102, 104–6, 108–9, 122
 and literary tradition 13–14
 The Love Song of J. Alfred Prufrock and Other Observations 21
 'Milton 1' 108–9
 and repression 16, 17–18, 100, 110
 and sonority 108–9
 and the symptom 110, 112
 and Thomas 12, 13–14, 16–18, 21–4, 59, 60, 64, 100, 102, 104–9, 110, 112, 120, 122, 128
 The Waste Land 17, 21–2, 38, 95, 102, 104–6, 108–9, 110, 112, 122
Ellman, Maud 38, 95, 102, 104–5, 108–9

Emig, Rainer 7, 90
Empson, William 87
ephebe, the 32, 35–6, 63
'Especially when the October wind' 51, 80, 113–14, 116
Evans, Caradoc 49
Evans, Dylan 37
events, poems as 71–2, 79, 80, 91, 92–4
excess 13–14, 15, 17, 32–3, 45, 61–4, 67–8, 71, 85–91, 113, 118, 128

Fantasia of the Unconscious (Lawrence) 92
fathers 24, 30–1, 35–6, 60–2, 64; *see also* imaginary father; Oedipus complex
female body 95, 102, 104–8; *see also* womb, the
'Fern Hill' (Thomas) 78–9
'Find meat on bones' (Thomas) 57
Fink, Bruce 74–5
Finnegans Wake (Joyce) 69, 118
fragmentation 25, 34, 37, 71, 110
free verse 13, 32, 40–1
Freud, Sigmund
 Bloom's application of 23–4, 30, 127
 Freudian interpretations of Thomas 2–4, 9
 Lacan's re-reading of 7, 25
 and literature 5–7
 Oedipus complex 5–6, 23–4, 34–6, 64
 and the phallus 44, 86
 reality principle 74
 and the symptom 110–11
 Thomas's manipulation of 9–10
'From love's first fever' (Thomas) 12, 26–30, 86
'Function and field of speech and language in psychoanalysis, The' (Lacan) 8

Gilbert, Sandra M. 23
Goodby, John 1, 4, 8, 22, 48, 52, 54, 56, 62–3, 73, 108, 109, 120, 123, 125

INDEX

Gothic 48–9
Gramich, Katie 112
Grosz, Elizabeth 99, 104
grotesque 48–9, 102, 106, 110, 123
Gubar, Susan 23

Hawkins, Desmond 22–3, 64
high Modernism 12, 14, 15, 16, 23, 70, 71, 100, 110, 128
Hitchcock, Alfred 117–18, 121
Holbrook, David 2–3, 4–5, 9, 11, 122
hommelette, the 14, 40
Hopkins, Gerard Manley 90
'How shall my animal?' (Thomas) 16, 46, 80–3
Hoy, Mikita 97
Hughes, Trevor 62
human body 11, 16–18, 57, 95, 99–109, 110–13, 118–24, 128
hybridity 22–3, 56, 59–60, 62, 63–4, 70, 128

'I dreamed my genesis' (Thomas) 17
'I in my intricate image' (Thomas) 115
'I see the boys of summer' (Thomas) 112
ideal ego 13, 47, 54, 57
identity 25, 27–8, 34–41, 43–4, 54, 76–7, 92, 102–5
'If I were tickled by the rub of love' (Thomas) 17, 123
imagery 3, 9–10, 41–3, 46–7
Imaginary, the 11, 13, 16, 25, 27, 30–1, 32, 36–7, 49–50, 60, 81, 127
imaginary father 13, 24, 61–2, 64
Imagism 41–3, 46–7, 57
imitations 39–40, 49, 55
In Country Heaven (Thomas) 67
'In the beginning' (Thomas) 8, 91–3
infancy 12, 13, 26, 36–8, 102–3
influence, theory of 12, 23–4, 30, 35–6, 38, 49, 50, 64, 127
internal rhyme 57

Jameson, Fredric 68, 94
'*Je est un Autre*' (Rimbaud) 76

Johnson, Pamela Hansford 17, 57, 77, 100–2, 119, 122
Jones, Gwyn 126
jouissance 10, 12, 14, 25, 32–3, 61, 62, 71–2, 95, 111, 117–18, 125, 127–8
Joyce, James 83, 84, 106, 111, 112
  Finnegans Wake 69, 118

Kant, Immanuel 68, 74
Korg, Jacob 53–4
Kristeva, Julia
  abjection 16–18, 95, 102–9, 119, 120, 128
  affect 45–6
  Black Sun 64
  on desire 45, 61–2
  the imaginary father 13, 24, 61–2, 64
  the loving third term 13, 31, 61–2, 64
  on poetic language 85
  Powers of Horror 106–7
  the Semiotic 11, 33–5, 106, 108–9, 113, 117
Krutch, J. W. 7

Lacan, Jacques
  on alienation 43–4, 54–5
  on desire 44
  on the ego 37–8, 40, 43–5, 54
  ego ideal 13, 61–2
  exclusion from academic theory 125
  the Father 24, 30–1, 60–1
  'The function and field of speech and language in psychoanalysis' 8
  the *hommelette* 14, 40
  ideal ego 13, 47, 54, 57
  the Imaginary 11, 13, 16, 25, 27, 30–1, 32, 36–7, 49–50, 60, 81, 127
  jouissance 10, 12, 14, 25, 32–3, 61, 62, 71–2, 95, 111, 117–18, 125, 127–8
  and language 7–8, 25, 27, 29–30, 74–5

and literature 7–8
méconnaissance 38, 43–4
mirror stage 25, 37–8, 43–4, 102
the Mother 24, 29–30
Oedipus complex 24, 36–7, 60–1, 64
and origins 7–8, 12, 25–7
the Other 13, 39–40, 43–5, 51, 60, 111
on the phallus 24
the pre-Symbolic 11, 26–7, 39–40, 74–5, 78–9
re-reading of Freud 7, 25
the Real 13, 14–16, 25, 74–84, 90, 121, 127
Seminar on the Purloined Letter 7–8
sinthomes 17–18, 110–13, 115, 116–18, 125, 127
the Symbolic 13, 16, 25, 29, 30–1, 32–3, 49–50, 60–2, 64, 80–2, 118, 127
symbolic interpellation 12, 13, 25, 44, 51
the third term 13, 30, 60
'Lament' (Thomas) 115
language
  acquisition of 27
  and excess 17, 61, 67–8, 71, 85–91, 94, 118, 128
  and Lacan 7–8, 25, 27, 29–30, 74–5
  materiality of 8–9, 12, 16, 33–4, 59–61, 99–100, 108–9, 110, 113–19
  musicality of 33, 59, 108, 113, 115
  and origins 7–8, 91–3
  plurality of 28–9, 85–91, 115
  and psychoanalysis 7–8
  and the Real 15–16, 29–30, 74–5, 79–84, 90
  and the Semiotic 106, 108–9, 113, 117
  and the *sinthome* 111–13, 115, 116–18
  Thomas's use of 8–11, 50–1, 59–60, 71–2, 85–91, 112–19, 129
  and the unconscious 7, 111
Lawrence, D. H. 41, 92

Leavis, F. R. 5, 87, 122, 124
Lewis, Saunders 49
Lifeboat (Hitchcock) 121
'Light breaks where no sun shines' (Thomas) 16, 17, 73
literary tradition 13–14, 29, 30, 32–3, 63–4, 125–8
literature
  and abjection 106–7
  and psychoanalysis 5–8
  and spirituality 124
  and the unconscious 6–7
Love Song of J. Alfred Profrock and Other Observations (Eliot) 21
loving third term, the 13, 31, 61–2, 64
Lyotard, Jean François 14, 65, 68–9, 89–91, 93–4, 121, 128

McAfee, Noëlle 103
McKay, Don 63, 67, 87–8
Malpas, Simon 68
Map of Love, The (Thomas) 39, 46
masturbation 112, 118–20, 123
materiality (linguistic) 8–9, 12, 16, 33–4, 59–61, 99–100, 108–9, 110, 113–19
Maud, Ralph 3, 26, 40, 42, 46, 53, 54, 58, 63, 73, 74, 80, 82, 92, 119
méconnaissance 38, 43–4
Miller, J. Hillis 76, 77, 79
Milton, John 108–9
'Milton 1' (Eliot) 108–9
mirror stage 25, 37–8, 43–4, 102
misrecognition 38, 43–4
Modernism
  and the body 16, 17, 100, 102, 106, 108
  and the grotesque 49
  high 12, 14, 15, 16, 23, 70, 71, 100, 110, 128
  and the Lacanian ego 38–9
  and masculinity 17, 106, 108, 110
  and postmodernism 68–71, 94, 120–2
  and the Real 83
  and Thomas 12, 14, 15, 21–3, 38–9, 59, 60, 62, 68–71, 83, 87, 100, 102, 125, 128

Welsh 49
Moruzzi, Norma Clare 104
mothers 24, 29–30, 34–5, 61–2; *see also* womb, the
Moynihan, William T. 3
musicality 33, 59, 108, 113, 115; *see also* sonority
'My hero bares his nerves' (Thomas) 17, 118–20, 123–4
'My world is a pyramid' (Thomas) 34–5
Myers, Tony 75–6, 125

narcissism 13, 45, 107, 108, 123
Neuberg, Victor 55–6
New Country poets 22, 51–2, 55, 56, 60
New Criticism 3, 72
New Signatures (Roberts) 51
Newman, Barnett 71, 90–1, 93, 94
Nonconformism 51, 54, 124
nonsense poetry 14, 62
nostalgia 15, 65, 67, 69, 71, 79, 83–4, 128
'Now' (Thomas) 14, 62–3

obscene object, the 17, 120–3
Oedipus complex 5–6, 23–4, 34–6, 60–1, 64
Oedipus Rex (Sophocles) 5–6
Oliver, Kelly 61, 64
'Once it was the colour of saying' (Thomas) 8
origins 7–8, 12, 25–7, 91–3
'Osiris, come to Isis' (Thomas) 41
Other, the 13, 39–40, 43–5, 51, 60, 111

Palahniuk, Chuck 75–6
para-rhyme 57–8, 63
parody 12, 14, 16, 17–18, 56, 62, 63, 70, 110, 120
Patton, Paul 65
Perloff, Marjorie 70
phallus, the 17–18, 24, 44, 61–2, 86, 119–20, 123–4
plurality 15, 27–8, 30
  linguistic 28–9, 85–91, 115

Poe, Edgar Allen 7–8
poetic development 12–13, 26, 32–47, 51–64, 106, 127
'Poetic manifesto' (Thomas) 112
postmodern sublime 14, 68–9, 71, 90–1, 93–4, 128
postmodernism 14–15, 67–71, 83, 90, 94–5, 108, 120–2, 128, 129
Pound, Ezra 24, 38–9, 70
Powers of Horror (Kristeva) 106–7
pre-natal, the 17, 34, 60–1, 76, 79, 83, 92, 106, 107–8
pre-Oedipal, the 26, 28–9, 36–7, 74–5, 78–9
pre-Symbolic, the 11, 26–7, 39–40, 74–5, 78–9
process poetic 13, 26, 52–6, 58–60, 72–8, 86, 94
process problematic 78–84
puns 111–12, 115–17, 119, 123

Rabaté, Jean-Michel 111–12
Read, Herbert 22
Real, the 13, 14–16, 25, 74–84, 90, 121, 127
reality principle 74
religion 52, 54, 64, 123–4
representation 64, 69, 70–1; *see also* unpresentable, the
repression 9, 11, 16, 17, 83, 100, 103, 109, 110
rhyme 35, 51–2, 55, 57–8, 63
rhythm 10, 50–1, 113, 114
Rimbaud, Arthur 76
Roberts, Harri Garrod 28, 101–2, 104–5, 114, 122
Roberts, Michael 51
Romanticism 15, 54, 67
Royle, Nicholas 71, 124

Saussure, Ferdinand de 7
Seminar on the Purloined Letter (Lacan) 7–8
Semiotic, the 11, 33–5, 108–9, 113, 117
sexual awareness 12, 26
sexual imagery 3, 9–10
sexual union 16, 82, 83

Shaw, Philip 91, 93, 94
Shelley, Percy Bysshe 53
sinthome, the 17–18, 110–13, 115, 116–18, 125, 127
Sitwell, Edith 22
Sitwell, Sachervell 42–3, 45–6, 55
slang 115–16, 119
slant rhyme 35
sonority 11, 50–1, 85, 108–9, 113; *see also* musicality
Sophocles 5–6
speech acquisition 27
Spender, Stephen 22
Stein, Gertrude 62, 69
Stevens, Wallace 32, 84, 87, 129
sublime, the 14, 68–9, 71, 90–1, 93–4, 128
surrealism 10, 63, 83, 125
symbiotic unity 11, 32, 39–40, 74–9
Symbolic, the 13, 16, 25, 29, 30–1, 32–3, 49–50, 60–2, 64, 80–2, 118, 127
symbolic castration 11, 26, 29, 75, 80
symbolic interpellation 12, 13, 25, 44, 51
symptom, the 17–18, 110–13, 115

Taig, Thomas 57
Tender Buttons (Stein) 62, 69
'That sanity be kept' (Thomas) 55–6
'The force that through the green fuse' (Thomas) 16, 77–8, 80, 126
'The hand that signed the paper' (Thomas) 70, 72
third term, the 13, 30, 60
Thomas, Dylan
  'Altarwise' sequence 72
  'And death shall have no dominion' 13, 51, 52–5, 58
  'Before I knocked' 17, 55, 59–61, 107, 118
  biographically-based criticism of 1–4
  and the body 16–18, 95, 99–102, 105–9, 110–13, 118–24, 128
  'Ceremony after a fire raid' 76
  'Do not go gentle into that good night' 126
  'Do you not father me?' 44–5
  'Ears in turrets hear' 57–8
  18 Poems 17, 21–2, 39, 43, 55–8, 72, 85, 105, 109, 120, 127
  and Eliot 12, 13–14, 16–18, 21–4, 59, 60, 64, 100, 102, 104–9, 110, 112, 120, 122, 128
  'Especially when the October wind' 51, 80, 113–14, 116
  and excess 13–14, 15, 17, 32–3, 61–4, 67–8, 71, 85–91, 113, 118, 128
  'Fern Hill' 78–9
  'Find meat on bones' 57
  'The force that through the green fuse' 16, 77–8, 80, 126
  as 'Freudian exemplar' 9–10
  Freudian interpretations of 2–4, 9
  'From love's first fever' 12, 26–30, 86
  'The hand that signed the paper' 70, 72
  'How shall my animal?' 16, 46, 80–3
  and hybridity 22–3, 56, 59–60, 62, 63–4, 70, 128
  'I dreamed my genesis' 17
  'I in my intricate image' 115
  'I see the boys of summer' 112
  'If I were tickled by the rub of love' 17, 123
  and the image 41–3, 46–7
  imitations 39–40, 49, 55
  In Country Heaven 67
  'In the beginning' 8, 91–3
  'Lament' 115
  letters 14–15, 17, 47, 57, 80, 100–1, 119, 122
  'Light breaks where no sun shines' 16, 17, 73
  and the literary tradition 13–14, 32–3, 63–4, 125–8
  The Map of Love 39, 46
  and Modernism 12, 14, 15, 21–3, 38–9, 59, 60, 62, 68–71, 83, 87, 100, 102, 125, 128
  'My hero bares his nerves' 17, 118–20, 123–4

'My world is a pyramid' 34–5
Notebook Poems 9, 13, 32, 40–7, 48–9, 51–61, 67, 127
'Now' 14, 62–3
'Once it was the colour of saying' 8
'Osiris, come to Isis' 41
poetic development 12–13, 26, 32–47, 51–64, 106, 127
'Poetic manifesto' 112
and postmodernism 14–15, 67–71, 83, 90, 94–5, 108, 120–2, 128, 129
'A process in the weather of the heart' 16, 17, 74, 107–8
process poetic 13, 26, 52–6, 58–60, 72–8, 86, 94
process problematic 78–84
'A refusal to mourn the death' 80
'That sanity be kept' 55–6
'Today this insect' 70, 85–90
Twenty-five Poems 39, 58, 70, 72, 85
and the unpresentable 14–16, 70–84, 94, 128
use of language 8–11, 50–1, 59–60, 71–2, 85–91, 112–19, 129
and Welsh identity 49–51, 126–7
'When like a running grave' 115–16, 117
'When once the twilight locks' 17, 105–6
'Where once the waters of your face' 16
working methods 9, 10, 112
Thomas, Gareth 79–80
Thomas, M. Wynn 50
Thurston, Luke 111
Tindall, William York 3, 87, 88
'Today this insect' (Thomas) 70, 85–90
tradition 13–14, 87–9

Treece, Henry 47, 80
Twenty-five Poems (Thomas) 39, 58, 70, 72, 85

uncanny, the 10, 14, 62–3, 125
unconscious, the 6–7, 60, 111
unpresentable, the 14–16, 64, 65, 68–9, 70–84, 94, 128

vers libre 13, 32, 40–1
Vice, Sue 7
Vine, Steve 6, 61

Wardi, Eynel 1, 4–5
Waste Land, The (Eliot) 17, 21–2, 38, 95, 102, 104–6, 108–9, 110, 112, 122
Watkins, Vernon 14–15, 57, 67
Waugh, Patricia 79
Welsh identity 49–51, 126–7
Welsh Modernism 49
'When like a running grave' (Thomas) 115–16, 117
'When once the twilight locks' 17, 105–6
'Where once the waters of your face' (Thomas) 16
Whitman, Walt 73
Wigginton, Chris 1, 4, 8, 49, 61, 71, 90, 105, 108, 118–19, 125
Wolfreys, Julian 103
womb, the 17, 34, 60–1, 76, 79, 83, 92, 106, 107–8
Wright, Elizabeth 121

Yeats, William Butler 41, 47

zaum 14, 62
Žižek, Slavoj 13, 17, 91, 116–18, 120–3, 125